Life isn't about "finding" fulfillment and success—it's about creating it. Why, then, has creativity been given a backseat in our culture? No longer.

Creativity is a force inside every person that, when unleashed, transforms our lives and delivers vitality to everything we do. Establishing a creative practice is therefore now our most valuable and urgent task—one as important to health and well-being as exercise or nutrition.

The good news? Renowned artist, author, and CreativeLive founder, Chase Jarvis, reminds us that creativity isn't a skill—it's a habit available to everyone: beginners to lifelong creators, entrepreneurs to executives, astronauts to zookeepers, and everyone in between. Through small, daily actions we can supercharge our innate creativity and rediscover our personal power in life.

Whether your ambition is to pursue a creative career, complete a creative project, or simply cultivate a creative mindset, *Creative Calling* will unlock your potential via Jarvis's memorable "IDEA" system:

- **IMAGINE** your big dream, whatever you want to create—or become—in this world.

- **DESIGN** a daily practice that supports that dream—and a life of expression and transformation.

- **EXECUTE** on your ambitious plans and make your vision real.

- **AMPLIFY** your impact through a supportive community you'll learn to grow and nurture.

Praise for *Creative Calling*

"I have always believed that you will enjoy life and be more successful if you focus on creating amazing experiences; businesses, and relationships. *Creative Calling* is an engaging handbook for doing just that, from a man who, in CreativeLive, has followed his passions and created a company to inspire others."
—*Sir Richard Branson, Virgin Group founder*

"There is a wild, untamed connection between our inherent creativity and our yearning for a meaningful, purpose-driven life. Chase's experiences and his commitment to creating make him the perfect guide as we set out on our own adventures to learn how creativity has the power to change everything."
—*Brené Brown, PhD, author of the* New York Times *#1 bestseller* Dare to Lead

"*Creative Calling* is a trail guide for anyone stepping onto the path of creativity, whether for personal fulfillment or as a career aspiration. You won't find a better resource to unlock your true potential and scale the heights of the creative economy."
—*Jimmy Chin, Oscar-winning director of* Free Solo

"Chase Jarvis is a remarkable creative spirit. His new book, *Creative Calling*, is proof positive that creativity is both an art and a practice. With great candor and deft insight, Chase debunks the myths surrounding what it means to be a creative person and proves that anyone and everyone can be creative. *Creative Calling* will wholeheartedly change the way you think about how and why humans create, and it will provide you with the inspiration to make a bigger life than you ever thought possible."
—*Debbie Millman, artist and chair of the School of Visual Arts master's in branding program and host of the* Design Matters *podcast*

"Everyone has a dream. In *Creative Calling*, Chase Jarvis gives us the closest thing there is to a road map for pursuing that dream—and succeeding in the process. It's a must-read for any creator or entrepreneur."

—*Daymond John, star of ABC'S* Shark Tank, *founder/CEO of FUBU, and CEO of the Shark Group*

"Relentlessly generous and endlessly creative, Chase is challenging us to see the shifts in our culture and media as the opportunity of a lifetime. If you care about making things better, this book is here to help."

—*Seth Godin, bestselling author and entrepreneur*

"This book isn't about your creativity calling, it's about your creativity *screaming* from inside you—fighting to be heard and to be ready to change the world."

—*James Victore, artist, activist, and author of* Feck Perfection

"Good design helps and delights others. Chase Jarvis shows you how to do it."

—*Stefan Sagmeister, designer and founder of Sagmeister & Walsh*

"Chase Jarvis is my favorite person to go to for advice. I'm sure he's tired of me calling him. He was one of the first people to recognize the power of the Internet for artists, and he still has the best insight for anyone looking to follow a creative path. He's taught me so much. This book reads like a long, intimate conversation with Chase. And there's nothing more valuable in the world."

—*Brandon Stanton, creator of Humans of New York and* New York Times *bestselling author*

Creative Calling

Also by Chase Jarvis

The Best Camera Is The One That's with You:
iPhone Photography

Seattle 100: Portrait of a City

Creative Calling

Establish a daily practice, infuse your world with meaning, and succeed in work + life.

Chase Jarvis

HARPER
BUSINESS

An Imprint of HarperCollins*Publishers*

HarperCollins books may be purchased for educational, business, or sales promotional use. For information, please email the Special Markets Department at SPsales@harpercollins.com.

FIRST EDITION

Designed by Bonni Leon-Berman

Library of Congress Cataloging-in-Publication Data has been applied for.

ISBN 978-0-06-287996-7

19 20 21 22 23   LSC   10 9 8 7 6 5 4 3 2 1

To you, reading this right now.
I hope this book helps you shape this one,
precious life you've got.

And to Kate,
the person who has shaped my life the most.
All my love.

Contents

Read This First!

You can't use up creativity. The more you use, the more you have.

—MAYA ANGELOU

Ask yourself: Is the way you're working *working*? Is the way you're *living* working?

This is a book about creativity, but in a larger sense it's about life and how you live it. It's not just about starting a creative practice or becoming a better designer, writer, photographer, or entrepreneur—though it will supercharge all of your creative skills. It's about living a richer, deeper, more rewarding life than ever before. Embracing creativity in your life is like that moment when Dorothy steps out of her black-and-white Kansas house into blazing Technicolor Munchkinland.

Think about what led you to open this book today, at this moment. What are you seeking?

If you're confident that you're living your highest calling in life and fulfilling your potential to its fullest, great. If you bring generosity and playfulness to everything you do, not just to creative tasks but to every area of your life, fantastic. If the spirit of creativity and invention infuses every day and all of your important relationships with joy, inspiration, and vitality, you've already learned anything I can teach you. Whatever you're doing, it's working. You're living the dream. Go back to creating your day. The world needs what you have to give. Please give this book to someone who needs it.

Still reading?

Okay, here's the other possibility: you're not, in fact, living your dream. Far from it, maybe. Instead, you're seeking. You might be burned out, run down, stuck—or you might just suspect that life on Earth could be more than just *this*. Something's missing. You may or may not think of yourself as a "creative person"—whatever that means—but something about this book piqued your interest. You might not know what it is yet. You might not be willing to admit it if you do. We'll get to that. Rest assured, though: this book is for you.

Or maybe you do identify as a creative person, but you don't actually, you know, create anything. Much of anything, anyway. You used to take photographs, code, write, or play an instrument, but somehow the practice that once excited or fulfilled you slipped away. Funny thing is, you can't seem to get back into the groove no matter how hard you try. This book is for you, too.

Or you do make stuff. You write, dance, sing, or start business after business. It could be a side gig or your full-time job, but you create regularly and you've been successful with it. Now, however, you're unsure how to keep going—or even *if* you should. Maybe your current project is on the rocks, your client is driving you nuts, and you're ready to call it quits. Or you felt a void inside after your last show. In fact, maybe you've even been considering—*gasp*—settling.

If your creative practice isn't everything you'd always dreamed it would be by this point, isn't it time to give up?

Not so fast.

Without a resilient creative practice, supportive creative peers, a thriving community, and a powerful mindset, life just does not have the same vibrancy. Even a successful professional can flounder. This book will help you find what's missing. The creativity inside of you—right now, at this moment—is the lever we will use. To quote Archimedes, give us a place to stand, and with this lever, we will move the world.

There is one final possibility: everything about your creative practice looks good on paper, but you still feel unmotivated, even apathetic, about continuing. This happens. It's happened to me. Everything can look right from the outside and still leave you feeling hollow.

The solution here is to remember why you started creating in the first place. We find the path forward by tracing it back to its beginning. Something inside of you called out to be expressed. Whether you started by dusting off the guitar you used to play in high school or signing up for an open-mic night at a comedy club, that inspiration—that joy, that life force you once felt in such abundance—is still available to you. You just have to hear the call and follow your path.

Wherever you find yourself, every new day is an opportunity to tune in to your creative calling.

The beauty of the path we walk is that no action is ever wasted—through all the twists and turns, you're never truly lost no matter how far you've wandered. This is the nature of the creative process: It all matters. It's all meaningful. The frustration, boredom, or resentment you might feel now is just your intuition's way of telling you that there's a turn up ahead. Will you be ready?

A good life is designed. Created. And this book is about living a better life *through creativity*. By expressing yourself regularly in small ways, you will discover the agency and drive necessary to create the life of your dreams. Creativity is as essential to health and well-being as exercise, proper nutrition, and mindfulness. Only with this potent energy unleashed will you be capable of living your life to its fullest.

This book is for you.

Introduction

> There's no such thing as creative people and non-creative
> people. There's just people who use their creativity and people
> who don't. And not using it doesn't go without penalty. As it turns
> out, unused creativity is not benign, it's dangerous.
>
> —BRENÉ BROWN

Everything looked right on paper: I had "appropriate" ambitions
and a clear plan for achieving them. I knew what I was going
to do with my life and I had confidence that I could succeed at
doing it. But inside, I was lost. Unsettled, emotionally absent,
stuck. I couldn't put my finger on it, but something felt off. I was
struggling and I couldn't take another step forward—how was I
going to follow this plan?

It wasn't until I experienced the loss of someone dear to me
that I realized something: that plan sucked. Each action made
sense by itself, but the destination left me cold. The year before,
I'd quit the opportunity to pursue soccer professionally. Now I
was off to med school, plunging into another life I had no desire
to live. What was I doing? How had this happened?

All my life, I'd sought the approval of others, to achieve at any
cost. Becoming a doctor seemed like the obvious choice. The
only choice. I truly believed that. Then loss taught me otherwise.
My grandfather's unexpected death woke me up. Losing him reminded me that I'd only ever have one life. If I didn't pursue my
calling on this go-around, I never would.

If I wasn't going to heal the sick, though, where did I belong in this world? What was I supposed to do? What was my calling? I didn't know the exact shape or contours yet, but there was something inside of me demanding to be let out. I found myself at one of life's crossroads, the "safe" path leading in one direction, uncertainty—and possibility—in the other.

Eventually I came to realize that a calling is just that: a whisper in the distance. Most of us don't wake up one day and decide we were born to be a horse veterinarian or an opera singer. That's a story we tell ourselves after the fact, once we've found ourselves wherever we happen to end up. No, a calling is an intuitive hint, a tug we experience when we're doing something that feels right: *This is awesome! I'm going to keep doing this and see where it takes me.*

If we keep listening to those hints and letting the tugs guide us, if we heed the call, we soon find that we're walking our own path. No matter where we're going, we're exactly where we're supposed to be.

So no, I didn't suddenly realize at the age of twenty-one that I wanted to be an artist, an action sports photographer, or the founder of an online learning platform. I simply decided to listen to my gut. I knew I wanted to take photos, simple as that. As long as I was doing what felt right, I figured, the rest would figure itself out—and it did.

This was the moment I summoned the courage to disappoint nearly everyone in my life. For the second time, I abandoned my plan for the future and took my first, hesitant step on a new path, the path in pursuit of my creative calling. I'm still on that path today, and I've never looked back.

Being creative doesn't mean quitting your day job, donning a beret, or moving to Paris. It doesn't mean dressing differently or making a whole new set of "artsy" friends. It doesn't mean trying on a persona or going through a phase. Forget everything you think you know about what it means to be a creator. Creativity is a natural, life-sustaining, human function that is essential to our health and well-being. It's as natural as breathing.

In fact, let's put it in perspective. Imagine a world where breathing is a shameful practice. They teach kids in schools: "Keep your breath down, children!" Kids never run and play because it would require heavy-duty exhalation. Adults don't get excited about anything for fear of sucking wind. Imagine living in that world, getting by on little sips of oxygen and always feeling dizzy and tired.

Then imagine being told that a nice, deep breath of fresh air, one that fills your whole belly, is invigorating, refreshing, and incredibly good for you. Imagine being told that your society is sick, not you. Imagine being told that breathing deeply will change the way you think and feel forever.

What would you do next?

We are all born creative. No matter your race, gender, sexual orientation, ability, or background, creativity welcomes you. The goal of this book is to invite you to embrace and enjoy all of creativity's benefits.

When we create, we tap into something powerful inside us. We don't control this energy as much as we channel it. The strength of this creative force in every human being is undeniable—I've seen it unleashed too many times to think otherwise. You have this power humming inside of you right now, whether you know it or not.

When we make something, this vast inner resource gets activated, even if the thing we make is simple and small, even if it's a halting, first attempt that is quickly abandoned. Our creativity doesn't care. It's awake now. Energy starts to flow in every direction. If we keep using our creative energy by making new things day after day, month after month, something incredible happens. We *feel* better: awake, fulfilled, whole. By creating regularly, we access a new source of vitality.

Turning an idea in your head into a tangible reality is one of life's great satisfactions, whether the end result is a story, a photograph, a meal, or a business. We're born with a reservoir for doing this, a dense little chunk of creative plutonium. This reactor contains more than enough fuel to power our creativity for a lifetime. In fact, the more you use its power, the more of it is available to you. But, like plutonium, creativity is dangerous. All that energy has to go somewhere. It must be released through a regular creative practice. Bottled up, it can go critical, become toxic. Unexpressed, your creativity can poison your life.

What Is Creativity, and Why Does It Matter?

Creativity is the practice of combining or rearranging two or more unlikely things in new and useful ways. That's it, though this simple definition has hidden depth.

More important than the what is the *why*: When we create, we give of ourselves freely, adding value and expecting nothing in return. To do it, we must tap into our true, authentic self. This means that creativity is the process of learning to trust oneself. When pure creativity is flowing through you, judgment can't grab hold. It's impossible. This book will show you how to let go of all judgment and trust in yourself completely. Everything you need is inside you right now.

Your future rests on three distinct premises:

1. You are creative by nature, endowed with a near limitless capacity to make and grow new things.
2. Accessing this capacity requires a kind of creative muscle that must be strengthened to achieve your full potential.
3. By identifying as a creative person, accepting the world around you as your canvas, and manifesting your ideas regularly, you will intuitively create the life you truly want for yourself.

In other words: yes, playing the piano makes you better at life. Cooking or coding or building a business changes your mind, instilling the notion that you can shape your environment and your experience. It gives you an unshakable sense of agency. The more creative you are day to day, the better you'll become at building the life you want. It's just creation at a larger scale.

We've never been taught any of this. Our society's narrative around "creative people" versus "the rest of us" is false and destructive. Once you let go of that distorted thinking, your mindset will change. Suddenly you'll understand that creativity is an immensely practical pursuit, one of the true sources of abundance in life. Unleashing your creative capacity is, in fact, your highest calling, the key to shaping the arc of your life. As powerful and dangerous as creativity can be, the only way you can really mess up this gift is by ignoring it as I once did.

I'm also living proof that the damage is reversible. I learned to hear my calling and found the way back onto my path. That's why I'm so passionate about helping others excavate and eradicate all of their toxic, limiting beliefs about creativity, how it works, and who gets to use it. At the top of that list is the belief that creativity is a rare talent limited to a select few. Nonsense! Creativity is a natural force. It's our culture that trains it out of us.

Creativity connects our default modes: thinking and doing, open and closed. When we're open, we're evaluating the possibilities and looking for ways to fit the pieces into a cohesive whole. When we're closed, we've got our nose to the grindstone and we're actively driving toward completion.

Being closed is fine. In fact, it's necessary—*if* we're completing the right thing in the right way. For example, if you're happy with the color and finish of that paint you've bought for the bedroom, don't just stand there. Roll up your sleeves and paint the damn wall. More often, however, we get stuck in the closed position. Usually, we're in such a rush to start that we don't give the color of our home a second thought. Until it's too late: "Ugh, everything is *beige*!"

We're taught from an early age to sit down, shut up, and do as we're told or risk looking weak, vulnerable, or foolish. As adults, the chronic stress and uncertainty of modern life keep us in that closed place, focused on checking off the next box on our to-do list. We get a kind of tunnel vision that prevents us from seeing the opportunities all around us. To thrive, we need to learn to weave back and forth between the two modes, open to closed and back again.

To be clear, by "creativity," I don't just mean "art," as in oil paintings and violin sonatas. Yes, art is a subset of creativity, but creativity itself isn't limited to specific crafts. It's the ability to make your ideas manifest in the world. It's problem solving. It's business and activism. It's raising a family. It's building connections, with others and with yourself, that make life worth living. Any creative craft practiced regularly—photography, coding, cooking—unlocks and activates your larger creative capacity. This allows you to see all the possibilities available to you and then choose among them to create the life you want.

According to the wildly creative actor, comedian, and author John Cleese, "Creativity is not a talent, it is a way of operating." To help you operate in this new way, I will draw on everything

I've learned about creativity—as an artist, entrepreneur, friend, husband, human being—to help you establish a rewarding and productive creative practice. Whether you create for a hobby, a side gig, or your day job, or even if you have no idea what you could make, this book might just save your life. I don't know where I'd be without this playful but sacred, silly but serious force of nature.

Pursuing My Own Calling

There's a reason it's so hard to follow our calling. The whisper of intuition telling us what we're meant to do and how we're meant to live comes from within, but it leads away into the unknown. Once I finally started listening to the call, I found myself on a new path. Not the path designed by my career counselor, encouraged by my parents, or suggested by society. My own.

It's a thrilling discovery to find yourself going where only you ever could. But hearing the call and finding your path are just the beginning. Next comes the doing. Walking my path took an epic amount of effort—hours of exploring, practice, trial and error—before there were any results. Money was a constant concern; I spent my first few years waiting tables on the side, eating ramen, and weighing paying household bills against the cost of buying film for my camera. Whenever I did have the opportunity to practice my craft, it was worth it—even if it meant hours spent clinging to the side of a snowy peak, clicking away with numb fingers.

No matter how tired or frustrated I became, I felt my feet on the path, and that made it all worthwhile. My intuition had been calling me all my life. Every now and then, I'd heeded it and experienced a rare sense of harmony and alignment without quite realizing why. Now I was listening with both ears and walking with both feet. For the first time, I was in tune with myself, and that made all the hard work more than worthwhile. Though it was nonlinear and nonsensical, my path made perfect sense once I truly started walking it. I'd finally discovered an outlet for everything that had been trapped inside me.

Eventually, the work paid off and I broke through. I started traveling the world to photograph campaigns for brands such as Apple, Nike, and Red Bull. Now it was coming together: my creative aspirations, my professional ambitions, the money. It was *working*. I'd found a wonderful and fulfilling career for myself and I'd grown tremendously as an artist—and then I heard another call to connect with other creators, to live a more collaborative, expansive life than the one I'd been leading. That craving for personal and professional connection led me to an entire ecosystem of like-minded people, each passionately following her own creative path. This global community existed in parallel to the workaday world. These were artists, entrepreneurs, builders, and makers of things who prioritized creation ahead of life's other demands. Many worked independently, others were free radicals operating inside large organizations. I found so much motivation just in knowing there were others out there forging their own destinies as I was mine.

In professional photography, people kept their techniques to themselves and viewed other photographers as competitors, not peers. Sharing and learning weren't part of the paradigm. I found this to be true in other creative fields as well. This had to change. Since each of our paths was fundamentally the same, I didn't understand why we couldn't travel our own paths yet stay connected along the way. The creative path is difficult enough; why couldn't we help one another learn and grow? Starting a blog, I wrote about my successes and failures as a creator. As the technology progressed, I started sharing behind-the-scenes videos about my work. By contributing to the creative ecosystem, I began to empower both myself and others. That rapidly led to a virtuous cycle of creativity, play, and discovery on the earliest social platforms, amplified by network effects.

Today, this kind of open sharing is normal for creative pros, but in the early days of social media, it was heresy. Old-guard photographers told me I was "destroying the industry" by sharing "trade secrets." Maybe I was putting myself at a disadvantage by giving away the knowledge I'd worked so hard to acquire, but hoarding what I'd learned didn't sit right with me. The opportunity to have an impact, create a community, and amplify my ideas seemed to outweigh any possible downside.

Disappointed—but not surprised—by the anger of my so-called peers, I pushed the criticism aside and doubled down on sharing. Deep down, however, I hoped other pros might eventually decide to share what they'd learned as well. I was still wrestling with "imposter syndrome," the feeling that "real" photographers knew it all and that I wouldn't be truly legit until I'd achieved complete mastery myself. Despite the substantial commercial success I'd already achieved, I still felt like a newcomer, an outsider, a fake.

As I continued practicing my craft and hurling myself at every emerging social platform and tool, I connected with ever-larger swaths of the worldwide creative community. They related to my work and my ideas because they were just like me—hungry for knowledge, stories, and experience. As engagement with my work grew, I realized that this phenomenon, whatever it was, was huge. Bigger than photography. Bigger, even, than art.

I didn't know it at the time, but the concept of sharing knowledge, building community, and empowering others to pursue their own creative dreams would lead me to CreativeLive, the online learning company I cofounded in 2010. Since then, more than 10 million students from every corner of the planet have consumed billions of minutes of video learning on our platform. We've built the world's best library of creative and entrepreneurial education, featuring more than ten thousand hours of the highest-quality learning. Our classes are taught by Pulitzer Prize, Grammy, and Oscar winners; *New York Times* bestselling authors; thought leaders; and game-changing entrepreneurs. Our classes, podcasts, and articles provide people with the inspiration and tools to unleash their own creative power and thrive in whatever they do.

The numbers still astonish me, but as I write these words some nine years into our journey, I feel certain we're just getting started. After all, the world has changed—we're long past the tipping point. Our species and our planet face a new set of challenges that only creativity can solve.

Who You Are

Right now, you might be replaying some of the things that have been said about your own creative capacity over the years. The words of parents, peers, teachers, and employers have a dramatic effect on our creative identities. A word of praise has inspired more than one creator. A word of negation has undermined many more.

How do you see yourself? Are you a novice, just getting started on the creative path and still skeptical that you have anything valuable to contribute? Have you been practicing a creative hobby for years but feeling the itch for a greater commitment to your craft—maybe even a full-time career? Are you an established creative professional struggling to make ends meet or to stay engaged with your work?

This book will help you regardless of where you are today:

- **AMBITIOUS PRO.** You identify as a serious, professional creator—even if your work isn't your primary source of income—and you want to take your work and its public reception to the next level.
- **STUCK CREATOR.** You want to make work, but you're not getting anywhere, whether because of conformity, economic pressure, or fear. You're open to a creative reawakening, but you're unsure how to light the fire.
- **DEVELOPING HOBBYIST.** You're content sticking with a day job that pays for your creative passions, but you want to increase your skills and develop a deeper and more productive creative practice.
- **CREATIVE CURIOUS.** You don't think of yourself as creative, but part of you wants to explore the idea that creativity is fundamental to human well-being.

Regardless of what camp you're in—full-time artist, entrepreneur, hobbyist, retiree, student, creator inside a company—this book will help you in ways you can't even imagine. That's the thing about creativity: You don't need to see the whole path. You just have to take the next step. And the next. The path of every creator takes many unforeseen twists and turns. That's its nature. The only way to "fail" at creativity is to stop walking the path altogether.

When it comes to creativity, no effort is ever wasted. Ever. Every unfinished manuscript, sunk business, crumpled charcoal drawing, or abandoned musical instrument represents another step forward. Once you understand that your entire creative journey—every clueless mistake, every stinging failure—is an essential part of your path, you will see that there is nothing to lose by taking the next step, no matter where it leads.

A New Way of Operating

Taken as a whole, *Creative Calling* offers a structured, robust, repeatable system for the creative process. Each chapter is carefully designed to build on the one before it. I've divided the chapters into four acronymic parts:

- Imagine what you want to create—without limitation.
- Design a strategy to make your dream a new reality.
- Execute your strategy and smash through obstacles.
- Amplify your vision to create the impact you seek.

IDEA is simultaneously a framework to create any successful project *and* a tool for creating the life you want. In large and small ways alike, it will allow you to manifest your creative inspirations—and reinvent yourself in the process.

Each element in this system is valuable on its own, but harnessing the true power of IDEA—and by extension this book—lies in committing to the complete process. For example, Imagining your most exciting outcomes and Designing a plan to get you there without taking action may feel temporarily inspiring, but ultimately it's just fantasizing. Similarly, Executing or Amplifying someone else's big dreams will leave you unfulfilled and perhaps full of regret. A full IDEA cycle where all the elements of the process work together, on the other hand, cultivates personal power and creates the results you seek. Whether they're aware of it or not, anyone who consistently drives successful outcomes—in specific projects and in their life in general—is using the IDEA process in some form to unleash their potential. By giving it a name, we can make sure we stick to this winning process in every area of our lives.

Once you've read through the book and implemented the suggestions that resonate with you, continue to rely on it as a trusted reference. Don't be shy, either. Scribble in it, reread it, dog-ear it, use it as a makeshift camera tripod in a pinch. Above all, take the recommended actions and see what happens. When I give you something to do, do it. Take this work as seriously as you would any process with the power to improve the rest of your life. A commitment to creativity will reward you many times over.

Along my journey helping millions of people pursue their creative passions, I have found that each and every one of us has been granted gifts. Yours are unique and specific. Job one is finding out what they are. Job two is bringing those unique gifts to bear. How? Pursue your own path, wherever it leads. Develop the skills to be successful in this pursuit. In moments of self-doubt, adopt a new mindset: stop avoiding the things you don't want and start chasing the things you do. The goal isn't to create a masterpiece; the goal is to make a masterpiece of your life.

Coming off the stage after a keynote speech at South by Southwest, the long-running conference and arts festival in Austin, Texas, I found a hundred or so people waiting for the Q&A. First in line was a woman in her forties who wanted to rekindle creativity in her life. She explained that she had always been passionate about design but that since leaving college, she had completely abandoned her dream of becoming a freelance designer. Not only had she chosen a "safe" career that left her unfulfilled, she had also given up all forms of creative expression.

When I asked her what was keeping her from going for it, she burst into tears. The demands of work, family, and life left her with no time or energy for herself. She felt completely stuck because her family relied on the income she brought in.

Without even realizing it, this woman had bought into a huge lie that so many of us accept. We internalize the idea that our calling is too risky, too impractical to even consider pursuing. That doing so would be selfish, deeply unwise. Deep down, we know we're selling ourselves out, so we carry this regret with us into each new phase of life. These faulty beliefs work their way into our bones as dogma, making it harder and harder to undo the damage as each year goes by. The only antidote, for this woman and for you, is to stop the madness right now. With love and empathy for yourself, gently summon the courage to make a change.

My answer to her was simple: Begin. Rekindle your creative craft for a few moments every day. Don't worry about the rest right now; simply sit down and make something. Once you've rekindled your practice, you can decide if you want to take it further and earn money on the side or even change careers. Conversations with family and loved ones will be easier when they see the passion and love you bring to your craft.

Hers is one of thousands of real-life examples that have inspired me to spread this message, whether through my podcast, *The Chase Jarvis LIVE Show*, on social media, or now in this book, the culmination of years of thought about the nature and importance of creativity in our lives. If you're in that woman's place, too, let this book and the community of like-minded people using the hashtag **#creativecalling** inspire and embolden you to take the next step.

When we say no to our creative impulses over and over again, they harden, like a bottle of glue with the cap left off. Thankfully, that hardened gunk can be softened again. The creativity within you is indestructible.

Every time a new batch of audience members arrives at CreativeLive's studios to participate as course students, I'm struck by the transformations that follow. People arrive on day one tentative, even closed off. A day or two later, they go home fired up to embrace new creative challenges. It's beautiful.

Knowing you have creativity inside of you is the key. Do you already see yourself as creative? If so, great. We'll build on that. If not, will you accept the identity you've been given or will you claim what's rightfully yours? Will you take ownership of your own life?

If you're willing to say that you are a creator, prepare to enter a world of possibility. There used to be a prescribed path for entering any particular career. This is no longer the case. Beyond a handful of professions, many of the most rewarding jobs today are intrinsically creative. They involve doing things that didn't even exist when the people doing them were still in school. The prescribed paths are crumbling away. The textbooks are moldering. It's never been more necessary—and *less* risky—to pursue your own path.

The world is at a crossroads, on the verge of a tectonic shift. Each of us must take responsibility for unlocking our own potential, no matter who we are or what we're trying to do. *Our creative calling is our highest calling.*

IMAGINE

Imagine what

you want to create—

without limitation.

1

Hear Your Call

No artist tolerates reality.

—FRIEDRICH NIETZSCHE

Put bluntly, too many of us spend years, even decades, in pursuit of someone else's plan for our one precious life. We're trapped: by our limiting beliefs, by the well-trod paths of others, by all our culture's "shoulds." But the trap is an illusion. The world would have you believe that a creative practice is an indulgence, an impractical waste of resources better invested in . . . something else, something more worthy. Watching the stock market? Performing science experiments? It's never very clear what you're supposed to do instead—only that pursuing creativity is lofty, selfish, or even naive.

But the truth is quite the opposite. Creativity is your birthright. Establishing a creative practice is the foundation for whatever it is you seek. Creativity is generous, life-changing, mind-altering, and practical as hell. In fact, it's only by creating in small ways every day that we come to understand that we can create big changes in our lives when we desire or need them most. It's only through developing a capacity to create *something* that we can create *everything*.

The System Is Rigged

The filmmaker James Cameron, writer and director of such films as *The Terminator* and *Avatar*, started coming up with movie ideas as a teenager. While the rest of the class memorized state capitals or studied biology, he scribbled notes about aliens and robots. Decades later, he's *still* turning some of those high school inspirations into colossal blockbusters. This is what I mean by a well of potential. It runs deep. (Imagine what he'll do as a director when he catches up to all the ideas he must have had in his twenties.)

But here's the thing: James Cameron isn't an exception in his capacity for creativity. All of us are born creative. Children are absolutely fired up to create, filled with ideas and eager to make them reality. Walk into any kindergarten classroom and ask if someone wants to draw you a picture. Every single hand will go up. Kids will be climbing onto their desks.

Unfortunately, it doesn't stay that way. If you make the same request in a fifth-grade classroom, maybe half the class will raise a hand. In a high school classroom? You'll be lucky if two teens risk volunteering. *That's by design.* Traditional schooling irons out our creative impulses in order to prepare us for the factory and the cubicle. Our educational system was made this way with the best of intentions, but that way of operating is wildly obsolete.

In second grade, I loved performing for my class: drawing, doing magic tricks, and telling jokes. One day, I overheard my teacher tell my mom that I was "much better at sports than I was at art." Inside, I cringed. But sure enough, at that moment I made a pact with myself to quit the stand-up routine and focus on sports instead. My story is all too common. We've been trained to avoid creative obstacles rather than risk trying to surmount them.

No more. Our natural creative instinct—our calling in life— doesn't go away. Whether you've maintained this spirit, recently recaptured it, or are setting out to rediscover it now, what's important is that this creative capacity still burns inside you.

Most of us have a gap in our lives between where we find ourselves and the life we actually want to be living. It's time for you to look at that gap, acknowledge it, and then use your innate creative capacity to close it. Stop acting out someone else's script and write your own: What do you want to make? More important, who do you want to be?

Hopefully, something stirred inside you as you read the introduction that preceded this chapter. (If you skipped it, go back and check it out.) Maybe you experienced a little itch, the faintest desire to pull a long-abandoned instrument out of the closet or dust off your hand tools. "Why not? Might be fun to savor a weekend afternoon without worrying about my to-do list for once."

Is this the call? Maybe. Or perhaps you've been hearing the call all along, but you've just been unwilling to act on it. Listening for the call is easy, but only if you know what you're trying to hear. Is it the murmur of the crowd—your parents, your peers, the tired cultural narrative as a whole? No. It's that quiet voice inside. Your intuition, your heart. You know the difference.

Intuition is the most powerful tool we have. You really can feel the truth of a situation in your body. Look back at the times when your gut told you to keep dating this person or finally leave that job: chances are it was telling you the right thing, even if you ignored its advice at the time, even if it took months or years to realize that your gut knew the right direction all along.

The "soft" intuition we've been taught to ignore is actually the most vital gift we are given, not only as creators but as human beings. After a lifetime of being conditioned to ignore your gut, however, it may be difficult to tap into and trust your intuition. Hard experience has taught me to pay close attention to mine at all times. When it warns me away or pulls me forward, it's always onto something genuine and important, even if it takes some additional reflection on my part to figure out what.

Listen closely to that inner voice. The answer is almost always right there in your gut, and science backs that up. Western culture has a long history of discounting the importance of intuition in favor of so-called rational thought. Only over the last few decades have researchers begun to discover that reason is far from perfect: everyday human cognition is limited, slow, and distorted by unhelpful biases. Meanwhile, intuition has increasingly revealed itself to be a mind-bogglingly quick, sensitive, and perceptive tool, rapidly picking up on subtleties and patterns in the world that the conscious mind isn't powerful enough to spot.

If you accept what I've said so far—that creativity is a boundless source of energy—then it follows that stifled creativity is an enormous energy drain. All that uncreated work and unexpressed self sit inside of you like a lead weight, dragging you down, sapping the satisfaction a healthy person finds in day-to-day life. In fact, you can consider yourself a really hard case if you're indifferent reading this right now. If your response to all this is "meh" and a shrug, you're bottled up *good and tight*.

On the bright side, that also means you've got that much more power ready to unleash. The only thing that matters is that you take action. Start creating.

The burden of tamping down your creativity every minute of every day is exhausting. It makes you sick, sure—stress and anxiety have proven negative health consequences—but it also drains your soul. Denying your creativity is like staying in a toxic relationship or a dead-end job because you can't imagine anything better. Sound familiar?

If you give yourself permission to trust the process and use these methods, you can obliterate whatever inhibits your capacity for sustained creative expression. The more you commit to the work, the more dramatic the results will be. It's a chain reaction: the more you give, the more you get. It won't be easy at first, but imagine how light you'll feel when you've finally begun making your ideas a reality, one after the other.

Being creative does *not* mean abandoning your career or throwing everything to the wind. That's a toxic myth. I'm not going to tell you to leave practical considerations behind. We all have our own path to a vibrant, rewarding creative life. How yours manifests is up to you. Whether you're looking for small ways to enrich each day, trying to jump-start a side hustle, or dreaming of a full-time career, creativity is a life amplifier. It's as fundamental to our well-being as physical fitness, proper nutrition, and mindfulness. Regardless of your intentions or where on the creative spectrum you fit, you are a creator and your creativity is not an indulgence or a luxury; it's required in order to thrive.

Your Words Make Your Mindset

Some people say, "Fake it till you make it." Forget that. *Make* it till you make it. Creators create. It doesn't matter who you know, what schools you attended, which parties you're invited to, or what you're wearing. Creators create. Action is identity. You become what you do. You don't need permission from anybody to call yourself a writer, entrepreneur, or musician. You just need to write, build a business, or make music. You've got to do the verb to be the noun.

The first and most powerful step in reopening your creative channel isn't learning a certain skill or uncovering a hidden talent. It's just identifying—remembering, really—one important thing: *YOU ARE CREATIVE.*

Words matter. If you aren't willing to think of yourself as a creator and declare that truth to other people, it doesn't matter what you *could* do or how much talent you *might* have hidden inside. When I finally admitted to myself that I wasn't going to be a doctor, I had some business cards printed up: "Chase Jarvis, photographer." I didn't even own a professional camera. All I'd taken were snapshots. But the business cards weren't really intended to convince potential clients. I needed those cards to convince *me*.

In conversations at parties, here in the United States, anyway, the first thing most people ask is "What do you do?" As embarrassing as it felt, I started answering the perennial question truthfully: "I'm a photographer." What people actually meant was "What's your paid, full-time occupation?" I no longer cared. It felt good to say who I wanted to be. Remember, *make* it till you make it. As soon as you start taking photos, you're a photographer in every way: conceptually, legally, in every practical sense. Sit down and paint: you're a painter. It's that simple.

This doesn't mean it's not difficult.

Once you stop sidestepping—or maybe even shunning—your creative identity, as I did when I was younger, everything changes. The formidable-looking barriers melt away. They were never real, they were always just words: talent, privilege, opportunity, luck. Sitting down and making real stuff has a way of clearing all that verbal cruft away.

Language is powerful. How you talk to yourself matters. When you are a self-proclaimed creator, you have an unbeatable advantage over those who are still ignoring their creativity.

Afraid? Even a little bit? That's a sign you're moving in the right direction. The very thought of putting something new into the world can be scary.

What if I'm not good enough?
What if this isn't the "right" thing to pursue?
What if no one likes me or my stuff?
What if I can't earn enough to make a living?

Fear is a gift, a precious instinct. Your primitive "reptile brain" is there to protect you and keep you alive. You can't reason with it; it learns through action. But if you take action *despite* the fear and survive, it learns a tiny lesson. Over time, action by action, the volume of the negative voices goes down. These might sound like the voices of unsupportive parents, critical teachers, cruel peers, and other frustrated creators you've encountered. But those people are not in this room with you right now. What you're really hearing is fear doing a table read. Your brain is just rehearsing lines from old scripts written by hacks, and the more you listen, the louder it gets. Ignore it. Write your own script.

Creative Obstacles and Hidden Strengths

I read biographies and watch documentaries to deconstruct the lives of the creators I most admire. Though the details are different, broad common traits emerge. Ernest Hemingway propped his Royal Quiet Deluxe on a bookshelf and typed standing up. Edith Wharton wrote in bed with a pen. But they both established creative rituals and stuck to them. They both worked steadily and published regularly. Pros go to work whether they're inspired or not. They allow for imperfection in their work. They finish what they start. They share their work when it's finished. The exceptions only prove the rule.

Struggling creators, on the other hand, struggle in different ways. The interesting thing is that each apparent weakness actually represents a misdirected or unharnessed strength in disguise.

Do you start many projects without actually finishing any? You may be a **Starter**.

Do you rework the same piece ad nauseam until you're sick of it? You may be a **Noodler**.

Have you been derailed by external forces? You may be a **Prioritizer**.

Do you object to the idea of being an artist? You may be a **Resister**.

Are you an active creator who isn't meeting some internal standard of quality, quantity, external recognition, or compensation? You may be a **Striver**.

You might relate to more than one of these personas. That's okay. Let's go through them and see what feels familiar.

The Starter

For Starters, the beginning of a creative project is an exciting time, a new romance filled with possibility. Whether you're envisioning a grand photo series on an important theme, the Great American Novel, or an indie documentary, there are no limits. You've got the run of your imagination, blue sky in every direction. There's no need to worry about budgets, timelines, collaborators, or—*gasp!*—finding an audience. Not yet, anyway. Just the bliss of pure imagination.

This part of any project can be intoxicating. For many of us, in fact, that's as far as we get. We buy the materials, order a stack of books, sign up for a class. Then something rises up inside of us and we veer, promising ourselves we'll try again, one day, when conditions improve.

A few of us push through the first wave of resistance and go further: take the first shots, type the first paragraphs, play the first few notes. Vision, meet reality. Right away, it's clear that the thing we're actually making doesn't match up to the idealized version in our head. Worse, we don't see a clear path to get from where we are to where we'd like to go.

Ultimately that's where Starters stop—after a few hesitant swipes of the paintbrush. Because you know what? There's a new, better idea to pursue.

> *Yes, I've taken a few good shots for the landscape series but a series of portraits would be much more Instagram-friendly.*
>
> *Yes, the first chapter of my novel is coming along, but I'd probably have more luck getting published if I wrote a short story instead.*
>
> *Yes, I have a few interviews in the can for my documentary, but by the time I'm done, this topic probably won't be as relevant to film festivals as this other one.*

Yes, we have a few paying customers for the web app, but it'll never be a unicorn. You know what might . . .

For Starters, the excitement about the next idea masks the reality: they are abandoning their current idea. Starters can put years, even decades, of work into a creative practice and come away with nothing concrete, nothing *done*. Worse, all those unfinished projects linger in their minds, taking up creative bandwidth. Over time, many of the "new" ideas start to look like variations on the old ones, though usually this is more obvious to everyone else than it is to the struggling Starter, who is constantly reinventing the wheel instead of, you know, rolling anywhere. In this endless chase of the new, things start to get old.

This weakness can be a strength. What is a Starter but someone bursting with passion and new ideas who hasn't yet learned to channel that passion and wrangle those ideas? If you identify as a Starter, you can learn how to focus on and fully execute your vision through any resistance, how to capture new ideas and act on them in a manageable way. That way, you can tackle them methodically, one at a time. The scale of the output that follows will be breathtaking.

The Noodler

Sometimes a flood of new ideas isn't the problem. As a Noodler, you're perfectly happy working on the project at hand. In your mind, you've uncovered a rich seam of material, and you plan to mine it. Starting isn't your problem. It's stopping.

When we pursue a creative project independently, there is no one around to tell us when it needs to be finished. As creators, we're always going to be far more aware of the flaws in our creation than others are, and some of us have a particularly hard time grappling with imperfection. *It's not ready yet*, we think. *One more draft. One more week of color correction. One more scene in the can.*

Underneath all of this is usually a fear of sharing the work. Sometimes, though, it's less about perfectionism than the urge to tinker. After all, we create because, on some level, we enjoy doing it. Saying that something is done means we don't get to play in that particular sandbox anymore. That can create its own fear.

A Noodler is a potential master who lacks certain skills. The greatest creators have the same capacity to stay with a piece and steadily develop it to its fullest. They achieve greatness not because they accept less than their best but because they have learned to recognize when they have reached the point of diminishing returns.

Work wants an audience. Sharing your creations is a powerful part of the creative process. Although each medium differs in its time requirements—and of course some projects do take years to complete—there is always a point at which more fiddling begins to eat away at the vitality of the work. Learning when to accept that you've done all you can is a key creative capacity. You will develop it.

The Prioritizer

"Hey," you're thinking, "I wish I had these problems. I've always been productive—when I sit down to work. If it weren't for my [family/medical diagnosis/financial problems/etc.], I'd have buckled down and finished my [creative goal] long ago."

Maybe that's true. But for that chronic illness or colicky first child, you might have stuck with your passion and even have gone pro. There's no denying that life gets in the way. This syndrome is particularly thorny because we *have* to prioritize in life. It's a matter of survival. We have a limited amount of time on this planet and if we don't learn how to put things in their proper place—financial security, health, family, and so on—we're never going to get past square one.

It is possible, even necessary, to prioritize your creativity alongside other essentials, such as your health and your family. You don't have to postpone creating until you're 100 percent ready or until conditions line up perfectly. Those things will never happen. Life is messy, and without creativity, it's incomplete. Creativity is not a nice-to-have, it's a must-have. Think of it as putting your own oxygen mask on before helping others in your row. If creativity keeps getting bumped, it's flawed prioritization.

Most of us don't have a coach standing over us telling us when it's time to throw in the towel and when we need to stand our ground. Without a single-minded focus, even obsession, it can be hard to justify spending time in the studio when you have a new baby at home, a work emergency, or a bad cold. The problem is, once you start prioritizing other areas of life over your creative needs, it gets easier and easier to keep doing so.

The lives of great artists reveal that for every lucky jerk with perfect health, an endlessly supportive spouse, and unlimited financial resources, countless more have faced obstacles at least as heavy as whatever sent you to the bench. The difference is, each of them persisted. Why? Call it grit, resilience, or sheer stubbornness. They understood the secret: working on what you love is like salt, it makes everything taste a little better. They weren't forcing their creativity out of grim determination but zestfully infusing their time on this planet with playfulness, joy, and whimsy. They brought creativity into their lives and life into their creativity.

Prioritizing creativity elevates everything you do. If you're a Prioritizer, the passion you have for performing at your best and supporting the ones you love will be your superpower—once you accept the value creativity has to offer.

The Resister

In *The Hero with a Thousand Faces*, the comparative mythologist Joseph Campbell described the stages of the archetypal journey faced by heroes across religions and mythologies. Those stages are universal, whether they describe Esther saving the Jewish people from Haman, Aphrodite intervening in the Trojan War to rescue her son Aeneas, or Luke Skywalker blowing up the Death Star in *Star Wars*. In Campbell's view, each of us is the hero of our own story, which is why these myths resonate with so many of us.

The hero's journey begins with a call to adventure. You felt that call when you realized you had something special inside of you that wanted to be expressed. Next, the hero refuses the call. When Obi-Wan Kenobi asks Luke Skywalker to join him in helping Princess Leia, Luke says no—even though he's been dreaming of leaving home for years. It isn't until Stormtroopers destroy that home that he becomes willing to heed the call.

Who knows why you've refused your own call? Maybe your parents worked their fingers to the bone to provide for you, so pursuing your passion feels self-indulgent. Maybe you have a fixed idea of what "creators" look or act like and don't want anything to do with that image. Maybe you worry that you have nothing of value to offer or that your art will never be good enough to share. Whatever the reason, you've hesitated at the gates. As a Resister, you are stubborn, pragmatic, rational. These are phenomenal attributes when facing down a creative challenge. Once you escape your limiting beliefs, there will be no stopping you.

The Striver

You may have a solid creative practice and a substantial community; you may even support yourself entirely with income from your creative efforts. You're reading this book because you're not where you think you *should* be. This dissatisfaction may be driven by your resentments against fellow creators. *Why did he get that award and not me? How did she get that grant while I applied eleven times?* It might be driven by a relentless inner critic. *This could be so much better. Why can't I do this as well as my creative idols do?* Impostor syndrome almost certainly plays a role.

For whatever reason, you don't have *enough*: talent, recognition, money, time, followers.

Some of these deficiencies can be addressed through strategy or hard work. Chances are, however, that there's a hole inside of you that will never be filled. Until you change your mindset, you will never be satisfied with your creative work—or your life.

Who is a Striver? Someone with a burning ambition to be farther along than he is right now, to grow and change and perform to his full potential. Isn't that beautiful? Once you escape the trap of "compare and despair," once you realize that the only path to walk is the one right in front of *you*, your progress will catch up with that limitless ambition.

Did you see your own creative identity in one or more of these personas? Great. Use that as a lens to help identify solutions throughout this book. If not, you may be a combination of two or more. That's fine, too. Hopefully, these categories will help you better understand your blocks as hidden strengths and recognize the skill gaps that are preventing you from capitalizing on those strengths. Now it's time to develop your skills. The strategies in this book will help you harness your strengths, not tamp them down. You need to bring everything you've got to the table if you're going to make your best work.

The Creative Revolution

Creative lives and creative careers are each *designed*. They happen intentionally. The so-called lucky ones, the people who live wildly creative lives or are paid to do what they love, *built* what they have deliberately and strategically. They created a vision and worked toward achieving it. Every one of them started exactly where you are now—or even farther back.

It's time to put your work boots on and start kicking some ass. No matter where you are today, you can design a fulfilling creative life for yourself. It's not important whether you're already a professional artist or simply "creative curious." Start from scratch. Ask yourself how you would truly like to express your creativity, not just in one bucket list item such as "finish that novel" but every day for the rest of your life. If you're a working photographer, maybe it's time to segue out of shooting weddings and start doing the fine art photography work that really fulfills you. If you're a pro in one discipline, that doesn't mean it has to be your only outlet of expression. Once the bills are paid, what makes your heart sing?

Don't judge it by commercial potential. In something like calligraphy, you may find an activity that not only engages you creatively but also deepens your primary practice. Steve Jobs credited the calligraphy classes he took in college for the strength of his design philosophy at Apple. (Plus, calligraphy is economical: you'll never have to buy another greeting card.)

Likewise, gardening is the embodiment of creative expression. You're given constraints: a plot of land, a specific climate, certain conditions of light and soil. It's up to you what to do with them. There is no "right" garden, only the one you choose to design, plant, and tend. If that isn't an art form, what is?

Regardless of what our culture will try to tell you, your age, gender, appearance, and background don't matter. Every aspect of you is fuel for your creative fire. If you want to act, you don't need to look like Halle Berry. We already have Halle Berry. Somewhere out there, films and plays need *your* face, *your* voice, *your* body. Likewise, a clothing designer doesn't need to wear all black and a poet doesn't need to live in a cabin in the woods. Let go of all your ideas about how a particular kind of creator looks or acts.

You are not your art. The greater the separation between your ego and the products of your creative efforts, the happier and more productive you'll be. So let go of all your assumptions and think. Ask yourself what creative activities you might enjoy. Don't worry about the product yet or where it will go. If you enjoy creating amazing dinner party experiences for others—at least some of the time—that's the important thing. It doesn't matter at this stage what you wish you had cooked or who you would like to have hosted. You don't have to be good at anything yet. You can learn. In fact, you'll begin to see the process of learning as a joy, not an obstacle. The only question that matters here is, what would you be excited to try?

It's time to start the gears turning and roll the possibilities around in your mind. Anything is possible: blacksmithing, ceramics, composing music, dancing, fiber crafts, filmmaking, flower arranging, gardening, glassblowing, jewelry making, joke writing, leathercraft, coding, painting, paper crafts, photography, playing an instrument, singing, or starting a business. It's the habit that matters.

This list just scratches the surface. The question isn't "Where will I end up?" but rather "Where should I begin?" The call rarely comes in the form of a ready-made career ladder with an internship to get you started. Your intuition provides directions, not destinations. Listening to the call will point you toward your path. It's your job to walk it.

2

Walk Your Path

Does this path have a heart? If it does, the path is good; if it doesn't, it is of no use. . . . One makes for a joyful journey; as long as you follow it, you are one with it. The other will make you curse your life. One makes you strong; the other weakens you.

—CARLOS CASTANEDA

Imagine a world with only two possible paths to travel. One is the path of reason and certainty. Well trodden, well mapped, it is a path of averages: average pleasure, average pain, average joy, average sorrow. Above all, average results. Along this road, you are certain to experience an aggregate blend, a mean, the middle of what's possible.

The second path is *your path*. Springing from within and obeying your heart's compass, it is unique to you. Your path isn't devoid of reason and certainty, but it's not trapped by them, either. It's not average because there is no data set to establish an average. Just you. At every intersection, you choose the direction using all your faculties, not just reason: intuition, instinct, heart.

This might seem like the risky choice, but it's far riskier to play it safe. Safety is an illusion in the realm of following your heart—a lie sold to us by suckers who are invested in protecting small lives and thoughts. On *your* path, nothing you do is perfect, but all of it is right. You're doing the best you can with everything you have, in tune with your authentic self. Because of this, nothing you do is ever wasted. Every experience contributes to the journey.

The world pushes us onto the first path because it's the easiest one for everyone else to understand. It's designed to produce consistently average results no matter who walks it. By contrast, you design the second path as you go, creating a life only you are capable of living. This leads to a much wider and richer range of possibilities. To follow this path, you simply have to hear the call and start walking toward it.

Even if you're not on your path now, you've intersected with it in the past. Trace your history. Look closely at times in your life when you were productive, fulfilled, and alive. You'll see moments—however fleeting—when you heard the call and actually *listened*. However briefly, you were on your path.

In chapter 1, you acknowledged that you are a creator. That label opens up a world of possibility. In this chapter, I ask you to accept that inner truth about what you'd really love to create with your life or experiment and play enough to find out.

Once you're able to tune in to this calling and take action to follow your own path, amazing things will begin to happen. First, you'll feel a new power. You'll be swimming with the current, instead of against it. Second, you'll understand why no one else could tell you what your calling is. Only you could ever hear it. Third, you'll start to trust yourself in a new way. You'll realize that going after what inspires, intrigues, or interests you will always lead to the progress and growth you seek.

Starting on the Path

At this point, you may be feeling some combination of excitement and fear. Excitement, because you're seeing new creative possibilities on the horizon. *Are you saying I could actually do some of these things? Get really, really good? Even transform my life?* Fear, for two reasons. One, maybe you're afraid you're going to have to quit your day job and live in poverty to pursue your dream. Two, maybe you're afraid that I'm going to make you choose just one dream. You might even feel both fears at the same time.

Take a deep breath. You don't have to downgrade your lifestyle to pursue creativity. Instead, you may find that you begin to value things differently, that with your creativity awakened, your idea of the good life becomes very different.

You don't have to limit yourself to a single creative discipline, either. David Lynch is known for directing films, but when he isn't on set, he paints, sculpts, and takes photographs. For almost a decade, he wrote a comic strip for an alternative weekly newspaper. A surprisingly high proportion of successful creative people express themselves across several mediums this way. Often, they find their "secondary" modes of expression just as fulfilling as the one that brings them money and acclaim. Gwyneth Paltrow hasn't quit acting to run her company, Goop, or write cookbooks, but the variety keeps her creative fire burning.

Life is about choices. Choosing to pursue every creative interest is equivalent to abandoning them all. We know where that road goes: ordering a bunch of how-to books and equipment, feeling overwhelmed when they arrive, putting them into a closet to deal with "someday," and going back to watching TV. Instead, choose one or two creative practices to pursue first and hold off on the dozen remaining ideas for the time being. Once you've made some progress along your path, pursuing additional areas of interest might be the perfect way to take a refreshing break from your primary discipline. Ultimately, committing to one area of focus for some period of time will help you later on.

Of course, your first choice may not be the one for you. That's okay. If you really aren't suited to it, you're free to go back to the drawing board (maybe literally). But commit to finishing a few pieces of work before moving on. You will learn something about yourself in the process. Each and every step along the creative path is a step forward; there are no wrong turns for an artist, only branches in a continuing evolution as you learn to express your point of view.

What matters is that you start. All you're deciding to do is to *try.* Do whatever you can with what you have. It will never feel like the right time. You will never be "ready." Avoid preparing too much. Start before you are ready. Start with fear. Start with uncertainty. This is one of the biggest secrets of the most creative, happy, successful people: Just start.

My Winding Path

I grew up in Seattle, an only child. In my household, I couldn't rely on video games to entertain me, so I spent a lot of time with my imagination. Something was always brewing in there. At the age of seven, I realized that "it" was a movie.

The neighborhood kids and I wrote a screenplay together. Luckily, there was a Super 8 camera at a friend's house down the street. Film was expensive, however, so we washed cars to raise funds. Then we assembled costumes and props, blocked out our fight scenes, and shot six thrilling minutes of footage, all chronologically composed in camera with only a few cuts and no edits.

When *Sons of Zorro* was ready for its debut, we plastered the neighborhood with flyers. Charging admission for the basement screening, we sold candy bars to our audience of parents and friends—everybody knows that concessions drive the lion's share of movie theater profitability.

While the Academy snubbed us in every category, we made thirty bucks on a film that cost fifteen bucks to make. A 100 percent profit—not every first-time filmmaker can claim that! More important, that early experience established a blueprint for creative living that serves me to this day. I remember thinking, "I wonder if there's a way that I could just do this forever."

The thing is, I stopped. Making and sharing my work meant putting myself out there, which was not something I was all that excited to do. We lived in a comfortable but vanilla suburb where sports were king. If the school system and the culture of our town had celebrated creative expression, it might have gone differently, but I was taught that creativity was something you did in art class using Popsicle sticks, pipe cleaners, and glue.

Putting the Super 8 camera back in its case, I joined the soccer team. It might have been better if I'd struggled at sports and been denied that social escape route, but I turned out to be pretty good, so sports became my identity for years. After *Sons of Zorro*, well over a decade passed before I picked up a camera to create, inspired by my father and his old Canon.

As a teen, I discovered skate culture, a world in which you can be both athletic and creative. Skate culture hummed with personal expression, from spray-painting the deck of your skateboard to consciously designing your entire lifestyle. It was a gift, the intimation of a path. But before I knew it, I was off to college, attending on a soccer scholarship.

I can see now that I had no heart in my half-baked plan to attend medical school. I just wanted to please my family. Social convention and family dynamics made my options clear: pro athlete or doctor. Mine felt like only one of many votes being cast.

Then, just a week before my college graduation, my beloved grandfather passed away from a heart attack. Devastated by the sudden loss, I learned to my surprise that my grandfather, an enthusiastic amateur photographer all his life, had left me his camera collection. My grief found a new direction. Losing my grandfather on the cusp of a career path—a life—I'd never wanted set me free. I felt pulled to take pictures as both he and my father had.

At the time, this idea seemed to come out of nowhere—I hadn't touched a camera in years outside of a photography class in high school. But the notion struck a deep chord and I committed at an entirely new level. You see, a burst of sudden inspiration isn't a goal or a strategy. Inspiration fades. Something major can happen in our lives and convince us that we *really* want to be X, Y, or Z, but if we don't follow up on that intuitive hint with *action*, the feelings will evaporate and we'll be right back where we were.

Into action, then. I packed up my grandfather's cameras and left for Europe with my then girlfriend, now wife, Kate, and what little savings we had. We'd backpack around while I taught myself the craft. For a backdrop, I had everything from the Swiss Alps to the sandy beaches of Greece. For a subject, I had Kate. I was surrounded by beauty.

At ten bucks a roll of film and twenty to develop, we'd camp out, eat beans and tuna fish out of the can, do whatever it took to see the results of my work. The process could take a while, so I'd keep careful notes about every shot to remind myself of the choices I'd made: "Frame 2 of St. Peter's Basilica, f/8, $1/250$ of a second on the shutter, overcast." Six weeks later in Budapest, I'd finally get to see whether I'd made the right calls back in Rome.

After months of this regimen, I felt as though I'd cobbled together a basic understanding of composition. That perfect alchemy—six months of freedom, adventure, new love, and my grandfather's cameras—catalyzed a period of incredible creative growth in my life. I started to come into my own. This, I realized, was what I'd been missing. Since *Sons of Zorro*, anyway.

Returning from Europe, I decided to explore action sports photography. The mix of sport, culture, and a free-spirit lifestyle was seductive, bringing me back to my days as a young punk in the skate park. At the time, I didn't see how I could ever make a living, but we were determined to defer "real life" a little longer. Why rush into a traditional career before giving photography a shot? So we drove to a mecca of action sports: Steamboat Springs, Colorado, headquarters of some of the best ski and snowboard athletes in the country. What better place to enter the community and practice the craft?

As soon as we arrived, we found jobs: Kate in a restaurant and me in a ski shop. Though we worked hard, we still had more time than money, but we didn't care. Each night, Kate would put her tips into the rent jar, and once we felt pretty confident about the rent, the rest went to film. I had to shoot selectively. Often it came down to taking photos or eating something other than ramen again. It wasn't always fun and none of it was easy, but it felt right, as though I were gradually zeroing in on . . . something.

You couldn't ask for a more astonishingly beautiful natural environment: towering snowy peaks, sweeping vistas in every direction. I befriended skiers and snowboarders while working in the shop, tuning their boards during the day and hanging out with them at night. Despite my amateur kit, no one seemed to mind being photographed. I wasn't even documenting per se—we were collaborating to create the images we wished we could see in the magazines. That meant countless frozen hours crouched on icy mountain slopes before returning home to develop negatives in my bathroom-turned-darkroom.

At a certain point, I realized I'd gone beyond what I could do in a bathtub. That's when a friend attending the local community college serendipitously offered to give me a tour of the fully equipped darkroom on campus.

I didn't have enough money to take the class with him as he'd hoped, but I was *very* interested in seeing the darkroom.

Not my proudest moment: I jimmied the lock on a window before we left. The following night, I crept back in and spent the next few hours blissfully developing and printing my photos. Just before dawn, I tidied up, put gaffer's tape over the latch to keep it open, and sneaked back out. Given the relative success of the operation, I made a habit of it. Same routine each time: I'd let myself in through the window around 1 a.m., develop and print feverishly for four hours, tidy up, and sneak back out around five. Now that I'd acknowledged my creative passion, I was willing to go to any length to make my work.

Questionable behavior aside, the dedication paid off with my first professional sale. The marketing team for a ski brand came to town to take some promotional images. I took the opportunity to show them my portfolio. To my surprise, it surprised them. On the spot, they offered me five hundred dollars and a pair of next season's skis to use one of my images in their campaign. It was the first indication I'd received from the universe that I could actually get paid to make the work I loved.

As time passed, I started piecing together even more sales. Again, I'd like to be able to say that I took that momentum and catapulted myself into a full-time photography career. But no,

I veered again. I was still too invested in the cultural narrative about "starving artists." Thinking I could square that circle and reconcile my creative yearning with my desire to make my family proud, I applied to a PhD program in Philosophy of Art at the University of Washington. Even though I had tasted the joy of pursuing my dream, even though I'd figured out how to get paid doing it, I found myself leaving the path.

I was never under the illusion that a doctorate in philosophy would guarantee financial security. In school, however, you're *safe*. You're back on the smooth, socially acceptable track leading through elementary school to higher ed to a nine-to-five job. In school, you know where you are and where you're going. You know what you have to do to "succeed": just check the right boxes.

Of course, I hadn't moved on completely. It was no coincidence that I chose to study the philosophy of art. Clearly, I was still feeling the pull in another direction. To pay the bills while I was in school, I got a job at the brand-new REI flagship store in Seattle, once again embedding myself as deeply as I could in the action sports industry even as I prepared for the life of an academic. I couldn't help but cringe at the images decorating the store: inauthentic, outdated, soulless. With very little to lose, I approached the merchandising manager and showed her my portfolio. Why not? I was a philosopher in training, after all, spending my days discussing Hegel, Husserl, and Heidegger. There was no risk involved whatsoever if she laughed it off (I told myself). To my delight, however, she offered me ten thousand dollars to license a handful of photos.

Ten grand. That was how much I'd earned *the entire previous year*. And I was doing what I loved.

Now it hit me. PhD or no PhD, it was time to get serious about my photography. The money went toward upgrading my gear.

My free time went toward improving my skill set. Self-taught, I had a long way to go toward professional mastery. Continuing the program of study I'd begun in Europe, I began deconstructing the work of experienced photographers in the action sports industry. Every spare minute between photographing, working, attending classes, and writing academic papers, I reviewed photos in magazines. (I couldn't even afford the magazines, so I'd just stand in the bookstore for hours with a notepad.) Conveniently, each image featured the name of the corresponding photographer, allowing me to connect the art with the artist.

For each image, I'd ask myself: What are the elements that make this good? Why did someone choose this image over the hundreds that must have been available? Technique was critical, that was obvious, but at this level, technique was a given. What elevated an image?

The first and most obvious element was the location. The photos were nearly always taken in well-known or aspirational places—you'd see the background and think, *I've always wanted to go there.* That factor alone winnowed out many aspirants. Most would-be action sports photographers don't have the time, money, or dedication to get themselves to those remote, often international, locations to fill their portfolios.

The second element of each winning photograph was the subject. It's common sense that famous athletes would feature prominently in magazines and ads. But so many aspiring photographers can't, or won't, figure out how to find and photograph these icons. Most dismiss the notion as impractical and photograph friends or random strangers instead. Then they wonder why their amazing images don't sell. The answer is simple: magazines don't want to buy photos of anonymous snowboarders.

The final element was the action happening in the photo. It had to be impressive, even astonishing, to work. Nobody wants a photo of the latest snow hero on a bunny slope.

Clearly, I needed to get into the pro scene to assemble the winning elements. Once I'd reached the aspirational locations, I'd find the top-tier athletes. Once I'd found the top-tier athletes, I'd have to connect with them somehow to capture one of them in action.

That method of deconstructing what works into its component elements has been the key to my success as a creator and an entrepreneur. You put the elements together in the best way you can and see what happens. Remember what works, forget the rest. Keep homing in until you've figured out the winning formula. Then use that formula consistently.

It sounds simple, but it's shockingly powerful:

Deconstruct
Emulate
Analyze
Repeat

DEAR for short.

I started going out on the circuit. Red Bull events, the X Games, anywhere the greatest athletes would be competing, I'd go, come hell or high water. I'd get up in the middle of the night and drive for hours or I'd take the cheapest, longest flights with the absolute worst itineraries—whatever it took to get to the location. Then I'd ascend the mountain before dawn and sneak into the area reserved for pros. Sometimes I'd actually stick my camera through the fence designed to keep me out in order to get a shot that *looked as though* it was from the same spot established photographers could access.

Being on location like that provided another benefit: community. At each event, I'd introduce myself to athletes, other photographers, brand reps, and magazine editors. As soon as I got home and developed my shots, I'd know exactly where to send the winners. Lo and behold, my photos started selling. I'd been chasing the dream on and off for years, but to the action sports world, it was as though I'd come out of nowhere.

"Dude," they'd say, "we've never heard of you, but these shots are awesome. Where have you been all this time?" "Oh, here and there," I'd reply. "I've been shooting for REI, mumble mumble, commercial work, mumble mumble. This editorial stuff is new for me, though." I was carefully tap-dancing around my limited experience.

My bona fides didn't matter because my photos stuck to the winning formula. They sold and sold. Usually, you'd spend years working for a star photographer to learn the ropes and enter the scene. Everyone would get to know you as "Fred's assistant" before you were given permission to go out on your own. I'd jumped the line, going from anonymity to two-page spreads without spending a day assisting anyone. That wasn't the accepted path to a professional career, but I quickly realized it didn't matter.

The negative voice in my head tried to tell me that I hadn't earned my stripes, that I should be ashamed. In turning away from that voice, I was proud, less about what I'd accomplished than about the way I'd accomplished it. I'd found my dream destination with a compass, not a map, a compass that had led me along my very own path. Yes, it was an awkward, circuitous one, but in the end it had landed me at my destination years ahead of the "traditional" timeline despite all the detours and painful lessons along the way. In fact, it was while taking that idiosyncratic journey that I began to understand my creative self and the agency I had to write my own script and walk my own path.

It would serve my ego nicely to rush through my own struggles on the creative path to get to the part where some magical epiphany told me exactly what I was about and what I wanted to do with my life. It was never that simple. It still isn't. I'm on the path with all its twists and turns, and I always will be. Sometimes it's hard and confusing. On a handful of occasions, yes, an epiphany has given me more clarity—but never the whole answer. I'm still seeking, just like you, but I'm grateful to have learned enough to help other creators make some sense of their creative calling.

It comes down to your values. What is most important to you in life? There's something about creative work that brings our values, or lack of them, front and center: "Do I quit or do I keep beating my head against the wall until I make it work?"

In creative expression, unlike any other arena of human behavior, there is no objective measure of success, no One Right Way to do something. This means we're always vulnerable to the lure of the easier, safer road. It's counterintuitive, but if you value money, comfort, or convenience over your own creativity, you jeopardize all four.

The path I took through Europe and Steamboat Springs and my early professional career revealed my core values. What truly matters to you? However you define your values, your creative work belongs very high up on your list, if not at the very top. Creativity is essential to your health and happiness. When you are creatively fulfilled doing work you believe in, you become a better spouse, parent, sibling, employee—it feeds into it all. Those who are willing to prioritize their creativity reap endless rewards in every area of life. It's transformed mine.

Effortless Hard Work

A few decades ago, the right path was clear: graduate from college, get a "good job" at a company working forty hours a week for forty years, and get the gold watch. Today, there are any number of paths leading to an unimaginable array of destinations that are changing all the time. What's so exciting about this moment in history is that the gatekeepers no longer hold the keys. Your career is less about the options at the job fair and more about exploring the call you hear when you lie awake at night, staring at the ceiling. When you hear the call, follow your path, and begin to arrive at dream destinations, it doesn't matter how you got there. No one questions your pedigree, whether you went to the right school or know the right crowd. All that matters is what you've done—and that you did it in your own weird, unique way.

Following your own path is like writing a script for a film. You can decide to write an indie flick or a summer blockbuster. Set modest goals or the loftiest ones imaginable—it's your world to create. *You* establish the settings, *you* develop the characters, and *you* work out the plotlines.

Since that's the case, my question to you is: Why settle for anything less than a glorious surround-sound epic? As a photographer, I quickly learned that selling my work for a hundred dollars took about as much effort as selling it for ten thousand— the difference was who I was selling it to. The limiting factor was my vision and ambition, not the infinite world of possibilities around me.

Do you want to go pro as a macramé artist or create an abundant life inking web comics? Who says you can't do those things? And what have those naysayers ever done themselves? It takes hard work and persistence to achieve *any* goal, so why not reach for the stars? There's an old Chinese proverb: The person who says it cannot be done should not interrupt the person doing it.

Two things happen when you stop holding back and start pursuing goals you actually want to achieve:

- **PEOPLE WANT TO HELP YOU.** When other people start to see how much you care, they want to join in. You find your tribe this way. We need other people, a community, to help us create the work and life we want for ourselves.
- **THE PATH WILL PULL YOU.** When you're on your chosen path, you'll find that you rarely need to push yourself to work. Instead, you begin to experience the joy and excitement of being pulled toward your objectives.

If you've never felt the pull before, this may sound too good to be true. But it's legit. Going after your authentic dream is a massive accelerant. There's nothing more invigorating than pursuing your true calling instead of settling for adjacency: writing instead of editing, acting instead of agenting, being your own boss instead of working for someone else. You may truly want to be an editor or a talent agent or a manager—and that's great. You simply have to figure that out for yourself. Just don't tell yourself that settling for less than what you *really* want is the smart choice. It's a fool's bargain. That's because you don't even know what's possible. Listening to what's calling you and deciding to follow the path makes anything feel possible. Once you've felt that pull, you'll never want to push again.

I moved to the mountains of Colorado to defer graduate school, to get away from a life I wasn't sure I wanted to live. As I tapped into that part of myself, however, something shifted inside me. I went from "getting away from school" to "moving toward what I loved." It was as if I realized I'd been walking in someone else's shoes for years, right down to the blisters. By comparison, photography felt like a custom pair of Chuck Taylors, broken in and comfy as hell. I didn't come to that realization by buying cameras, reading books, or thinking about what life as a photographer might be like. I just *did the thing that sounded like fun*—the thing that was calling me. It wasn't always a monumental trumpet from the mountaintops. Sometimes it was as quiet as the click of a shutter. Indulging my curiosity, I walked the path and felt the pull. I became hooked. That was all I needed to keep going.

There was fear, of course, but fear never goes away when we're trying something new. Insecurity and discomfort are integral to the growth process—to creating art and creating yourself. You just learn to trust your fear and let it guide you. Keep making marks on the page, following that internal unease, until you've written something true. When you do stumble off the path by ignoring your creative calling for a while, it's okay. Your only job is simply to get back to it.

If you're familiar with meditation, this process might sound familiar. Nearly every meditation tradition involves directing your attention—to your breath or a mantra, for example. When your attention wanders—to your grocery list or a song you heard on the radio—your only "task" is to realize what is happening and redirect your attention to your focus. Pursuing your creative calling is the same. By regularly practicing, you will realize when you go off track so you can bring your attention back to realizing your dream. The creative call is always present no matter how faint or how far off the path you wander.

You'll encounter failure along the way. But so what? It's an illusion that society's plan for you is any safer. This is the riskiest time in history to play it safe. "Go to college so you can get a good job and enjoy financial security ever after"? Audiences will accept superheroes and monsters in their action blockbusters, but they'll never buy that absurd fantasy again. Absolute economic safety has always been a myth, but the promise of stability in a soul-sucking, full-time job you hate has never been more obviously false. The problem is that the human brain evolved to keep us safe, not happy—it will resist your efforts to walk your own path because creativity challenges certainty. It will even accept the comforting illusion that there is certainty along the traditional path. It's a lot harder to ignore the risk when you're being creative. By necessity, you're trafficking in the new, the unknown.

In fact, the creative path is far more resilient and ultimately safer than any soul-sucking job. Creators learn to mitigate risk, make smart bets, and always protect the downside. In practicing their craft, they learn to be flexible and proactive in all aspects of life. With their ingenuity and drive, it's impossible to keep them down for long.

The Big 3

While traveling along the path you've chosen, you'll certainly feel moments of effortless success—the pull of creative flow, joy, and ease—but you're also guaranteed to encounter struggles along the way. Though the details of any struggle will be particular to your situation, the fundamental challenges are pretty much universal. As such, I'd be remiss not to share what I call "The Big 3." These challenges crop up in nearly every creator's journey: money, creative control, and the company you keep.

Money

Start talking about money and creativity in the same sentence, and you're bound to piss people off. I can tell you until I'm blue in the face that you don't need to make money from your creative work to consider yourself a creator. That I wrote this book for every single creative person whether aspiring, amateur, or pro. That you're free to ignore anything I say that relates to the commercial application of your work. Regardless, no matter how many caveats I throw at you, I'll still get angry tweets and reviews telling me I got it wrong for talking about money in a book that aims to help you unlock your creative power.

Forget all that. I'm here to give it to you straight. At some point along your path, money is going to come up, even if it's simply to buy supplies that serve your hobby. So what? Money is not, in fact, a dirty word. Whether or not you *choose* to make a living through your creative work, I'd like to call attention to your unexamined beliefs about money. These common distorted ideas hold creators back from achieving their full potential.

The stubborn myth of the "starving artist," the threadbare but exuberant poet who has to choose between ink and food, isn't just false, it's toxic. Notions like this drain your energy and either get you chasing dollars for all the wrong reasons or encourage others to take advantage of you by undervaluing your work.

Textbooks and Hollywood biopics usually gloss over the everyday financial dealings of great artists. As a kid, you never hear about Michelangelo haggling with the Vatican over pricey lapis lazuli paint for the Sistine Chapel ceiling or, more recently, Kathryn Bigelow fighting for top-tier budgets. No one tells you that Ansel Adams wasn't too proud to accept a payment of 25 cents for allowing his photos to be printed on restaurant menus—and that the decision didn't scuttle his career.

In the end, it's no wonder that our feelings about the intersection of money and art are complex. And it doesn't matter whether you just want a creative boost in your life or you're trying to turn your side hustle into a full-time gig. Ask yourself whether the ideas you cling to about money and art are based on reality or are part of society's script. If the latter is true, have those limiting beliefs held you back from the prosperous, productive creative career of your dreams? Or even from making a little extra scratch with your hobby?

If they have, why are you holding on to them?

We want our Michelangelos and Bigelows to get paid for their sculpting and filmmaking so they can keep on doing it. And we acknowledge that Ansel Adams might have made the right call to take the quarter at that point in his career.

No matter what you've heard or read, creators can make it work financially if they don't get precious about doing it. When artists can't figure out how to pay the bills, we all lose. Without money, how are creators supposed to eat between their feats of transcendent communion with the Muse?

There is nothing noble, edgy, or cool about being a starving artist. Starving sucks, plain and simple. Believing in the myth of the starving artist is also a self-fulfilling prophecy. When aspiring artists have this distorted belief, they accept little or no money for their work, the rest of society gets creative work done too cheaply, and as a consequence other artists have a harder time charging appropriately.

If you don't want a job that involves your art, find one that supports it. Whether you decide to just get by financially so you can spend time making as much art as possible or you reduce your time commitment to art to keep it stress free and keep your steady paycheck rolling in, you're making your work, and that's what matters.

The fact is, creators hold wildly different attitudes toward money. Begin to examine yours. Don't get precious about it. Have an open mind when it comes to cash and creativity, and do what is in alignment with your calling—and your path to getting there.

Creative Control

Whether you pursue a creative practice for personal expression, professional success, fame, or simply to bring joy and inspiration to others, you will eventually have to stand up for your work, your vision. Creative control can become an issue whenever you work with other people. It doesn't matter how successful you become. Movie directors fight to have the "final cut" of their films. Stars are written off their TV shows. Founders of startups strive to retain control of their companies.

Advocating for your work can also mean setting healthy boundaries, from negotiating with your spouse or partner for time to practice with the band to drawing a line in the sand when a client pushes you in a direction you're not willing to go. The questions you want to answer now are: What matters to you about your work? How much does it matter? And why?

Contrary to the beliefs of some beret-wearing *artistes*, it's not required that you know everything about where you stand on your art, memorize your responses, and be prepared to defend them at a moment's notice. It's fine for your values to grow and evolve over time. Just know that unless you're a Buddhist monk, at some point you're going to need to negotiate with others and advocate for your vision. You don't have to be willing to die for your art, but you do need to begin the process of deciding what matters to you and why.

The Company You Keep

When you begin to embrace your creativity, you'll notice that the people who love you the most will react in all sorts of unexpected ways. Your friends and family may be the first ones to tell you that you shouldn't walk *this* path, that you need to be "safe" by going back to operating in ways they can easily understand and pursuing goals that make sense to them.

In cases like this, Kermit the Frog gives the best advice: "When you decide what your Big Dream is, you'll be bursting with enthusiasm and want to share it with everybody. Most everybody will give you one of those 'Okay, that's nice, now please pass the ketchup' looks. Some will scoff, suggesting that whatever your Big Dream is, it's too big for you. And a select few will whisper words of encouragement. My advice is this: Pass the ketchup. Ignore the scoffers. And remember those words of encouragement 'cause they're the only ones that matter."

Have some empathy. Acknowledge that it's scary to watch someone you care about change in significant ways. It's even worse to watch the person you love go where you've always been afraid to go yourself. It's understandable that other people want you to be safe, but that doesn't mean you should let them deter you from pursuing your dream. You can love your family. You can trust your friends. You can listen to their encouragement. You can hear their concerns. But in the end, you must decide what works for you. Your life is *not* a democracy.

Ultimately each of The Big 3 has everything to do with your values. You will encounter each one at some point as you walk your path. In my career, I've witnessed the many ways people use money or power to exert their will on others. I've been guaranteed unlimited creative freedom—even in contracts—and had that control yanked from my fingers. I've been shown the door when my ideas were judged too difficult, weird, or expensive. I've disappointed family members who thought I'd gone astray. I've stood my ground and given up large chunks of money to protect my integrity. I've also compromised when I needed to put food on the table. It never stops. All you can do is become clearer about your values over time.

Though you may make some bad decisions along the way or even lose some battles that really hurt, you have to win the war. Just remember that "winning" simply means seeing a positive slope over time. Know thyself, and you'll be just fine.

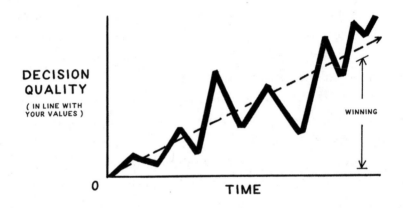

Be the Hero of Your Own Life

To begin the hero's journey, Joseph Campbell told us, we must follow our bliss. Once we heed that inner call and take the first step in a new direction, we're on our way. But becoming a hero requires crossing a mystic threshold at the start. In most myths and stories, that threshold is protected by a fierce guardian.

For most of us, the guardian of the first threshold isn't a deadly sphinx—it's whatever is getting in the way of your starting down *your* path: your fear, your current job, your priorities, or even the people who love you the most.

According to Campbell, the threshold guardian isn't necessarily the hero's enemy. In fact, it can often turn into an ally. But early on, it will test your resolve. If you are able to push through your fear and continue the process of growth and transformation, you may look over to realize that the once-fearsome guardian of the threshold has become a trusted helper at your side.

Be the hero of your own life. Walk your own path. When obstacles arise, go over, under, or around them. When you lose your way, listen for the call. Your heart will always lead you.

3

You Stand Out

The things that made you weird as a kid make you great today.

—JAMES VICTORE

What if you gave full rein to your imagination for once—and envisioned for yourself the life of which you've always dreamed? Then doubled it?

Sure, there's a line between imagination and fantasy. The problem is, none of us is very good at drawing that line. We dismiss and deny our wildest aspirations to avoid even the possibility of failure and rejection. In doing so, we extinguish all the passion and vitality we might have brought to the field of play. Whether we dream big or small, we will encounter our fair share of failures in life. So explain to me, where's the glory in failing to get something we never really wanted? If we're going to get a dose of failure along our path, shouldn't we taste it while going after what we really want in life?

In this chapter, which is dedicated to envisioning a more creative life for yourself, it's time to face reality—then bend it to your will. What is truly possible for you? Whatever your answer is, whatever success, accomplishment, or fulfillment you've only imagined might be within your reach, let's pause to acknowledge that you're likely thinking too small. *We all do that at first.* Small is comfortable and familiar. It feels safe—even though it's anything but.

To rise up, you must stand out, and proudly. This isn't about making a scene just to be seen. It's about being truly and completely authentic to yourself. When you bring your genuine self to bear on what you do and how you do it, you can't help but stand apart from everyone else. There is only one you—*you* are the highest value you can contribute.

Standing out like this can feel exhilarating—or exposed and vulnerable. It depends on your mindset. Adopting a creative mindset is what this chapter is all about. The more comfortable you become at being completely authentic, the more you'll distinguish yourself from everyone around you.

Isn't it funny how we try rebelling to stand out? One generation rebels by wearing leather jackets and riding motorcycles. Suddenly everyone's wearing leather jackets and riding motorcycles. Another generation turns to tie-dye and Birkenstocks to escape conformity. Next thing you know, there's a run on Birkenstocks and every concert you attend is a sea of psychedelic T-shirts. The cycle never ends. Rebellion is always a reaction. That means it's just another form of control—you are controlled by the thing you are rebelling against. It's not a choice; it's a trap.

Instead of rebelling or conforming, simply choose. *Choose yourself.*

Don't kid yourself, though. Being yourself is difficult. No matter how far you go as a creator, it will always be a challenge to remain authentic. It takes bottomless courage and confidence to become vulnerable and to stay in that place of discomfort in the face of both successes and failures. You have to learn to be okay with sticking your neck out over and over again.

From another perspective, standing out is the easiest thing in the world. You never have to pretend or do anything out of character. There's no sophisticated strategy. You just have to do as you do and get used to doing it. It's scary as hell, but it's not complicated.

Here's the thing about fear: when we let people see how weird and different we are—and, to be clear, we're all weird and different—we're taking a risk. What if they don't like what they see? In contrast, hiding feels safe. The truth is that hiding to fit in is the biggest danger of all. We're entering a new era where creative thinking will be the most important, most valuable skill anyone can possess. You simply can't do it while blending into the crowd.

This doesn't mean we can't mitigate the risks involved in being ourselves and standing out. There's an art to being an artist without becoming so vulnerable that you crumple in your first fender bender.

We'll get around to managing the risk. But first we have to tap into our authentic selves—no matter how deeply they've been buried.

Follow the Fear

Creative thinking can be hard. It takes energy—your three-pound brain burns 20 percent of your entire body's calories—and the new ideas we generate are disruptive to the people around us. Most of them are just trying to "get things done." That's why the Industrial Age had no time for creative thinking by the mass of individuals—it would have lowered the efficiency of the factories.

All schools are prep schools in a way. They prepare you for Industrial Age careers. Your teachers and parents meant well, but our educational system was designed using a twentieth-century factory as a model, with efficiency in mind, not creativity or diversity of thought. Being told over and over to sit still, raise your hand, and use a number-two pencil has an effect on you. From an early age, we spend seven hours a day, 180 days a year, in a classroom. If we head to college, we've been head down at our desks for well over fifteen thousand hours. If it takes ten thousand hours to achieve mastery of a subject, what skill have we mastered in all that time? Not being disruptive, and doing whatever it takes to make the grade. After all that training, it takes a hard nut to come out the other end with her vitality, whimsy, and originality intact. The rest of us are going to need to excavate. We have to relearn how to access our unbridled creativity by tapping into the raw part of ourselves that gave us joy before society pasteurized it.

To find that buried vitality, just follow your fear. Ask yourself: What makes you weird? What are the things about yourself that you are most unwilling to share? What are the parts of yourself that you find ugly, distasteful, scary, or unacceptable? It could be that you're resentful of the sister who always got your parents' attention, even though she's always been good to you. It could be that you're not sure you're in love with your spouse anymore. Maybe, for all your talk about beauty being internal, you wish you were ten years younger and you're considering plastic surgery. Whatever it is, pull it out. Tap into those painful areas— that's where the magic is waiting, the authentic, vulnerable parts that are jet fuel for your most creative work.

Take Steven Spielberg, for example. The guy has long been a creative genius. He transformed cinema with blockbusters such as *Jaws*, *E.T.*, and *Jurassic Park*. But it wasn't until he tackled his own personal struggles with culture, identity, and religion that he was able to make *Schindler's List*, the masterpiece that elevated his stature and earned him his first Academy Award for Best Director.

You see, this isn't about skill. Spielberg was a terrific director before *Schindler's List*, and he remains one despite having made *Indiana Jones and the Kingdom of the Crystal Skull*. This is about revealing your authentic self. Even in a movie about aliens, dinosaurs, or swashbuckling archaeologists, all the audience wants to receive from us is truth. The deeper you go, the closer they will come.

James Joyce once said, "In the particular is contained the universal." Your story is unique, weird, *particular*. When you share your truth with others, they connect with a universal truth within the particular. That's the real reason it resonates with them.

Zero In

The more you narrow your creative focus, the faster you will learn and the more effective your work will become. Think about your favorite artists and entrepreneurs. They may do many different things now that they have the freedom to do so, but how did they stand out in the first place—through a focused approach or a scattershot one?

Zero in. If someone will give you money to learn something new, take it, but don't put a section full of dog photos on your website if you don't want to be a dog photographer. If you want to be a dog photographer, then include *only* those photos. William Wegman built an entire career out of photographing one breed.

You can't boil the ocean. No matter what your creative calling, breadth is helpful only when you're exploring. Chances are you're great at one thing, okay at three others, lousy at five. Four good photos beat a mix of three great ones, three mediocre ones, and one stinker. To the outside observer, the negatives substantially outweigh the positives. Focus on the winners.

Once I was walking my path, once I'd found my creative niche, my photography—and my life—had focus. The difference was dramatic. Suddenly I went from wandering the woods to sprinting like a track star. I dropped out of grad school and went from my first few local clients to working with some of the world's biggest sports brands. Before I knew it, I was doing major photo shoots with renowned celebrities and athletes in remote locations of astonishing beauty. Focus made it possible.

I'm not saying you know where that focus should be just yet. You'll find it through doing the work. Once your intuition tells you that you're moving in the right direction, however, focus *ruthlessly*.

Wake-up Call

Despite all my experience and extensive backcountry and avalanche training, I had butterflies. It had been storming in Alaska for days now; the snow was measured in feet, not inches. Then we'd had a break in the weather and we were going to take it. Would the conditions hold?

With the owner of one of the top heli-skiing operations as our guide and a cadre of some of the world's best skiers, we were setting out to capture some epic photographs. The images we created that day would serve as ads for Nike, as magazine covers, and in editorial spreads for the top action sport magazines.

Once we started out, my jitters evaporated. The conditions were perfect. The athletes swept down steep, untouched mountain faces. They leapt off cliffs, cornices, and snowy spines with grace and power. The pictures flowed as easily as the snow under our skis.

I'll never forget one particular peak. The helicopter touched down on a knifelike ridge, and the guide hopped out and shoveled out a small flat area so that the three other athletes and I had a place to gather atop the ridge. As the chopper pulled away . . . *wop* . . . *wop* . . . *wop* . . . we were left perched atop the snowy peak in silence with two thousand vertical feet of fresh snow below us.

With avalanche precaution protocols complete and an agreement on the route of descent, the first athlete dropped onto the face of the mountain. My camera shutter blazed as she ripped one turn, then another, and finally a third before dropping out of sight behind a snowy spine and descending to the valley floor. I changed positions as another athlete dropped into the line, and another one after that.

With just me and the guide left up top, we radioed the others that I'd get into a new position and pause in a "safe zone" adjacent to the prime ski line to capture some images of our guide, a legend in the industry. With my photo gear tucked safely away, I dropped into the steep face to move into a new location. One turn, then another.

And then it happened. The avalanche.

I heard a loud and deep *whump* that I'll never forget. For a moment, time stood still—even though I was traveling at a tremendous pace. Then I was in what avalanche survivors call the white room, named after the color of the snow. But it's not white to the victim—it's pitch black as you're pulled under the surface. Tumbling, blind, swept along with a million tons of snow and

Volkswagen-sized chunks of ice—slowly at first, then twenty, thirty, forty miles an hour.

Footage of avalanches can make them appear deceptively slow, like a gentle white tide sweeping in from above. No. When you're in an avalanche, everything is obliterated in an instant. You can have all the training and take every precaution; you're still extraordinarily vulnerable to the power of an avalanche.

My thoughts raced even as my body tumbled. I recalled the size of the peak, the depth of the fracture lines, the several feet of snow that had fallen over the previous several days, the un-forgettable *whump* sound; the entire mountain face must have ripped off. Almost immediately, I recognized that I was very likely going to die. If I was going to cheat death, I had less than five seconds to do so.

And somehow I did.

Through a blend of skiing techniques, avalanche survival pro-tocols, luck, and an adrenaline rush that produced some super-human strength that's still hard for me to explain, I escaped with my life intact.

Thankfully, no one else was caught in the slide, and my injuries were minor. The one thing the avalanche did obliterate that day was my complacency. So often, a new call sounds at a turning point in our lives. In an ideal world, we'd spur reflection and shake ourselves out of comfortable, old routines by way of a vipassana retreat or a solo road trip with a blank journal and a nice cup of coffee to reevaluate our priorities and set a new chal-lenge. But if we don't choose this in the normal course of events, we might just get flung down a mountainside, narrowly avoiding death. That can work, too.

That night, I lay awake and thought for hours. Only five years earlier, I hadn't even been a photographer. Now it seemed as if my career was at its peak, but in the moment when all of it was nearly taken from me, I'd felt small and self-centered. As successful as my life might have appeared to others, living *my* dream, I knew I could create orders of magnitude more impact if I became willing to take real risks again. I'd learned my craft, I'd surpassed my ten thousand hours of training, I'd built a great career as a photographer. But I was still playing it safe because I wasn't listening to the call. I'd become complacent.

Sure, I was willing to risk my life—case in point, putting myself on a snow-loaded slope in Alaska. But coming so close to death in pursuit of an extraordinary photo forced me to recognize that I craved more than success in commercial photography. I wanted to create extraordinary impact. The next step on my path would be to embrace my unique, curious, adventurous self in all my imperfection and work to help others achieve their biggest dreams.

Every period of creative growth in my life before that had coincided with a risk: abandoning the security of medical school, taking my grandfather's cameras to Europe, moving to Steamboat Springs to try action sports photography. The moment I'd experienced success, however, I'd started to shy away from risk. Before, the only thing at stake had been a life I didn't want. Now I had things to lose: security, a career, a community. If I wanted to stand out, I would have to be willing to ante up everything I'd gained and more.

Developing as a creator meant accepting the possibility of making something people didn't like or saying something people didn't want to hear. It would be much easier to keep my head down, make my clients happy, and keep cashing checks until I was too old to hold a camera steady—or until my luck turned, as it almost had that morning.

Lying in bed that night with the cold of the day still in my bones, I realized that the prospect of taking genuine creative risks in my career had seemed a whole lot scarier *before* I had faced down a massive wall of snow.

Your life has two big arcs. The first is about acquisition; acquiring knowledge about yourself and the world—figuring out how to meet your own needs. What am I going to do to make a living? Will I get married? Buy a house? Have kids? The second arc is about contribution. You start thinking about how you can serve others and make a lasting impression on the world. We take, and then we give.

The avalanche sparked a major transition for me. It expanded my circle of awareness from simply meeting my own needs to extending my contribution to the world. I started thinking about ways I could pass on the gift I'd been given, the gift of creative expression. How might I inspire and empower others to pursue their own creative aspirations?

That tectonic shift in my thinking ultimately led to writing my blog, sharing my online behind-the-scenes videos, building a worldwide community of creators, developing the Best Camera app, and eventually building CreativeLive. It all started on that slope in Alaska.

As we move through life, it's easy to see how really big events—the births of our kids, a diagnosis, the loss of a job, or a close call with death—grab our attention and force us to take stock. But in reality the call that we're meant to heed—the wake-up call—is always there for us, if we're just willing to listen more carefully.

The Rules Are Meant to Be Broken

School teaches us that life is a game to win against our peers. We're graded on a uniform scale no matter our background, our strengths and weaknesses, or our future goals. Sometimes we're even graded on a curve relative to our peers. This inane, pointless system of competition is baked into the twentieth-century educational model. We're taught that life is a game of musical chairs and that if we don't hustle, we're going to be left standing without a seat.

This in-it-to-win-it mentality is the polar opposite of a creative mindset, which is abundant, resilient, and full of potential. Aiming to be "better" is a dead end because it means you're walking in someone else's footsteps and trying to catch up.

Life gets so much easier once you decide to play your own game. Don't just try to be better. Be different.

I learned to put more of myself into my work while experimenting with video. On the surface it might have seemed like a distraction from my "real" work in photography, but it became a catalyst for my career. My early experiments with video were shorts about my personal exploration of my photography, about what it was like to be an up-and-comer, finding my personal style while traveling the world. In making and sharing those videos, several things happened. First, I became a better storyteller. There is a synergy between moving and still pictures; work in each benefits the other. My learning curve steepened. Second, in opening up about my personal creative journey, I helped others by sharing techniques of the trade that were hard to learn in books: my lighting tips, my business strategies, and the methods I used to get my best shots. Third, because all those behind-the-scenes videos were so radically different from the norm, I immediately created an awareness about my work in the market.

None of the established photographers was doing this. In fact, they found the whole idea of sharing methods sacrilegious. It was "against the rules." After all, if you show people how to take professional photos, you're going to have to compete with more professional photographers in the world. That never worried me. Skill is just one way to stand out in a crowd. In pursuing my genuine, authentic curiosity about video and storytelling and transparency, I found a different way to stand out from my peers. That was eye opening to me back then, but it makes a ton of sense to me now. Following your call and pursuing your own path? That can only be you. I started playing my own game back then, and that made the difference.

"Think different" isn't just a slogan. It's a credo, one that made Apple the most profitable company in human history. People accused Steve Jobs of creating a "reality distortion field," but he understood that *reality is already distorted.* Apple would never win by trying to build a better mainframe computer. That would have been playing by IBM's rules. Instead, Apple created a *personal* computer because that was what it wanted the future to look like. The blue suits at IBM laughed because those cute little boxes couldn't beat their room-sized business beasts. But Jobs was playing a *different* game—his own. And today, in large part because he played his own game from the start, his company sells millions of phones that can outcompute any of those old IBM behemoths.

It turns out that the so-called rules—"work your way up the ladder," for example—were put into place by someone aiming to keep you distracted from following your own path and keep you focused on following someone else's. Follow the rules at your peril.

When we tell our parents or peers about a creative aspiration, more often than not we're told to face reality. "You can't be an X, Y, or Z. That's a pipe dream." Listen up: There is no such thing as a "real" reality for you to accept. When people say "that's the way things are," they're revealing a big, fat limiting belief that is standing in the way of everything they've ever wanted. Think like Steve Jobs. Forge your own reality. If others can do their own thing, why can't you?

Whenever you get yourself caught up in the "not me" trap, the sense that you'll never "make it," whatever "it" happens to be, you're chasing someone else's tail, maybe without even realizing it. Ask yourself whether you're working on a project that fires you up or creating something you think other people will like. Would you listen to this album? Would you use this website? Would you sit through this talk?

Make meaning, not money. Pursue your values. Pluck something straight from your own authentic weirdness and share it with the world. Forget about some blogger's three criteria for commercial viability. The zeitgeist is not something you chase, it's something you create.

Yeah, werewolf movies with a strong female lead might be hot now, but movies take years to make between brainstorm and box-office smash. By the time you've decided to jump on the bandwagon, a zombie script written out of genuine love of the reanimated dead will be entering production, destined to send the zeitgeist spinning off in a new direction.

No more bandwagons. In blazing your own trail and leaving your own footprints, you are far more likely to make something better—effortlessly, through the joy of exploration and discovery. When we love what we're making, we lean into it. We progress so much faster. And people will love it not because it's more of the same, executed perfectly, but because, however rough, it's a breath of fresh air. Even if your genuine expression doesn't shift the mainstream or your vision fails to create commercial success—if that's what you sought—could you ever really have made something worthwhile if it hadn't come from your heart? The answer is most likely no. The road to recognition is lined with the souls of those who chased recognition alone. Ironically, the people we celebrate as cultural heroes are those who blaze their own weird and winding trails.

Labels Stick

Sun Tzu's legendary treatise *The Art of War* offers a strategy for defeating your enemy, whether it's another general on the battlefield or a rival startup muscling in on your business model. The strategy I offer you in this book is designed to help you win the battle in your head. When it comes to creativity, you are your own worst enemy.

One of the simplest and most effective ways to get unstuck and start making the best work of your life is to let go of all the negative labels you've attached to yourself over the years. "I'm not an artist, I'm a surgeon, a mother, a practical person . . ." Our brains are incredibly tuned in to labels. If you think of yourself in a certain way, your mind will do its best to make sure you become that thing, body and soul.

Take "weird," a word that is often affixed to openly creative people. In our society, "weird" has negative connotations, but what is it even in contrast to—normal? What could be more boring? Who wants to be an extra in someone else's movie?

Yet I fell for that trap. I was a weird kid. I liked to do magic tricks, breakdance, and perform stand-up comedy for the class. Those things were not "normal" for my town. As soon as I was old enough to understand that my interests were weird, I ran as far as I could in the other direction. Looking back, that is one of my few big regrets in life.

Labels come at us out of nowhere, often from completely unexpected directions. That's what makes it so hard to defend against them.

One day, I awoke early to go for a run. Two steps out of bed, I collapsed onto the floor, unable to see straight or move without throwing up. Viral labyrinthitis had attacked my inner ear. It's not an uncommon condition, but my case was so severe that my doctor said that my dizziness might never go away, I'd likely be sick for the rest of my life. Wow. Talk about a label. Sick for the rest of my life? That really got into my head. Though I did recover over the course of several months, I was scarred for years. Long after the virus was out of my body, I experienced the symptoms of PTSD. Anytime I'd move my head quickly or lose my balance for a moment, I'd have a panic attack, thinking the virus had returned.

Through therapy, I came to understand that it was *my acceptance of the doctor's label*, not the infection, that had done the real damage. Overcoming the label of "sick person" and getting back to being me took a tremendous amount of work. This is the power of labels to steer us off course. Think about some of your own labels, the ideas you have about yourself or that others have put on you. A few unexamined words can stand in the way of your becoming the person you want to be. You tell yourself either that you're creative or that you're not, and that will be your reality. Accepting the wrong label is debilitating. You have to be aggressive about rooting out negative labels and limiting beliefs.

You are creative. Say it out loud. Write it down a hundred times. Whatever it takes to force your brain to accept its new programming. The label matters.

Trying to Be Liked Makes You Less Likeable

Growing up, we build up layer after layer after layer of protection to keep ourselves safe. Every time we say something weird in class and the other kids laugh at us or we get picked last for a team, every time we put ourselves out there and fall flat on our faces, another layer of scar tissue is added. Eventually our real selves, and everything that makes us worth knowing, are buried.

The *central relational paradox*, a concept developed by the noted psychiatrist Jean Baker Miller, is simple but profound: we all want close, intimate relationships. That means we need people to like us. The problem is, we worry that they won't like *all* of us, so we hide the parts we consider bad or just different. When our true selves are hidden, other people find it very difficult to connect with us. They can tell we're closed off, and they don't feel safe opening up to us. Therefore—cue the paradox—we end up without any close, intimate relationships. See the problem?

Nowhere is this paradox more visible than in the arts. It's obvious when artists make art to please others. You can tell they're projecting a certain image of themselves—cool, edgy, hip, whatever—instead of revealing what makes them "bad or just different." When an artist is willing to show us her truth, to be vulnerable, it's so real and authentic you feel as though you've known that person your whole life, even if she was born five hundred years ago on the other side of the planet. When we hide what makes us unique in order to get people to like our work, we neuter our work.

The self-defeating desire to be liked does more than hobble our creativity. We hide in all sorts of other ways; we'd rather be invisible to friends than be seen in a negative light by a stranger. We become allergic to the very idea of rejection. When a friend tells you he has given up on getting his novel published—the novel he spent years writing—because of a handful of rejection letters, you're watching this allergy in action. If you've spent years, months, or even a few days creating something, why wouldn't you invest an equivalent amount of time in finding an audience? Again, it's our desperate desire to be liked at all costs that prevents us from connecting with people who will love the work.

It's all ego. That's why it's helpful to call it "*the* work." That simple "the" helps separate the stuff we make from *us*. I can take a bad photo without becoming a bad photographer or, worse, a bad person. (Illogical as it seems, it can sometimes feel that way.) Some work is better than others, and I'm able to see that—and get better—because I don't see any one photo as a statement about me, Chase. Chase deserves unconditional love. Some of my photos, not so much.

This self-protective hiding takes many different forms. Sometimes, making a lot of different things at once is a way of hiding. If we scatter our energy and never finish anything, we never have to share our creations and risk rejection. Even if we do finish things, having many different projects going at once can be an attempt to lessen the sting of rejection. If you submit ten photos to ten different competitions, any individual rejection won't hurt as much. I'm all for doing tons of work and getting yourself out there, but don't let fear turn you into a dilettante. Be willing to zero in on one thing you want to do next. Focus, improve, and take your ego out of it. Stop hiding.

Take Risks to Keep Growing

It's simple: you can't stand out and fit in at the same time. If you never make anything, if you make only what you're comfortable making, or if you make but you never share, you're *hiding*. Once you start hiding, you stop growing. Part of you goes to sleep. Even as I reached what I thought was my creative zenith, it took an avalanche to reveal an even deeper level of authenticity. I meet so many people who get stuck at such a point without even realizing it.

To take creative risks not only once but again and again requires getting out of your head and tuning in to your heart and gut. Our survival instincts evolved to keep us safe from sabertoothed tigers. News flash: they're extinct. We no longer face mortal danger on a daily basis. Instead, our brains turn their attention to the things that *feel* life-threatening: public speaking, for example, or asking someone out on a date. In a misguided attempt to protect us, our brains tell us to fit in, make friends, get "likes." Being an artist means standing out, revealing yourself, becoming vulnerable to others. Art is truth, and the truth cuts both ways.

If you've read along up until this point, you may already be on board with the idea that creativity is a core human function that plays a fundamental role in our health and well-being. If we don't rev our creative engine regularly, something inside us withers. This is true both metaphorically and practically. "Use it or lose it" is true of both Muses and neurons.

Creativity requires risk, real risk—something has to be at stake *for you*. What you're doing has to matter. Mistakes should hurt. All those bruised hips and scraped knees taught me how to ride a skateboard. If you know what the outcome will be before you start working or you don't care what happens either way, where's the lesson? Where's the growth? We improve as artists by taking chances. If you never fail to do what you set out to do, you're not learning and you're not growing. Mistakes are a sign that you're pushing yourself to your limits by tackling meaningful challenges.

At home and at school, we're taught that mistakes are "bad" and that people who are "good" at things don't make mistakes. The truth is that the best performers in any field are the ones who routinely take risks, the ones who are willing to face rejection and gamble the money and the acclaim to keep growing, to stand out.

Even if we accept the idea that a safe life is a small life, many of us reassure ourselves that we'll take the real risks later, one day, when we're rich enough, successful enough, popular enough. In other words, we'll take risks when it's safe to do so. I can tell you from personal experience that that magical day will never come. You will begin to take risks only when you realize it's more dangerous not to. Success only raises the stakes, making risks harder to stomach. Once you have popularity and money, the necessary creative risks become scarier than ever. Worst of all, this trap is a gilded cage. To everyone else, and even to yourself, it can look as though you have everything you ever wanted.

I'm grateful for that avalanche. Looking back, I can see that if I'd continued on my path by making one safe choice after another in the hope of preserving my newfound success, my creativity might have slowed to a stop as I lost touch with what had motivated me to work in the first place. You've got to be willing to risk what you've got or you risk losing it.

Now's the time to decide: What price are you willing to pay to live your best life?

Manage Risk Like an Entrepreneur

I've had the opportunity to meet and work with a number of the world's greatest venture capitalists. Good VCs understand risk. Most startups will fail, but the ones that succeed can more than make up for all the rest. That's how the game works. Anyone with some money can become a VC. Remaining a VC? That means weighing the risks properly so you can keep your seat at the table. It's just like Vegas: once your pot is empty, you have to go home.

Creators can learn a lot from VCs. We are the capital *and* the venture. Again and again, we slide our chips—time, attention, and reputation—into the center of the table and wager them. To stay in the game as creators, we want to make lots of bets when the stakes are low. But often we measure the stakes all wrong, valuing our dignity far too much and our integrity far too little. A creative failure doesn't cost you much beyond a little embarrassment; selling out for a quick buck can cost you everything.

Seth Godin and I once talked on CreativeLive about his childhood experience of going bowling with friends. His mom had given him enough money to play a certain number of games. Each game offered a certain number of rolls. That meant each and every one mattered—you didn't mess around. You kept it simple and rolled as straight as you could. No trick shots, no play, no experiments, no funny business. He contrasted this with the "unlimited bowling" offered by the era we're in today. On the internet, for example, you're in an arena where you can try things, build things, and share things as many times as you like and take endless creative risks without remorse. I love this concept—it reminds me of the freedom offered by digital cameras over film. I can take as many risks as I want with my camera. Unlimited exposures.

There is no reason to hide. Be bold. Take smart risks. Embrace failure like an old friend. People respect a wrong move made with confidence far more than a correct one made without conviction. If you're writing a blog post, improvising a scene, or putting together a new and unusual service offering for your business, the stakes may feel high, but they aren't. Go for it. If you fail, learn from your mistakes and move on.

But what about when the stakes *are* high? Does that mean

you shouldn't try? People get stuck in dualistic thinking here. It's either risk it all or play it safe. Successful people got where they are by taking huge swings, right? So if you're not willing to take out a second mortgage on the house to fund your startup, you might as well give up. That's a false dichotomy! The most successful performers weigh the merits of every risk before taking it and *they protect their downside*, often invisibly.

If you're playing roulette in Las Vegas, your goal—if you're smart—is to have fun for as long as you can. You know that the house always wins. Once you've decided how much you're willing to bet, the trick is to maximize your time at the table. You might feel like a big shot putting everything on red, but that gives you a 50 percent chance of heading back to your room to watch TV all night. Make an array of bets and you get to play longer. Serial entrepreneurs have the same mentality. The people on the covers of magazines are almost always more risk conscious and risk averse than you realize. You might get lucky once or twice with a big bet, but your luck will always run out. If you want to stay at the table, you have to learn to assess risks and anticipate problems.

To get Virgin Airlines off the ground, Sir Richard Branson made a deal to buy a used 747 from Boeing. When it comes to risky moves, starting an airline is up there. So is investing a hundred or so million dollars in any new business venture. But Branson has been successful over the long haul because he knows how to hedge his bets. When he bought the first plane, he prenegotiated a deal to sell it back to the manufacturer and recoup most of the money if the airline didn't take off. That part of the story is usually glossed over by the magazines. Think big *and* be prepared to mitigate any losses. Remember: if you bet everything on red and lose, you're going back to your room.

Be honest and clear about the risks you're taking. Figure out what things cost and how long things will take *before* you move ahead or call it quits. When you consider a new project, take out your notebook and answer the following questions:

What is the goal of this project?
Why am I doing it? What do I hope to get out of it?
What is the worst thing that might happen if I fail?
What steps can I take to reduce risk and mitigate failure?
Is it worth it?

Every big creative project calls for a risk assessment because most of us risk too little to truly stand out. It's only once you sit down and write out all the worst-case scenarios that you realize that the shadowy fears circling around your head aren't really all that concrete or overwhelming. They're just manageable obstacles.

Yes, if you take some money out of your savings to buy gear for your streaming video channel, you might get into financial trouble down the road if, for example, you and your spouse lose your jobs at the same time. On the other hand, the channel is a major goal for you that lines up with your creative interests and aspirations. What are some things you can do to cut costs? Consider bartering, sharing gear with another videographer, renting more expensive gear instead of buying it, and so on. What are some things you can do to mitigate the risk? If the channel doesn't take off, you can always try a different channel concept. You can offer your videography skills and gear to local companies as a side hustle. You can sell the gear on eBay to recoup some of your investment. And so on. Once you've labeled your risks and your plans to deal with them, your outlook will change. What felt impossible will feel doable, exciting, filled with promise.

Today, time is a more common limiter to our creative ideas than money is. Thanks to technology, we have movie cameras in our pockets and recording studios in our laptops. We can publish books with the click of a button and start profitable, robust online businesses with shockingly inexpensive digital tools. Best of all, we can learn how to do all of it for free. It just takes time, and lots of it. How much time can you afford to invest in making something that matters to you?

Time is precious. Never risk it blindly. Do a risk assessment there as well. Let's say you want to write a book but between work and family obligations, you never have time to do it during the day. One risky choice would be writing at the office while pretending you're working and hoping you don't get caught. The risk there is your livelihood—it's substantial.

As an alternative, why not get up at 4 a.m.? Not forever, that's an ungodly hour, but just until you've achieved your creative goal. If you get up early to write every morning for two years and publish a best-selling book, that's a clear win. You can now afford to quit your day job and write full-time. If your book bombs, what's the downside? You'll have given up a little sleep and a little time on the couch at night without sacrificing important family time or your day job. You'll have proven to yourself that you're able to set a creative goal and meet it, which is absolutely invaluable. You'll have become a better writer. Creativity is about reps, about building your creative fitness. You've worked your conditioning to peak levels. Now you can continue getting up early if you enjoy it or try something else for your next bet.

Smaller Risks = More Creative Possibility

Hedging your bets frees you up to play. For example, I go into each commercial photo shoot with a crew of professionals to assist me and hundreds of thousands of dollars of photo equipment. Those are big bets for everyone involved, so it's very difficult to take real creative risks while on set. Contrary to what you might think, big shoots are usually about the execution of a previously conceived idea. There is very little creativity involved. You have to produce something that looks a certain way. There's very little joy in checking the boxes; it's all about executing according to the brief.

By 2007, the rigidity of the process had started to get to me. I loved my work, but I also needed simple, open, free creativity in my life, without formal limitations. It was around that time that I got the new iPhone. Its camera couldn't compare to the ones I used for work, but hey, it was in my pocket. That phone became an incredible creative escape during my shoots. I'd walk around during breaks and take the pictures that interested me: a manhole cover with an odd pattern, an imprint left by a boot in the snow. In that way, photography became carefree for me again. Just play. Can you imagine me dragging my crew and $100,000 in camera gear to go take a picture of a boot imprint? The iPhone let me be in the moment for a few minutes of whimsical experimentation. None of the photos had to *be* anything.

Ironically, that new hobby led to one of my greatest professional successes. Living life with a camera in my pocket, I saw that the world was about to change. We were all going to have these cameras with us at all times. We'd never miss a picture of a kid's first home run or first recital again. Once we all had smartphones with decent cameras, we would photograph everything and would want to share it all. That insight led me to create the Best Camera app, which kicked off the mobile photography craze. Keeping things small and simple brought me to a gigantic milestone in my career.

Something similar happened when I discovered a service

called Ustream. Entrepreneur Brad Hunstable and his talented team built an app for broadcasting live video on the web in order to help military service members overseas stay in virtual face-to-face contact with their families back home. This is cool, I thought. Why not use it to give aspiring photographers an inside look at a professional photo shoot? With only a little bit of effort and practically no risk, I was able to show 25,000 people exactly what I did to photograph a punk band for its album cover in real time. The success of that zero-stakes experiment led to my podcast, *Chase Jarvis LIVE*, and then, ultimately, to CreativeLive. I didn't play with Ustream to launch the Next Big Thing or raise venture capital. I just tried it because the tech was there and it seemed like a worthwhile experiment. Damn. Who knew? Whimsy and play sparked two of my biggest professional successes.

In my experience, it's the small risk taken to satisfy a creative whim that is more likely to lead to a real-world success than the triple-down, bet-the-house investment with some enormous hope at the other end of it. If you're struggling to get a big project off the ground, you may need to lighten up and try something smaller.

Signature Style

You will never reach the next level as a creator if you don't develop a personal style. Unearthing authenticity and expressing it in high fidelity is the most valuable thing, the single most important creative aspiration you can have. You can learn how to make stuff really, really well. That doesn't mean you will know who you are as a creator. As a musician, you may be able to make beats, build songs, and perform live, but until you've found a way to make your work *distinctive*, you will never have a lasting hit. As a screenwriter, you might be able to craft a perfect three-act structure with a clear protagonist and a clear antagonist—but until you know what *you* are about, any movie you make will be a snoozer.

It's like a fingerprint. Two or three measures into one of Adele's songs, you know exactly who you're listening to, even if that particular song is new to you. It goes beyond brand to the very DNA of your work and your process.

So what's your special sauce, the flair only you can bring to a creation?

"Wait," you're thinking, "what about variety? I get bored easily. I want to bounce around between making different kinds of things and trying different styles." If you spend your valuable time chasing other people's styles, you're going to be miserable and burn out quickly. The world doesn't need another Adele. Of course you can't help imitating at first, that's how we learn, but what you *should* be doing when you borrow from other artists is testing things out, trying things on, and gradually building your own tool kit. Let your style become more and more authentic to you, not what you think it should be. Fluency as an artist boils down to developing the skill set to make things look, sound, and feel the way only you can.

If you keep making lots of stuff, you will develop your style. It always goes back to your authentic self, the stuff that makes you weird. Forget better or even different. Think *only*. There's only one of you. Only you have lived your life. Only you have *your* point of view. Figure out how to share it with the rest of us. Your point of view is the highest value you can bring. Once you can create work with a distinctive and recognizable personal style over and over again, the world will unlock itself for you. Even if your work is not recognized, you will have unlocked something precious in yourself.

Incremental improvement is valuable, but the only way to stand out is to double down on *you*. Always look for more ways to bring yourself into your work. There are no shortcuts to doing this, unfortunately. It takes time. The best way to discover and cultivate your signature style is to make lots and lots of the same kinds of things. You can't force it, and you can't bounce around in search of your style in some external source. If you try to *instill* style into your work, it'll ring false. It'll just be your idea of what your style *should* be. Style has to come from within, from your work, from the way you approach your process. Don't sit around and think about it. Work and work and work, and your style will arise naturally, organically. Make it till you make it.

Let go of that voice telling you that you have to try everything. Focus. You can't be all things to all people. If you try ten different styles at once, you'll never become distinctive enough in any of them to be recognized. Make ten things in the same genre. Once you've made ten, make a hundred. Once you've made a hundred, look back. Lo and behold, you'll catch a glimpse of what makes your work truly distinctive. Keep at it, and people will start to be able to pick your work out of any lineup.

Some people find their unique truths in the trauma they've experienced. If that's not you, don't go digging for it. Find the universal in the particular. Your unique genius might lie in the way you see the everyday annoyances of life in the office or something else that looks banal on the surface but simmers with richness and detail. This is why repetition is your friend. Instead of trying for a certain style, just make your work and let your style emerge from the things that move, inspire, and energize you. What are you curious about? What made you weird as a kid?

Find yourself. The deliberate cultivation of your signature style should be a key priority in your journey. Focus until you've developed it and in the process you will achieve a degree of mastery. The act of mastering one thing will enable you to master many others.

Fight Uphill Battles

At the end of the day, you are all you've got. If not you, who? If not now, when?

Standing out isn't easy. There's a reason people push back against the new and different. New is hard, risky, uncertain. Make no mistake: Steve Jobs was a very difficult person to work for and with. Simply doing it better than last time was never going to be good enough for him. It had to be different.

I'm not saying you have to be an insensitive jerk to achieve your creative vision, but you do need to develop inner steel. Assert yourself. If you don't advocate for your ideas, who will?

About a decade ago, Jeff Bezos declared that Amazon was "willing to be misunderstood for long periods of time." It was expanding from selling everyday goods such as books and brushes to selling "cloud services." Talk about castles in the sky. What the hell did Amazon know about "Big Data"? The collective reaction was: "Stay in your lane, Bezos. Leave this brainy digital stuff to companies like Google and Microsoft and go back to selling lawn mowers."

Similarly, Sara Blakely was told so many times that her idea for Spanx wasn't worth investing in, and yet she painstakingly led the company toward her vision, regardless of what everyone shouted from the sidelines. When factories declined to work with her on the seamless undergarments, she refined prototypes on her own. Now, billions of dollars later, we're able to clearly understand both Spanx and Amazon, thanks entirely to the stubborn visions of these founders.

In short, anything that bucks the status quo—whether on your team inside a big company, at a startup, or within a personal art project—will be an uphill battle. *These are the battles worth fighting.* If you put something out there and it meets no resistance, chances are it isn't as vital and worthwhile as you think it is. When it generates a reaction, you know you're onto something. Then the job becomes nurturing that little spark, *especially* when some of those around you are trying to blow it out. The haters will be your compass.

My friend Alex Calderwood created the Ace Hotel chain, re-defining what a hotel could be and leaving an indelible mark on the hospitality industry. We met for coffee one day in London and started talking about branding; he was a master. I explained that my philosophy was always to work on things that were deeply personal to me and on either end of the spectrum: gritty, cheap, and raw or polished and precise. To me, everything in the middle—"best practices" and "industry standards" and "whatever the competition is doing"—created forgettable results.

I felt pretty insightful until Alex revealed that he'd called his hotel the Ace because that card is simultaneously the lowest and highest in the deck. Genius.

Who wants to be another nine of hearts or six of clubs? You're an Ace. Play your card.

DESIGN

Design a strategy
to make your dream
a new reality.

4

Develop Your Systems

Our goals can only be reached through a vehicle of a plan, in which we must fervently believe, and upon which we must vigorously act. There's no other route to success.

—PABLO PICASSO

If creativity is connecting unlikely ideas in novel ways, following a structured approach to it can feel contradictory or even counter-productive. You can't put borders around spontaneity! Making an actual plan for how you're going to be creative can feel just plain *wrong*. But by developing basic strategies, systems, and frameworks to support your output, you'll relieve yourself of the burden of waiting around for lightning to strike. In the process, you'll become much more effective. Trust me—I wish I'd learned this sooner.

Throughout my childhood I had more guidelines than I could handle on what to do and how to do it. Nothing unreasonable by itself, but I always had a curfew, a slew of daily chores, and a laundry list of rules to follow around the house: keep the heat at 62 degrees even in the dead of winter, put dirty dishes in the dishwasher a particular way, set the table just so—you get the picture. My parents are lovely, and they are fastidious.

The same held true with the team sports I played. Football and soccer each came with plenty of rules. So did academia, of course, all the way through graduate school. Though I appreciated the consistency those boundaries provided, many of the rules struck me as arbitrary, unnecessary, or designed solely in the interests of someone else's convenience. I rarely saw them as providing any value for *me*. Ultimately, I began to see all rules, rituals, and systems as little more than disguised mechanisms of control and oppression.

Fast-forward a few years, and—naturally—this disdain for structure and frameworks hindered my early creative career. You can't program creativity, I thought. It should be spontaneous; I'd work only when I felt inspired by magical forces from above and do whatever I wanted with the rest of my time. Creativity wasn't about discipline—it was about freedom, right?

Looking back at that undeveloped view of creativity, it's obvious to me that my beliefs were informed by the dominant cultural narrative around artists as wild mystics, people who go off into the woods or a loft in Soho or some other sacred place and return with a finished masterpiece—somehow. In reality, this romantic myth has next to nothing in common with the true working methods of professionals in any field, *especially* the creative ones.

Today I know what gets results: establishing a consistent creative practice and sticking to it. Building even a basic framework for creative work will save you a lot of disappointment and put you on the fast track to the success you seek.

The Power of Consistent Action

After flunking out of college in Georgia, Brandon Stanton moved to Chicago, where a friend in finance helped him land a job as a bond trader. Finance wasn't an area of passion for Stanton, but he was thrilled to be making real money in a respectable position—it felt good to be able to show friends and family that he was making something of himself. So good, in fact, that he became obsessed with the job. He grew emotionally dependent on the identity it gave him and the lifestyle it made possible. He started working nonstop, spending every waking minute thinking about the markets.

Though his day job took up most of his time and all of his attention, Stanton occasionally took a few minutes to photograph urban landscapes or capture portraits of strangers while riding Chicago public transit. It was a form of pressure relief, an opportunity to spend a moment of his day not thinking about money. But he told himself not to get distracted by the pretty pictures. Photography might have been more interesting to him than fixed-income securities, but his own security came first. If everything went according to plan, he'd make a fortune trading bonds. Once he'd signaled his success to the world—and insulated himself from financial peril—he'd be free to pursue his real passion.

That belief kept him going for two years. Then he was fired. Leaving the building that day and returning to the streets of Chicago, he had an epiphany. After two years spent obsessing over money, a subject of no personal interest whatsoever, his mind was suddenly *empty*. He could fill it with anything he wanted. Likewise his time—he could go wherever and do whatever he wanted. The sense of freedom that inspired in him was intoxicating. He never wanted it to end.

It was then that Stanton made a bold decision, but one that would eventually create value for millions of people around the world. He made it his goal from that moment forward to spend his time doing what brought him joy. He was tired of promising himself that he would get to be creative and live the life he wanted to live "one day," once he'd built a financial buffer. Instead, he'd begin living the life he wanted then and there, fresh out of a job and with no buffer at all.

He struck on the idea of a photo project: taking street portraits of ten thousand New Yorkers. To fund the trip, he sold landscape photos to his friends. Upon arrival in New York City, he slept on a mattress on the floor of a sublet apartment in Bedford-Stuyvesant, Brooklyn. Comfort and security took a back seat. He had work to do.

If you're familiar with the photo blog Humans of New York, you'll barely recognize the first images on the site. There were no likes and no comments. The photos didn't even have captions. After spending a couple of months posting portraits every day, all for a following numbering well under a thousand, something crucial happened. Feeling stymied with only one lackluster portrait in the queue for that day, Stanton remembered something the subject, a woman wearing green, had said to him: "I used to go through different stages. But then I found that I was happiest when I was green, so I've been green for 15 years." He decided to post that caption with the photo. It became the most engaged-with photo he'd ever posted. Following his intuition this way, Stanton stumbled on the missing piece of the formula: the story. He'd already lost any fear about approaching strangers after months of daily practice, so he simply started talking to his subjects about their lives and condensing what he learned into a caption below each image.

Early social media traction led to interest from a literary agent and a book deal. Today, Stanton has more than 20 million followers, multiple best-selling books, and a video series on Facebook Watch. Beyond achieving more wealth than he'd ever hoped for as a bond trader, Stanton has also raised millions of dollars for charities around the world. Through the structure of a daily practice, a willingness to embrace hard work and risk, and a readiness to follow his intuition, he has become one of the best-known and most prolific living photographers.

How did he start? First, he decided to believe that he could change his own situation through creativity. Next, he identified as a photographer, a creator. Finally, he took regular, consistent action toward his goal. The simple but intentional act of heading out in the morning with his camera created all his staggering momentum. Small daily actions, outsized results.

Accept These Truths

This chapter kicks off the Design section of the book. These three chapters will help you develop a creative mindset and establish a set of habits to shape your work and your life. Before we get into specific tactics, however, I'd ask you to consider the following principles.

Your Mindset Matters Most

As the philosopher and Roman emperor Marcus Aurelius said, "The happiness of your life depends on the quality of your thoughts." As true today as in Roman times. The state of your mind, body, and spirit is the direct result of all the decisions you've made in your life up until this moment. Physical health, cognitive performance, happiness, and well-being—these are driven almost entirely by our beliefs and behaviors. Day after day, choosing to exercise *or* watch Netflix, pull an all-nighter *or* get some sleep, eat clean *or* binge on mint chocolate-chip ice cream—all these decisions create our days, and our days create our lives as a whole. Each of us faces unique physical and mental challenges, but no matter what hand you've been dealt, your mindset makes a massive difference.

To achieve a new mindset and transform your life, you have to believe two things: Your situation—whatever it is—is changeable for the better; and you are capable of making that change happen.

What needs to change? How can you design your best life? To help you figure that out, I'll share a few key ideas and some proven practices. You can experiment with these to find out what works best for you and then design an approach according to *your* ideal mode of being and doing.

The Benefits of Quitting

If the elation and joy we experience when we're doing what we love feed us, it only follows that being out of alignment with our authenticity drains the vital energy required to make and share creative work.

Once upon a time, trying to be something I wasn't took a major toll on me. A professor from my philosophy PhD program once called me an "armchair sociologist"—the kind of insult you hear only in grad school—simply because I wanted to engage with ideas in the living world around us, not just parse Aristotle and Plato all day.

My feelings weren't hurt. He was only telling me what I already knew deep inside: that I was just going to school because I was afraid to chase my real dreams and that I didn't care enough about grad school to do work that was anything more than superficial. I left the university not long after. Little did I know at the time that I was developing a rare but powerful tool: quitting stuff I wasn't meant to do. This is a tool you must wield to create the life you want.

Though deciding to quit was a difficult decision, quitting itself felt good. I soon realized that grad school had taught me as valuable a set of lessons as any I'd learned in Europe. Through just a few pivotal experiences, I'd been given a master class in *What Works for Chase*. Designing my life from that point forward became much easier. By analyzing my unsuccessful experiences to identify what had drained me and held me back, I was able to make decisions that would steer me clear of those pitfalls moving forward.

Joy Is the Way

I know what you're thinking. "Hey, Chase. Thanks for the nice stories, but I can't quit grad school or move to a ski town, let alone fly off to Europe to teach myself photography."

Not my intention. No vision quest necessary. What this is really about is listening to your gut and understanding the consequences of *not* following your intuition. The path is different for everybody. The important thing is to figure out what works for you and what doesn't. Then do more of the good stuff and less of what turns you off. How very hedonistic, you might say. To that, I'd respond that far too many people these days die with the regret of not having done what they wanted for a career, let alone having lived the life of their dreams. Don't let this happen to you.

Doing more of what you love doesn't have to mean dashing off to Paris. You can have a lovely experience at the local museum or by paging through a coffee-table art book you purchased to provide a few moments of quiet inspiration now and then. If you once felt completely empowered in the peace and quiet of a spiritual retreat, try integrating some natural solitude into your day with a walk through a nearby park on the way to work. The goal is to cultivate activities that will resonate with you and bring you joy. By constructing a practical blueprint for what nourishes you—pursuing creative paths that brought you joy as a kid or writing in a journal before others in your household wake up, for example—you'll give yourself the chance to see your life and your personal agency in new and powerful ways.

Your job is to figure out which behaviors feed your soul and which leave you running on empty. By the end of this chapter, you'll have a set of habits and routines to fan your creative spark and accelerate your progress toward becoming the creator and human you want to be.

Building a Creative Mindset

In the previous chapter, we looked at creating a healthy relationship with risk by developing the distinction between *real* risk (losing your house when you quit your job without a plan) versus *perceived* risk (sharing your work on Instagram). Only by learning to overcome irrational risks—that don't threaten anything but your ego—can you become your authentic self and begin to stand out as a creator.

A creative mindset is not only about managing downside risk; it's also critical to use your mind to go on the offensive. How can you keep your mind open, happy, and positive? Because, let's face it, the quality of your life is determined by what you think and feel.

Science tells us that positive thoughts are healthier—they makes us feel better and are tightly correlated with flow states and improved performance. We simply cannot ignore the role that mindset plays in creating everything we want for ourselves—whether a gorgeous illustration, a sonata, a thriving business, or the life we envision. I like to think of mindset as the ground floor, the bedrock. The wrong foundation crumbles quickly when loaded with challenges, and we become trapped in the rubble. The right foundation can support a rocket launch. The core principles of a stable creative mindset are:

You are a creative person.
The world is abundant and full of possibilities.
Your situation can always be changed.
You can use your creativity to create the change you seek.
Creativity is natural and healthy but requires practice.
Creativity is ultimate personal power.

Unfortunately, you can't adopt a creative mindset just by reading this book. *Repetition of corresponding actions* is necessary to develop it. Changing your mindset requires the consistent effort of putting this set of beliefs to work. Think you're creative? Great, then prove it by creating something: today, tomorrow, and the next day.

Only when you commit to a program of creative development will your old ideas about talent and destiny start to melt away. Beware: the stronger your creative muscles get, the deeper and richer your work—and, by extension, your life—will become. This is potent medicine. The creative mindset is the launchpad for a virtuous cycle.

Goals

Your goals are mile markers along your path. Therefore, it is essential that they align with what you truly want in life. No "shoulds." Goals with a meaningful *why* behind them energize us. Whether your goal is building an app, becoming a surgeon, learning to dance, or earning all your income from your freelance passion—it's creativity at work. In small, daily actions, you're creating outcomes for yourself and, by extension, creating your *life*. So you must be clear about what you want those outcomes to be.

Entire books have been written about goal setting, but to get you started, here are a few key principles.

1. Write your goals down and refer to them regularly. Every day.
2. Keep your goals few in number—three or four at most—so that you can focus on them.
3. Assign each goal an appropriate window of time. The clearer the goal, the more likely you are to achieve it.

So instead of "Learn to dance," try "Dance the Macarena at my wedding." Or, if you want to up the stakes, try "Land a spot on *So You Think You Can Dance* by next year." To quote a fortune cookie I once ate, "If you don't know where you want to go, how will you ever get there?"

Habits

Habits are nothing more than behaviors that have become automatic through repetition and reward. The strength of a habit has nothing to do with your inherent worth as a human being or any sort of natural talent. Habits get stronger when they're reinforced—it's that simple. The important part to remember is that you must approach all habits in a healthy way, from a place of self-care and love, not self-negation or masochism. Any habit can become unhealthy when the effort is coming from a place of "have to" or "should." With small but consistent effort, anyone can build a new habit. Then the behavior simply happens when it's supposed to, without much conscious thought. You find yourself automatically writing in your journal first thing each morning, reaching for water instead of soda, and so on.

Creativity itself is a habit. It's a behavior like any other, and it can be strengthened, even made automatic. If your creative work were an effortless, joyful experience of perfect flow every day, I don't think you'd be reading this book right now. Either you'd be off creating something magical, or you'd be out there enjoying the rest of your life—radiating that special glow of creative fulfillment. But you're not. And that's okay. We're all in this together.

Imagine that a friend comes to you for advice. He says he's having trouble bending pipes in half and deadlifting huge boulders. (Never mind why.) Your first question would be, Are you strong enough to deadlift a boulder? Your friend may be a very nice person, but he has never set foot in a gym and eats Pop-Tarts for breakfast, lunch, and dinner. He has arms like hot dogs, and you've seen him faint after opening a tightly sealed jar. Boulders will have to wait.

Sure, it's an absurd image, but people are even more naive about what goes into being creative. Lady Gaga has the hulking creative muscles to have written and recorded several multi-platinum albums. She's invented and reinvented herself a half-dozen times. She's a queen of fashion and music. Now she's a movie star. This is not just talent. Her creative muscles have creative muscles thanks to years of steady effort. Yet countless aspiring musicians expect to sit down and write a song in the same amount of time, with the same practiced ease, and with the same excellent results as she does on the first try. If they can't do that, they think, it somehow reflects upon their inherent lack of talent or character, not their undeveloped creative capacity.

How do you build habits? Through consistent reinforcement. Habits are the path to your goals—whatever they may be.

The Creative Pyramid

I developed a simple image to help me understand the relationship among mindset, habits, and goals. I call it the Creative Pyramid.

A goal that is not supported by the right mindset or the necessary habits is just a pipe dream—it's never gonna happen. The Egyptians knew they couldn't build a pyramid without a base. Whether it's your goal to publish a best-selling novel, create the next unicorn startup, or simply develop a creative habit for the sake of enriching your life, you'll need a clear goal, the right habits, and a creative mindset.

Creativity Boosters and Zappers

Let's get something clear: all the "productivity" gibberish we read in our social feeds day in and day out is largely a waste of time. Productivity has become a self-help institution that deals with the symptoms rather than the cause of our problems. Are you busy? Busy isn't cool. Being busy shows a lack of priority. Instead of finding ways to cram more five-minute meetings into a day or accelerate the hamster wheel of emails flowing into your in-box, start thinking about how you can cultivate the state of mind and actions that will unleash your creative power. Creativity—the power to make your ideas manifest—is *never* a waste of time. It's the lever that matters the most.

Creativity Boosters are habits that feed and nurture our creative capacity. Creativity Zappers are habits that drain us and put our goals further out of reach. With habits, a little change goes a long way. Adopting even a handful of Boosters and letting go of a couple of Zappers could help move you from where you are now to where you want to be. As you experience some success with behavior change, you can return to this list and continue to improve your tool kit.

These lists of Boosters and Zappers are drawn from my own experience as well as the experiences of all the world-class creators, best-selling authors, and paradigm-shifting entrepreneurs I've hosted on my podcast. I'm including them here as guideposts to inspire you in your own journey. I like to begin with discussing Creativity Zappers because you will likely discover one or more that you can dispose of now to earn a quick win.

Creativity Zappers

From a life in the trenches, I've learned that the hard-living artist is mostly a myth. Some things contribute to your work and some just don't, no matter how romantic they might seem. Once you learn what helps and what doesn't, you'll see that there's very little that is counterintuitive about any of it. Abusing your body, partying too much, neglecting your headspace—this stuff wouldn't make you a better mathematician, plumber, or stock-broker. Why would it improve your graphic design skills or ability to build a business? Any temporary upside in ideation from reducing inhibitions is usually followed by a downside of low output and poor execution—aka the stuff that really matters.

We've witnessed the disintegration of many great artists in the name of inspiration for their art, but if you look closely, those periods of alcoholism, drug abuse, and other self-destructive behaviors were often tied to past trauma and rarely intersected with the productive periods that made those people successful in the first place. Let's agree to let go of the tired clichés we may have used in the past to justify bad decisions and unhelpful behavior.

You don't have to be unhappy or alternate between ecstasy and suffering to make great work. You need to stay in the game and *just keep practicing.*

Finally, behavioral science says it's really hard to just quit habits that don't serve us, and it's way easier to make new ones that will crowd out the old ones. Keep that in mind as you read through the following list of potentially toxic habits and, later in the chapter, the list of supportive strategies.

Bad Medicine

Take an honest, no-BS look at the things you put into your body to "help you cope with the day-to-day." Ask yourself: Do they really? This can be anything you consume to get some sort of effect, from excess food, sugar, or caffeine to hard-core drugs. I'm not saying you ought to live on kale and lentils. And this section isn't about debating whether your molly trip is "medicine" or an escape. Truth be told, I'm far from a saint. There are biological reasons we aim to alter our body chemistry from time to time, and I'd go crazy without ~~cheat~~, I mean *treat* days when I eat like I'm a teenager every couple weeks, or throw down for a party when it sounds like fun. That said, we know when we're our peak creative selves—showing up the best that we can for ourselves and those around us. It's when we're taking care of our bodies and minds. Stay honest with yourself about what works for you and what doesn't.

Social Media

Yes, social media plays an important role in how we connect with our community and cultivate an audience for our work. That said, we all know by now that the companies behind those services purposefully use behavioral psychology to trap and funnel our attention for their own purposes. As artists, our attention is a vital resource. We can't afford to squander that mental energy. Facebook will *never* have enough of you—Mark Zuckerberg will never say, "You've scrolled through enough updates for today, Allison. Better get back to writing." It's one thing to use those tools to share your work (more on that in Step IV); it's another to check if anyone new has liked your post fifty times a day in the hope of a quick burst of dopamine. Treat social media like junk food and be deliberate about setting limits. We'll discuss scheduling social media use in chapter 5. For now, try to be aware of how much you use the stuff, how it makes you feel, and how it affects your creative productivity. You'll be surprised.

News

I recommend you fast from news as much as possible. [Gasp.] The reality is that you will receive the news you need to. We live in a culture where the news is ubiquitous. So try this as an experiment. Stop seeking the news, aka the list of what went wrong today somewhere else. Try it for a week. I guarantee that by the end of seven days, you will still have been made aware of every major news story you would have learned about online, but without the constant sense of dread and despair that reading the news daily instills. That sludge of unending negativity takes a vicious toll on our creativity and overall well-being. If it makes you feel better, set up automatic donations to a few nonprofits in areas you care about. Let them put your dollars to work for climate change or prison reform. When an election rolls around, spend time carefully reading up on the issues and candidates, and vary the sources of your news for broadened perspective. The rest of the time, protect your mindset by governing the volume and quality of news you consume.

Email

Even the Luddites who angrily quit social media are stuck with email. Again, all you can do is become deliberate about how you use this tool so that it doesn't leech your energy. Do *not* check your email at the start of your day if you can help it. This is one of the biggest killers of critical morning energy and momentum. Email is a petition for your time; it's not a demand that you must respond to immediately. Rarely are there mission-critical obligations to address between 6 and 8 a.m., and, most important, it's up to you to train those in your life when you'll be available to respond and when you will not. I'm militant about getting through my morning routine without getting sidetracked by email. In fact, even after I complete my morning routine, I still avoid email until

I've attacked the most important thing on my list for that day, the one domino I can tip over that, if accomplished, will (a) help me consider the day a success and (b) possibly tip other dominos.

Overwork

Whether on your day job or your creative project, it's easy to overdo it and burn out. Pushing yourself to your limit can work here and there when absolutely necessary, but a creative life is built through consistency, not by lurching from one outsized explosion of effort to the next. It's better to learn to rest more often and keep going than outright quit.

Many creators struggle with both overwork and underwork. It becomes a vicious cycle: working on something until you're totally run down, then avoiding it as you try to recover. By the time you're ready to return to the project, you've already lost touch with your excitement. I fall into the overwork trap when I'm not careful. "Sprints" are fine, but only now and then, and you have to double down on self-care to compensate.

There comes a time in every day when you will begin to achieve diminishing returns. Use this section of the book to help develop this awareness. When you're truly sunk for the day—simply walk away. Rest can work wonders when we're stuck.

The Wrong Work

A common destructive element in the life of any creative person is doing the wrong work—in other words, spending too much of your time on things that don't matter or don't come naturally. We flourish by leaning into our strengths more than by "fixing" our weaknesses. Delegate, outsource, or avoid the tasks that call on your weakest areas. There is no benefit in being so stubborn that you do it all. Every client wants to work with the very best she can get at X, Y, *or* Z, not someone who is pretty decent at all three. When we try to do things that lie outside our expertise and inclination, everything becomes more draining. You may still not be ready to embark on a full-time creative career, but if you hate your job, how will you marshal the necessary enthusiasm for creative work? Find something you're better suited to do to pay the bills. When you're playing to your strengths at work, you'll be much more likely to have the bandwidth to embrace your creativity the rest of the time. When I get stuck in noncreative tasks at work, I experience increased anxiety, decreased appetite, and poor sleep. The lack of sleep and food leaves me tired and even more anxious, creating a snowball effect. It's a toxic cycle.

Creativity Boosters

At this stage in my life, it's become impossible to ignore the fact that the good days—when I'm feeling great and doing my best work—have common elements. For one thing, they're intentional. On those days, I'm in the driver's seat, with clear objectives in mind and a plan for achieving them, even if the objective is simply taking time to think through a problem. Over the past decade I've made a point of recognizing the behaviors that work for me and building them into my regular schedule. It might seem that such activities take time away from the "doing," but activities that expand your creative capacity are force multipliers in every aspect of your life.

Do I occasionally skip some of these habits in my daily routine? Absolutely. I'm so far from perfect with this stuff, it's laughable. But the fact remains that I've put serious effort into staying on track and that the more regular these activities have become for me, the more creative capacity I've developed. So start small. Use this list as a buffet from which to pick and choose. Select a few activities and experiment.

Craft

Duh duh *duuuuh*! Despite my qualifier above, this one habit is nonnegotiable. Whether you're a hobbyist or a pro, learning the technical skills of your craft is essential. And if you aspire to move into a creative profession, core skills are the price of entry. Practicing these skills once you've acquired them matters deeply and will unquestionably contribute toward creating the outcomes you seek. Become so good at the fundamentals of your craft that they become automatic and effortless, like breathing, walking, or chewing gum. That's when you'll experience the real fun and prizes of a creative calling. Take learning a foreign language. First you need a basic understanding of vocabulary, verb conjugation, syntax, and grammar. Only then will you be able to move beyond thinking about which word comes next in the sentence to expressing yourself in a dynamic and powerful way. Now you can have a real conversation. The same is true for any creative craft. The goal is to achieve fluency so you can finally speak your mind.

Creative Cross-Training

Regularly practicing your creative craft in your hobby or career is only part of the story. For every aspect of disciplined focus on your primary pursuit—mastering your knowledge of light for photography, hammering technique for blacksmithing, or color theory for painting—there is a need for and benefit to staying creatively nimble in a broad sense as well.

For example, even though photography is my primary area of mastery, I practice a daily habit of creating *something beyond photography* every day—whether it's writing three lines of poetry, scribbling three paragraphs for a blog post, or playing the three chords I know on my guitar over and over for a few minutes. By practicing a host of creative crafts beyond your chosen medium of focus, not only do you stay creatively fit, but you consistently and subconsciously remind yourself that you can take an active role in shaping the arc of your life.

Once you're actively creating a host of small creative acts each day, you develop a stronger sense of your own agency, creative capacity, and self-determination. If you can take a photo, write a paragraph, or sketch a still life, you can sure as hell forge your own destiny. Think cross-training: If you're a basketball player and you shoot only jump shots in practice, you'll struggle during a game because your cardio capacity—a baseline requirement—isn't up to par.

Meditation

Doctors, scientists, gurus, and performance experts have been advocating for a mindfulness practice for years. I, too, have gone on the record for my appreciation for meditation and the value it provides. It's easily had the most positive effect of any one "master skill" I have practiced over the past decade. As researchers continue conducting high-quality studies into meditation, the advocates are only banging the drum harder because of its benefits to good health and wellness.

If you're still on the fence about spending ten or twenty minutes sitting still when you have So Much Important Stuff To Do, ask yourself what your real objections might be. At first I complained about the time commitment myself, but deep down I was actually worried that meditating might dull my competitive edge. Yogi types always seemed too laid back to me. When I started meditating, it turned out that I didn't "lose" anything; rather, I gained clarity and awareness within a week of starting, and I've yet to find a single drawback in it.

Gratitude and Visualization

Both gratitude and visualization are well researched and have scientifically proven benefits. An attitude of gratitude helps us

stay in touch with the overall richness of life and acts as an antidote to any negative emotions we might be feeling. Visualization
is a powerful tool that high performers from myriad disciplines
use for programming their subconscious mind. Even the most
cursory online search will reveal a number of methods for each.

Except on a rare day with extenuating circumstances, I'll
follow my meditation with a three-minute gratitude and visualization practice. I begin with my eyes closed and make a short
list of three genuine and heartfelt moments I'm grateful to have
had in my life—and I relive them as if watching the experience
through my own eyes and feeling those moments as fully as
possible. They can be big life moments, such as my wedding
ceremony, or small delicate moments, like when our family pet
did something cute—any moment that brought joy or awareness
to how awesome life can be.

Then I transition into visualizing myself in a world where I
have just achieved my three most important goals. I live through
the feelings that come along with each achievement, imagining
all of it in as much detail as possible: sounds, smells, emotions.
What would it look, feel, taste, smell, and sound like to accomplish
those goals? The subconscious mind can't clearly distinguish
between visualized experiences and actual experiences, so by
focusing on the feelings in the body of achieving these visions,
we're priming our neurology for success.

Movement

Staying fit and getting your heart rate up during the day has been
shown in study after study to increase creative connections and
cognitive ability. My approach is to have a baseline practice that
keeps me physically fit. Ultimately, anything that gets my blood
pumping is good, and fresh air is a plus. It doesn't take a marathon to change your headspace.

In short, move your body, and your brain will follow. The neuroscientific data is clear: changing your physiological state changes your blood chemistry, which in turn drives your mood and mental clarity. All that jumping around at Tony Robbins's seminars? That's biochemistry in action. Movement is a creativity catalyst.

Cold Therapy

Admittedly, this is esoteric, but just a few minutes of cold-water therapy in the morning can be a game changer. In addition to the science that suggests it's a mood enhancer (not always at first for some people) and potentially even an antidote against depression, it's also a powerful stimulant for one's immune system.

The goal is simple: to get the body cold every morning as a mechanism for waking up and facing the day. The desired effect can be achieved by soaking in a deep tub filled with 45°F to 55°F water (expert level) or by finishing a normal morning shower (after hot water, cleaning, etc.) with two to three minutes of the coldest water you can get out of the showerhead—directly on the neck, shoulders, face, back, and chest. Either way, you'll be surprised by the sense of well-being that follows. (If you want to learn more, check out my Instagram feed and YouTube channel, where I occasionally post on these topics, and there's tons of literature about cold therapy online.)

Good Nutrition

Though I don't recommend switching to the latest fad diet, what you put into your body makes a big difference in your energy levels and concentration throughout the day. Eating unprocessed foods, consuming fewer carbohydrates, and keeping to regular mealtimes cover 90 percent of my personal regimen. I almost never leave the house without eating something, typically a protein such as eggs and a vegetable, within thirty minutes of getting up (based on Tim Ferriss's slow-carb approach). If I'm in a hurry, I get some good fats with half an avocado, a teaspoon of coconut oil, or some almonds and a protein shake. My lunches and dinners aren't remarkable; they're just simple, whole foods. Live your life as you will, but eating clean and reducing your consumption of processed foods and refined sugars will keep your energy levels steady throughout the day—and over the arc of months and years.

Proper Hydration

This is essential. I try to drink sixty-four ounces—roughly eight glasses—of water each day and more when I can. I find that if I kick off the day with two glasses of cold water immediately on waking, I feel revitalized right away and I'm much more likely to hit my sixty-four-ounce goal.

Creating Before Consuming

If the first thing you do each day is pick up your phone and cruise all your favorite creators and entrepreneurs for inspiration, you probably end up feeling anxious or depressed that you're not far enough along. The simple act of creating something with intention first, before consuming the work of others, alters the dynamic. This is a small-but-mighty behavior I learned from a podcast interview with my friend Marie Forleo, and I'm grateful for that wisdom every day.

Too many of us start our days consuming instead of creating: browsing the web, watching TV, whatever. We become audience members and critics. Our thoughts get sucked into what other people are doing, how well they're doing it, and the response they're getting from the world. This is supertoxic, especially if you haven't made any of your own stuff lately, and a surefire way to undermine all the creative mindset stuff I wrote about earlier in this chapter.

Creating before consuming is a seemingly minor shift that will have a profound effect on your daily outlook and creative capacity. So please, create first. Make something (and ideally share it), no matter how small.

Good Organization

One of those myths about creative types is that we're messy. Yes, plenty are, but plenty *more* keep things clean and organized. This isn't a recommendation to clean the entire house before engaging in your creative practice. That's called procrastination. I'm talking about staying organized as a means to your creative end. There's nothing counterintuitive about it, either: a good craftsperson knows where to find each tool and has it ready to hand. I'll talk more about setting the space for effective creative work in chapter 5. For now, it's enough to know that a chaotic work space adds cognitive load to your efforts and a more organized one can give you a creative boost.

Adventure and Play

Plain and simple, get off your ass and go have some fun! No matter how abstract or fantastic your work, it all has to come from somewhere in your psyche to have any value. Some quality input is required before you can create worthwhile output. Creators need some thrills, some experience with the work of others, some discomfort, excitement, fun, highs and lows, wins and losses. Living life is the very basis of our work.

Adventure is different for everyone. It might be travel, outdoor activity, or "living large" via nightlife. Cut loose. Have fun. Laugh more. Whatever fuels you in life will probably be good for your art. Of course, flying off to a foreign city or climbing a frozen waterfall can have a dramatic energizing effect. Do it if you can. But don't blow money on "getting inspired" or wait until you can afford a round-the-world tour to inject regular doses of adventure and play into your life. Embrace new experiences, and challenge yourself to get out of your comfort zone right now. If people ask you why you weren't at your desk, tell them you were gathering raw material.

Art

This is one of the creative industry's biggest secrets (that hides in plain sight). Creative inspiration comes from other inspired creations and creators. Diversity breeds growth, even if it's growing to understand what you don't like. And don't restrict yourself to popular masterpieces, either. Look at the work of other artists just starting out, people making work closer to your own level of success and impact. Get curious and explore.

It also helps to cross-pollinate. If you're a musician, consume film. If you're a web designer, attend the ballet. This is one tactic that helped me find my unique voice as an artist: most of my influences come from beyond the world of photography. To learn about light, I studied oil painting for years. To learn how to shoot lifestyle images, I studied balanced body positioning through figure drawing. The list is a mile long.

One of my favorite things about hosting my own podcast is welcoming musicians, artists, designers, writers, speakers, travelers, entrepreneurs, business titans, and more to chat for an hour at a time. This informs my art, my work, and my world and fuels new passions beyond my current comfort zone.

Knowledge of history—from art or contemporary pop culture—can be powerful. It's a well-trodden path to know the rules, master them, and then decide how and where to break those rules, whether in art, business, the humanities, or anywhere else. History builds context.

Quiet

Creative work is often assisted by living vibrant or new experiences. That said, great ideas do *not* usually come in the height of any daily grind. Neuroscience shows that creative thinking—the making of novel and useful connections between different concepts and ideas—happens best when the mind is at rest or, even better, lightly occupied with a quiet task. I've found this to be true over and over again. That's why I deliberately alternate my time between adventure mode and quiet mode. I go out into the world to seek inspiration. Then I go into the studio and let those experiences percolate quietly until something new bubbles up in my mind. My best business ideas have always come after intense work periods and radical play in areas unrelated to business.

There has to be a calm after the storm. This is why your best ideas happen in the shower, right before bed, or when you wake up earlier than usual. When there's less noise in your world and you don't have an important task to focus your attention on, magic happens. If you want to produce your best ideas, cultivate time like this. Trust me. Some of my best ideas have come from my hammock.

Sleep

This is last but far from least. For a long time—years, in fact—I was one of those people who claimed they didn't need much sleep. I went a decade on four or five hours a night. I figured it was genetic. It was a tool to get ahead, my edge. After all, I usually had a ton of energy all day. People occasionally warned me about the negative long-term effects of sleep deprivation but, again, I thought I had a special gift. Plenty of successful people, from US presidents to *Fortune* 500 CEOs, have been famous for the mere handful of hours they require under the covers.

Then, on a tropical vacation a few years back toward the end of that sleepless decade and after a period of incredibly heavy work, exhausted, I decided to try an experiment: no wake-up schedule and no alarm. I'd let my body sleep as long as it wanted to. I even used earplugs and an eye mask to create the best results possible. If my ability to forgo sleep were truly a genetic quirk, that would confirm it.

The result? Holy cow—I slept fourteen hours a night for six nights. Sleeping in was a treat, but the effect that sleep had on the rest of my day was eye opening. Suddenly I was smarter. Happier. More creative. A new man, in fact. Since that experiment, I've shifted gears completely. I'm still proud of working hard, but I'm embarrassed about my ignorant, sleep-deprived past. I started tracking my sleep a few years ago with the aim of optimizing its quality and quantity. I now aim to get at least seven hours a night. Get your sleep and, if you can, try waking up early. It's a simple way to create high-quality, uninterrupted time and space for your creative work.

Just Start

The punch line of this very tactical chapter is this: being creative is certainly an attribute we can possess, but that attribute cannot be manifested, enhanced, strengthened, or made better without *doing creative acts*. So this entire chapter is guidance to care for yourself in a way that will provide a reservoir of energy for creating. You can't just think your way through it. Put bluntly, since practicing makes you better, what's most important in your development as a creator is cultivating a regular—ideally daily—practice.

As we go deeper into this book together, consider letting go of the endless hunger for tricks or "hacks" to meet some particular creative goal. Remember, creativity is not a skill, it's habit, a way of operating. The more you operate that way, the more capable you are of doing so. The good news about creativity is that it resides naturally within you. The bad news is that there are no shortcuts, no one-line zingers that will unleash this power in you. The only "cheat code" is that once you become aware of your creativity, you can begin to manifest it toward nearly anything in life. And it does not have to feel like work. Cooking dinner tonight? Figure out how you can tweak the recipe to surprise your family for once, how you can create something that will be playful and joyful. It can be as simple as that.

Think back to Brandon Stanton's story and the creation of Humans of New York. Losing his job revealed to Stanton that he had agency over his own life. The right framework allowed him to create—and iterate on—his vision in small ways every day. Remember that his original work looks almost nothing like what ultimately worked for him. If he'd waited to conceive the "perfect" concept before actually taking any photos, he'd never have started. It was his daily creative practice—eliminating basic distractions and adding simple behaviors—that delivered his success, not some brilliant, detailed plan. *The process of creating became the success.*

The same will be true for you. Pursuing small, imperfect, playful habits today—having a regular creative practice—is far more important than chasing a long list of perfect things you want to create tomorrow.

5

Make Your Space

You don't build the life you want by saving time. You build
the life you want, and then time saves itself. Recognizing
that is what makes success possible.

—LAURA VANDERKAM

Let's say you have a time machine. (My book, my rules. Go with
it.) This time machine can transport you to any point in history.
Dial it to the day your favorite artist started working on something you loved: the movie that inspired you to be a filmmaker
or the song that changed your life.

Cue the light and sound effects, clocks flying through the air.
Okay, we're back in time. You are facing your creative hero. What's
your first thought? If you're anything like me, it's probably: *protect the creator's time and attention.* You want to make sure
that this important work actually gets created. Can you imagine
how easy it would be to steer things off course? "David Bowie,
big fan, love your work. This is a device from the future called

an iPhone. I put a game called Candy Crush on there, you're gonna love it." Good-bye, *Ziggy Stardust*.

On the day you visited, your favorite artist would be feeling just as much doubt about the outcome of his project as you do about yours. It wouldn't take much to disrupt his flow. If you were there, you would protect his time and attention with a vengeance.

If Frida Kahlo asked you whether her morning would be better spent painting *Self-Portrait with Cropped Hair* or taking the car to the mechanic, it wouldn't be a tough call for you to make. "First things first, Frida! Get to the studio. You can deal with the car while the paint's drying." In fact, you'd tell her that almost anything else could wait.

Yet when it comes to our own work, we fall into weirdly distorted thinking. The most mundane tasks suddenly weigh on our minds as more important than the pursuit of our creative calling.

Avoiding this trap is simple: *prioritize the work*. But it isn't that easy. Though prioritizing creative work for someone else, such as a boss or a client, feels straightforward, the situation always gets cloudy when it comes to our own affairs. Those household finances aren't going to tally themselves. Instagram won't update itself, either, come to think of it. If I don't post now, everyone will unfollow me, and then who will watch the video I'm . . . not editing because I'm fiddling with Instagram? Round and round we go.

The point of the time machine thought experiment is to reveal that competing priorities aren't competitive at all. *What you're really struggling with is the willingness to value as-yet-unmade work.* Whenever you find yourself on the fence about whether to stick to your schedule and follow your vision, ask yourself what you'd say if someone else's work were on the line, work you already knew was going to be worth the effort. This will break open that insidious emotional trap like nothing else.

Thought experiments and slogans are useful in a pinch, but they won't carry you to the finish line. You need structure to turn the future you imagined in Step I into reality. That structure begins with a schedule.

Your Schedule Is Your Friend

My younger self thought schedules were tools of conformity and repression, something for bankers and the military, not creators. The older, wiser people who kept telling me to use a calendar just wanted to keep my creativity contained. Maya Angelou didn't worry about her schedule, I thought—she was an *artist*. She simply waited for inspiration to strike and then wrote a brilliant poem on the spot—didn't she? No. Maya Angelou always made time for her work, established it and protected it. In fact, as related by Mason Currey in *Daily Rituals*, his book on the working habits of great artists, Angelou made a practice of booking a hotel room to work every day, arriving before seven a.m. and staying until well after lunch.

It only makes sense. A poet knows better than anyone the importance of timing and structure. Angelou never left her creative output to chance.

I've learned through surviving a career's worth of deadlines that a schedule is one of a creator's greatest allies. It's the most effective way to safeguard the time you can devote to creative work, protecting those precious minutes from all of life's other demands. It's also a powerful tool for ensuring that you invest the necessary time in rest and recovery, sharpening your skill set, and building your community. If you've ever wondered how the most seasoned pros manage to juggle all these functions, the answer is: a calendar.

This doesn't mean that you have to stick to a nine-to-five schedule with thirty minutes for lunch—only that you'll be happier and more creatively fulfilled if you set up a schedule in a way that serves your needs and then—*most* of the time—stick to it. It doesn't have to be perfect. "Pretty good" will get you farther over time than you can imagine. Whether it's writing first thing in the morning, playing music for a couple of hours after dinner, or going for a photo walk during your lunch break, keeping to a relatively consistent schedule of some kind will deepen and expand your creative output. The more you schedule your work time instead of waiting for inspiration to strike, the better.

All that said, you can't optimize art. That's why this book doesn't provide a "productivity method" for checking off more creative "tasks" in a certain amount of time. (Grace Hopper's list for 1944: "Invent computer code compiler. Check.") No, it's about becoming more intentional about the way you work, creating space not only to work but to play, to think, to dream. In order to create your best stuff, you have to put your creative needs ahead of countless other things that feel urgent in the moment but aren't actually all that important. This can be hard. It can feel selfish.

Well, good. You *should* create for yourself first. It's time to retire the tired idea that your creative practice is a "nice to have." This isn't just fun, healing, and restorative; it's also critical to your success and well-being. When you're creating regularly, you become a better lover, spouse, parent, employee, and friend. In the end, doing your work isn't selfish at all; you're doing everyone around you a favor as well.

This chapter is about improving the balance you strike between creativity and life's other demands. It's about building a new creative practice or developing the one you have into the one you've always wished you had. It will turbocharge your output and fulfill you in ways you can't even imagine—but it won't be a walk in the park. Along the way, you'll have to say no to old ways of operating that don't serve you so that you can say yes to what matters. This can hurt. Think of it like a new exercise routine: the first few workouts spent doing unfamiliar, challenging movements leave you feeling sore and tired, but if you stick to the schedule through all the aches and pains, you quickly find your groove.

We always want to find ourselves pulled into our work. Continuous pushing leads to burnout. The absence of any pull toward your work is a sign that you're pursuing the wrong thing. In fact, it's possible that the lack of a pull toward your creative project is one reason you picked up this book in the first place.

So my telling you to stick to a schedule does not mean push, push, and push yourself until it's done. Just understand that even in pursuit of things you love, some rigor and discipline are necessary. Setting aside time and space and keeping clear of distractions and interruptions will create momentum. Slowly but surely, your brain will begin to fill that time with ideas and the energy to work on them. If you're listening to the call—the hints provided by your intuition—then you're following the path. Over time, the pull will return.

In chapter 6, I'll explain how to establish an effective creative practice, a way of using time and space once you've got it. For now, stay focused on simply creating and defending that space. *Your space.*

Busy versus Effective

Let's be real: we give away too much of our time to things that don't serve us. Given that time is our most precious resource, it always surprises me how cavalier we can be with how we spend it. Growing up, I believed that busy people were important, impressive, and deserving of sympathy and special treatment. They had it rough! Once I quit grad school and went to work for myself full-time, "busy" became real for me. Suddenly I had a lot to do to pay the rent and put food on the table. It always felt as though there weren't enough hours in the day.

Over time and without consciously realizing it, I let this insidious "busy" mentality take hold. It was seductive. Whenever I told my friends how busy I was, they seemed impressed. Naturally, they asked me what I was so busy doing, which meant I got to talk about myself and how important my work was to me. It felt good. I was busy; I was important. I took that label and pinned it right on my lapel.

At the time, I didn't have much of a system for anything, let alone for how to do my creative work every day. I ran my entire business via a bunch of scribbled lists. Routines of any kind still felt like the opposite of creativity. After bailing on grad school, the thought of going back to a structured routine seemed absurd. What I imagined I wanted was a world where every day was a new adventure. And for a while, that was exciting. I woke up each morning never knowing what to expect. Sometimes I'd be insanely productive, just fired up and filled with amazing ideas.

Then the other kind of day would roll around. I'd get nowhere. Or I'd realize I had missed an important milestone, and now I was stuck. Eventually I looked around at the growing chaos, and something struck me. Most of what I was "busy" doing all the time was just noise. All bark, no bite. I was taking action after action but getting less and less in the way of results. I'm not sure I'd even been thinking in terms of results until that point. I was just a whirlwind with a camera and a dream.

Ultimately I realized that there was nothing noble or romantic about being busy all the time. It just meant I didn't have my shit together.

It was time to put the "pro" into professional photographer.

First, I identified the things I needed to do to move the needle, such as shooting the right photos for my portfolio, learning critical skills, promoting my work, and winning lucrative gigs. Those were the things that mattered.

Next, I tracked how I actually spent my time, hour by hour. It didn't take much data to show me that there was zero correlation between how much something mattered and how much time I invested in doing it. It felt fun to wander, to catch inspiration here and there. But fun didn't equal progress, and I actually wanted to make stuff, get somewhere. Tackling whatever caught my attention in an endless flurry of doing wasn't being creative, it was just prioritizing poorly. Though what I was doing felt good in the moment, it never amounted to much of anything.

It was after my third month of contributing nothing to the rent that I finally woke up. Lounging on the ratty futon in our apartment, uninspired and frustrated with myself, something inside me changed. In that moment, I finally decided to take charge. Step one? Stop glamorizing being busy. A hamster on a wheel is busy—where does it get him? I had grander ambitions. I resolved to stop doing whatever came up, whatever highly visible activity created a false aura of productivity and glamour, and instead to focus on being effective.

That shift made all the difference. I was still living a very full life, but I wasn't in a chaotic rush all the time, nor was I wasting time signaling my success to my friends. Best of all, I found that being focused was actually more fun and rewarding. Spending my time thoughtfully got results even faster than I'd anticipated; every week saw a new killer photo for my portfolio or a well-paying gig. I wasn't busy, I was on point. I was *effective*.

Since then, I've found that the most badass people I know, the ones who are the best in the world at their craft, are rarely busy in the way we've been taught to think of it. Being busy is a disease, a terminal one. It destroys your precious time. Being effective is about using every minute thoughtfully and mindfully as you make steady progress toward your dream. The biggest surprise to me has been that those people, those creators who are so deliberate and planned in the way they work, are also incredibly joyful and playful while they work. Planning and play aren't opposites; they complement each other beautifully.

It's time to make a change. Stop telling yourself everything has to be so hard. Pain in life isn't optional, but suffering is. Suffering is all about your attitude toward the pain, the story you tell yourself when things get difficult. By creating systems to manage my time and energy, I began to see progress. That progress helped me understand that all my goals were achievable without sacrificing myself at the altar of my creativity. I finally discarded the toxic belief that pursuing my ambitions had to be an epic, do-or-die struggle. By dropping the "busy" label, refusing to use the word and let it program my thinking, I became so much more effective at getting what I wanted out of life.

You know what's fun? Pursuing your true calling in life is fun.

Learn to prioritize. President Dwight D. Eisenhower often said that what is important is rarely urgent and what is urgent is rarely important. The author Stephen Covey turned that idea into a powerful matrix:

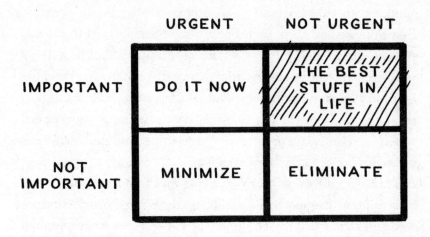

These four rectangles can change your life. I wish someone had shown me this diagram a decade ago. Of course, you need to tackle important, urgent tasks right away, but it is essential to carve out time for the important, not urgent, activities in your life; otherwise all your time will be occupied with unimportant tasks.

Conduct an Audit

Where does your time go? Chances are you spend much of it on things that feel productive but actually aren't. Do you spend hours scrolling through social media on your phone? It's easy to justify that as building your following. Sure, to a point, but without a specific audience-building strategy, you're not going to make much progress. More important, what good is a community if you've made nothing to share with it?

If you want to understand your true priorities, look at two

things: your calendar and your bank statement. Audit yourself. I do this regularly. For example, I recently suspected that I was traveling too much for work. This can sound like a first-world problem, but the reality is that many of us have to travel for work in one way or another, that it often isn't 100 percent necessary, and that it can suck up an extraordinary amount of our time. Traveling for work makes us feel important and busy—it's a classic time-wasting Trojan horse.

I always told myself how valuable and important every trip was and how productive I could be on the plane. Nope. My audit revealed that work travel alone was chewing up more than ten hours out of every week and that I was much less productive during that travel time than I'd been willing to admit.

For example, flying between CreativeLive's studios in Seattle and San Francisco always felt warranted as a way to get face time with my teammates, board members, and partners, but peeling back even the first layer of the onion revealed that a lot of those trips were unnecessary. They *felt* helpful, but when I analyzed them objectively, I realized I could hold a lot of these meetings as video calls. I was allowing my most precious resource to be squandered by what felt productive instead of what actually, measurably was. So I cut way, way down on the number of trips, and, lo and behold, I became more effective.

Now it's your turn. Here's a checklist to get you started.

Track your time using an online calendar or time-tracking app: Apple's Calendar app, Google Calendar, Microsoft Outlook— whatever tool you prefer. It doesn't have to be perfect—fifteen- or thirty-minute increments is fine. Put everything on there in categories that make sense for you, from meetings and calls to chores and commuting. Be brutally honest.

At the end of two weeks, add up the time you spent in each category. Then marvel at the madness.

Ask yourself: What do you have on the calendar that you love? And where do your hours feel wasted?

Consider your options: Are you commuting to work by car? How about taking the bus or train and using that time productively? Are you cleaning the house when you could afford to hire a housekeeper and spend that time writing? If you can't afford to send the laundry out to be done, why not take a sketch pad to the laundromat and draw instead of watching movies on your phone?

The purpose of this exercise is to see the disconnect between the way you spend your time and your core values. This isn't about becoming a robot. It's usually the trivial things we do unthinkingly that steal our time, not the big ones—no one's telling you to cut out date night with your spouse or skip preparing for a big job interview. It's the mindless use of time that needs to change, not the intentional, important stuff. By looking closely at how you spend your time, you can understand your current approach, continue what is working, and change what isn't. In doing so, you will free yourself up to do more of what you love, not less.

Managing your time is an art in itself. Your schedule is a creative work in progress that calls on your ingenuity just like the creation of any book, song, or drawing. By doing this exercise a few times every year, you'll find yourself spending less and less of each week on the stuff that doesn't matter.

Ever seen Warren Buffett's calendar? It's mostly *blank*. "Yeah, well, he's a billionaire," you might say. If you ask him, though, he'll tell you that his time isn't free because he's rich; he's rich because he made time for what mattered to him.

It's time to get creative about getting creative.

Plan to Be Creative

There is no one "right" way to establish a creative schedule because each medium makes its own demands. If you paint with oils, there will be times when you're on the paint's schedule, not your own. If you're trying to sketch out a business plan, simply getting your research materials organized may take twenty minutes, so an hourlong work session may just leave you frustrated. You'll subconsciously resist starting because of how fruitless your time will probably be. It's better to dig deeper and make sufficient time to get the work done.

My own preference is to set aside at least ninety minutes to tackle a small creative task. If I'm doing any heavy lifting, I prefer a three-hour block, at minimum. I aim for one three-hour creative push per day, more under duress—but then I have to double down on rest and self-care.

(Of course, this doesn't prevent me from grabbing a quick slice of time here and there if that's all I've got to create a photo or retouch something in Photoshop. In times of scarcity, grab what you can.)

We're all different. How much time will you need to accomplish what you want to? It depends on your ambitions. How much are your dreams worth to you? Your behavior needs to match your goals. This is not about productivity; this is about aggressively doing what you need to do to be successful as you define it. It's about showing up for yourself.

When you're establishing a schedule, there are several key factors to keep in mind. Let's go through them now so you can create a target schedule that works for you. Get proactive with your time instead of letting the world take it from you.

Set a Cadence

How frequently do you need to work to make real progress in your medium? This will vary depending on how far along you are in your creative journey and at what point in a project you might find yourself.

I recommend creating every day, even if only in small amounts. This daily practice doesn't have to be in your primary medium, either. No time to throw a pot on the wheel? No sweat. Write a blog post about a new insight. Journal. Sketch out some ideas you'll work on when you're back in the studio. Think of this daily creative practice like exercise or meditation: it's nourishing and necessary.

Separately from that daily practice, if necessary, establish regular work sessions to practice your craft. Inspiration usually visits us while we're working. So set a schedule of full creative sessions and stick to it. Then be thankful for inspiration when it arrives.

Start small. A routine that isn't sustainable isn't a routine; it's useless. If you plan to drag yourself into your basement studio six days out of seven right from the beginning, you'll find yourself skipping sessions at the drop of a hat. When you have only one or two opportunities to work full bore each week, you will be adamant about protecting each one from interruption.

Set a Duration

When I'm on an outdoor shoot, I take photos until the sun is down and the "blue hour" of twilight is past. In photography, light often dictates the duration. When I write, though, the matter isn't as clear cut. Sometimes I stop in the middle of a new thought so I'll be excited to pick things up in the next session.

Other times I'll catch a wave of creative flow and ride it until it runs its course.

Every medium is different, even for the same creator. It's more important to establish a consistent baseline and meet it (or exceed it, if you choose) rather than set an unrealistic expectation and then make excuses about why you have cut the session short. A weekly hour-long photo walk might be ridiculous if it's pouring rain, but you can manage fifteen minutes. This is how you build your creative muscles. Working through creative obstacles and across a range of conditions teaches us that nothing can truly get in the way of our creativity unless we let it.

For most aspiring creators, time is the resource we never seem to have enough of. If this resonates with you, the first question to ask yourself is, What is the smallest effective amount of creative work I can do? There is no one right answer. Your personality, preferences, and chosen medium all play a role. Experience is relevant, too. As you build your creative skill set, you get better at working effectively for long stretches *and* at whipping things together when time is short.

Batch Similar Tasks

Consider combining similar tasks and tackling them all at once. As a photographer, I'm responsible for location scouting, creative planning, color-correcting images, working with clients. As CEO, for fund-raising, driving company-level strategy, setting vision, holding meetings with direct reports. Though my worlds are very different, each role calls for certain types of tasks that can be tackled more effectively in sequence. Batching similar tasks makes everything more manageable and less daunting.

You might set aside a specific time each day for processing emails and one for making phone calls rather than allow these activities to proliferate throughout your day, stealing precious time from work that requires sustained concentration. On my podcast, the renowned designer Jessica Hische explained how she uses "Admin Mondays" to tackle all the small, miscellaneous tasks required of her freelance business in a single, dedicated workday. It requires discipline to maintain boundaries and not let other kinds of work spill in, but batching is a masterful way to protect creative work from the day-to-day interruptions that feel urgent but actually aren't and can easily wait until you're ready to deal with them.

Batching doesn't have to be limited to doing certain tasks at certain times of the day, either. The best-selling author Ryan Holiday writes his books in distinct phases: ideation, research, writing, and editing. Instead of looking at a creative project as a monolithic, overwhelming chunk of time that has to be filled with magical inspiration, break it down into different types of tasks, categorized by different demands. Only by getting specific and planning your sessions will you make the best possible use of the time, space, and headspace you create.

Work When You're Most Effective

Take a look at the results of your time audit and identify the open spaces in your calendar. Building a creative schedule should be as simple as laying out the sessions you want in slots of time large enough to accommodate them. But there's one more factor to consider: your personal rhythm.

In his book *When: The Scientific Secrets of Perfect Timing*, Daniel Pink looks at the body's natural rhythms and how they affect your work. Whether you're a morning person or a night owl, your ability to concentrate and make good decisions varies widely throughout the day. For most of us, focus becomes more difficult to muster in the afternoon, so scheduling a writing session an hour after lunch, even if you have the time available, may be self-defeating. In fact, I always ask the guests on my podcast about their schedules, and a majority consider themselves most effective early in the morning. Their Aha! moments tend to occur shortly after waking, before their pragmatic intellect has a chance to fully kick in.

This isn't true of everyone, but if you're not sure, start early. Listen to your body, and see how it works. You know yourself best. When are you most alert, most creative? Thirty minutes of morning "prime time" might be more productive for you than two hours of sluggish, lackluster effort before bed. As you lay out an initial creative schedule, place sessions that require intense concentration and focus where you will be most likely to have them, and place sessions of more mundane back-end work at the times of day when you aren't at your best.

Take what you can get. Your schedule will evolve over time as you learn your own preferences, as will the depth of your creative requirements. Also, expect your creative muscles to be extremely rusty if you've been out of the game for a while. If you haven't been in the habit of creating lately, you might feel sluggish and out of ideas for the first several sessions no matter what time of day you start work. Once a bit of time has passed, you'll be able to see the forest for the trees and make modifications based on your natural rhythms. Until then, stick to the schedule, whatever it is.

Sometimes you have only a small chunk of time available each day, and it isn't the time you'd choose. That's okay. Rather than give up on nurturing your creativity, think about how you might modify the scope. Do what you can in the time you have available. No matter how difficult things might be right now, circumstances change. Sick relatives get better. Small children grow up and become more self-sufficient. The chaos at the office quiets down. Bosses quit. Hell, you might quit. When things do get easier, having kept the fire burning through tougher times will make a larger practice feel easy by comparison.

Your approach will evolve over time. You don't have to figure it all out now. Just start sketching out the different kinds of work sessions you might create, their duration and purpose, and then, when the time is right, sit down to work.

Establish a Work Space

Now that you've given some thought to establishing or bolstering a creative schedule, it's time to establish or optimize your work space. This works best when you can block out a few hours and set yourself up properly with the tools, equipment, and supplies you need. Each creator is different, and so is each medium, but there are certain universal factors to at least consider.

Create Positive Headspace

The first space you have to set aside for your work is between your ears. It's the emotional and mental space you need to put down your other concerns and fully immerse yourself in the design and execution of your vision. Your enemy here is psychological clutter.

I once spoke with a CreativeLive student who was struggling with his family. They weren't supporting him in the pursuit of his photography side hustle. When I pressed him, he admitted that he'd never really talked to them about his dreams and why he needed time alone to do creative work.

"Have you spoken to your husband about how important this

work is to you?" I asked. "Does he know that your full-time job makes you miserable and that you light up inside when you land a photo gig?"

"No," he said. "I don't talk to him about it because I'm afraid he'll resent me if I change careers or reduce our family income."

It can be hard to express your creativity, especially in the early stages. But if you are willing to have this difficult conversation—and others that will surely follow—with honesty and humility, with love, care, and patience, you will free yourself of an incredible burden. Experience tells me that the conversation usually goes better than most creators expect. Creative work is hard enough by itself. You don't need the additional cognitive burden of trying to work when you're not in alignment with the other people in your life.

Whether the above is the conversation you need to have or not, identifying the psychological clutter that has you weighed down—and clearing it out—can free you to be more productive than ever.

Find a Good-Enough Space

I'm happiest clinging to the side of a mountain with one hand and shooting photos with the other. But as a photographer I still spend plenty of hours in front of a monitor. Chefs have to order food from farmers and set aside time to sharpen their knives. You will have time demands like this, too. So ask yourself, when you're not in the field, where do you need to work? More important, where could you work effectively if you had to?

The legendary actress and playwright Mae West began expressing her talents on stages at obscure churches in New York City. A century later, Matthew Patrick, the popular YouTuber known as MatPat, started his YouTube channel by filming in his closet. Now he has millions of followers. At first, do whatever it takes to find a place where your creative practice can begin to sprout. Do what you can with what you have today.

A large, airy, well-lit work space of your own—preferably with an ocean view—would be ideal. But highly productive artists everywhere hunker down to work in cafés, restaurants, coworking spaces, parks, empty college classrooms, and waiting rooms—not to mention buses, trains, subways, and planes. Don't get so finicky about where you can get some work done that you never do the work at all.

Today, mobile devices are sophisticated enough to perform nearly any task, up to and including professional-grade photo and video editing. Would you be able to make progress during your commute if, for example, you bought yourself a digital tablet to edit photos or sketch? Would investing in a pair of noise-canceling headphones make it possible to concentrate on the train or in the break room? If you can't afford them right now, what about a good old pair of earplugs?

A huge part of one's early endeavors—whether you're picking up a new creative craft, starting a new business, or transitioning out of a full-time job into a freelance career—is about flexibility. Think about modifications or purchases you might make to become "creative ready" in as many environments as possible. This might mean carrying a sketch pad in your bag at all times, investing in a mobile audio rig or a digital tablet, or renting a spot at the local work-sharing space. Instead of wishing for a twenty-fifth hour in the day, ask how a relatively small investment of money might make it easier to get work done when you actually have the time to work.

Reduce Friction

If at all possible, you deserve a clean and orderly physical work space. Do you have a spot in your home that can be dedicated to your craft? If possible, establish an area just for you and your work, where all your tools and supplies are close at hand and easy to find. You'll be much more likely to use your scrapbooking nook if you don't have to drag storage boxes full of supplies out from under the bed each time you want to work. You'll practice your violin more regularly if you can leave your stand out with your sheet music ready to go. I love to have a nice, big white-board available for visualizing my ideas. If you aren't able to set aside a dedicated space, create an orderly kit that can be easily transported to wherever you plan to work that day. Always aim to reduce the friction involved in starting.

Set the Scene

Everyone's needs are different. Some people are sensitive to any noise while they work. Others can't concentrate unless there's some chatter in the background. I already mentioned the idea of noise-canceling headphones. They're worth mentioning again. If you need to work in a shared area such as an office kitchen or coffee shop, consider investing in a pair. They are one of my favorite inventions of the past twenty years. On-demand silence has made my often nomadic professional life so much more manageable.

Music, of course, is one of the most powerful cognitive en-hancers available without a prescription, whether you prefer hip-hop, ambient sounds, or even white noise while you're working. I wrote 90 percent of this book listening to the Productive Morning playlist on Spotify. It was just the kind of chill background music I needed, with no lyrics.

Don't neglect your other senses, either. Visual clutter in your space can be creatively fertile or a huge distraction. You might be happier standing while you work or ensconced on a couch under a blanket. The novelist Mark Salzman's cats kept jumping into his lap while he worked, so he took to wearing an aluminum foil "skirt" to deter them. On the other hand, the designer and entrepreneur Tina Roth Eisenberg's cat jumps onto her throughout the day, and she considers those visits welcome breaks. Try to be mindful about the aspects of your environment that make it conducive to your work and those that disrupt your flow; then take concrete action to optimize your space.

Create Efficient Storage

You may need two different types of storage space: supplies and archives. Supplies can be anything from paper to canvas to guitar strings; the important thing is that you have enough, that they are of the appropriate quality, and that you can find them quickly. Archives are where you put your work when you're done. If you work digitally, you'll want to create an orderly system for organizing your output; I don't know how I would survive if I didn't have a very carefully considered system for archiving my photos. Now would also be a good time to establish a regular backup schedule, with copies of your work automatically funneled to at least two destinations, one of which is off-site, in the cloud. If you're producing physical pieces such as sculptures, you may need quite a lot of storage space; consider renting a storage unit nearby so your work space doesn't become unusable over time.

Your work space and your schedule will both evolve as your creative practice develops. For now, you have drawn clear lines around certain times of the week for your work and created a space to do that work. Next, you have to fill that time and space somehow. More on that in the next chapter.

Before I move on, though, let me make one thing clear: don't let the lack of ideal conditions stop you. I was a working pro making a living wage long before I had my own work space. We brainstormed CreativeLive v1.0 out of my photo studio long before it was a registered business, and our first class—attended by 50,000 people online—was launched from a rented warehouse in a gritty part of South Seattle.

Making space for your work is important, but it isn't the same as doing the work. Get yourself set up, give yourself the time, tools, and whatever space you can, and then, for the love of everything holy, start. Just start.

Troubleshoot

Whatever schedule you put into place, stick to it for a few weeks and take note of any obstacles. Once you've gotten some momentum, consider the following ways to bolster your efforts.

Overcome Creative Obstacles

When you're feeling stuck, recognize that you're not waiting to be able to create, you're waiting to *feel like* creating. That's a very different thing. The trap is that we often don't feel like creating until we're well under way. If you wait for the feeling to come before you start, you're going to be sitting there waiting a long time.

When the talented copywriter Cal McAllister was in advertising school, he went to his adviser's office to say he was stuck on an assignment. Clearly, it was a case of writer's block. "Cal," his adviser replied, "I'm going to tell you what you need to hear.

You're not good enough for writer's block. Not yet. Get back to work."

It was a blunt analysis, but creative blocks don't respond well to finesse. You've got to knock them out of the way. Ryan Holiday laughs this off: "Can you imagine having runner's block?" he said. "Go for a run."

When my motivation flags, I find it helpful to switch projects. Five is a number that works for me: one big, one medium, and three small ones, all going at the same time. When I run into resistance on one, I can switch to another, and it feels like a huge relief. Different kinds of projects work best: some calling for strategy, others using my hands, some playful, others mundane. I often find myself coming full circle and switching back to the first project, and suddenly I'm so pleased to be working on that one and not that *other* one. It's a mystery why this works so well, but it does.

Block Your Time

When I returned to CreativeLive as its CEO after a couple of years away from daily operations at the company, a tidal wave of meetings crashed through my calendar, obliterating my daily creative practice. I gave up a lot of freedom in order to learn the creative skill of building a business at scale. As soon as I could catch my breath, though, I had to do exactly what I'm prescribing here. I had to audit my schedule and realign it with my ambitions and values.

After the initial shock to my system passed, I relied more and more on batching, creating dedicated windows for meetings, email, calls, and other related tasks. Then I slowly found myself able to flex my creative muscles during the blocks of time I had created for myself this way.

Work in Microbursts

Let's not be precious, okay? If you aren't able to assemble the ideal amount of time to create each week, it's still up to you to be creative. Writing on the subway or speaking your ideas into a voice-recording app during a walk are ways of squeezing micro-bursts of creativity into your day no matter how busy things get. Posting a daily photo to social media or scribbling a haiku can be enough when things are particularly hectic. *The times we are most stressed are exactly when we need to keep our creative practice on point.* Microsessions of creative activity can be incredibly powerful if you're willing to reset your expectations. Again, make the most of what you can with the time you've got.

Quit Your Day Job. Or Don't.

Obviously this topic is enough for an entire book. The right approach to full-time employment is different for everyone. I do urge you to fully consider your options if an unfulfilling job is getting in the way of your creative ambitions. One of the most important gifts of a creative practice is the sense of agency and empowerment it gives us over our lives as a whole. Being creative at a desk or a canvas shows us that we are capable of making the life of our dreams a reality as well.

If you want to keep your job but it's impairing your creative practice, look at ways to constrain its impact. There are lots of books, blogs, and even classes on CreativeLive about this topic, so you have no excuses *not* to improve your approach.

Also, more companies than ever are open to the idea of remote work. Would it be possible to switch to a three- or four-day office week? Or to work from home entirely? Have that conversation with your boss. If flexibility isn't an option, consider using your vacation days strategically to give yourself mini-sabbaticals to create. Instead of taking a two-week vacation each year, spread five or even all ten of those days throughout the year to give yourself a day devoted to creativity every month or two. I find a day doing creative work much more restorative than a day spent drinking margaritas at the beach.

The legendary designer Stefan Sagmeister is famous for taking a one-year sabbatical every seven to recharge his creative mojo. He doesn't lose clients during that time, either. Instead, they stack up while he's gone, each one anxiously waiting for his return because they know he'll be so wildly creative once he gets back.

If your goal is to ditch your job and devote yourself to creative work full-time, treat your dream career as though it's your full-time job and treat your day job as though it's your side hustle. Flip your priorities completely. Then try to segue. Once your creative work starts to make enough income, consider doing part-time work to supplement it instead of letting it supplement a full-time job: wait tables, bartend, drive an Uber or a Lyft, whatever it takes to speed the transition to full-time creative work.

I give this advice often, but it's usually received with a furrowed brow. Transitioning gradually is counterintuitive to us only because we're sold a narrative in this culture that you've got to "go all in" to succeed at the highest levels. At some point, you may *have* to burn your boats to take the island, but in general this high-risk gamble is unnecessary. We have far more flexibility. We no longer have to move to a certain city to pursue a creative dream in most disciplines, and we can call on many more flexible work options to supplement our income than ever before. Don't quit your day job until you've designed and built a better one.

Guard Your Dreams

Whether we realize it or not, life happens. Interruptions and obstacles crop up: an implosion in your side hustle disrupts your day job, or a big challenge at your day job necessitates skipping creative work for several weeks in a row. Regardless of the external circumstances, clear values and a clear point of view will get you through *anything* with your creative practice intact. Establish them now, and trust them to guide you.

Again, remember the time travel thought experiment at the beginning of this chapter. Deep down, we know intuitively how to protect our most precious resources. We *know* where our time should be spent if we allow ourselves the time to think it through. So, *be a beast about it*. Guard your time savagely.

6

Do Your
Best Work

Inspiration is for amateurs—the rest of us just show up and
get to work. And the belief that things will grow out of the
activity itself and that you will—through work—bump into
other possibilities and kick open other doors that you would
never have dreamt of if you were just sitting around looking
for a great "art idea."

—CHUCK CLOSE

I'm calling your bluff.

For years, maybe decades, you've known you have something
amazing inside you, just waiting to get made. Whether your
dream project is a book, a business, or a play for the local theater
group, it just . . . hasn't happened. Whenever a birthday or other
important milestone rolls around—whenever you pause, step
back, and look at the arc of your life—it occurs to you that this
creative work, or even the life you really want to be living, is still
there, on hold until "someday."

Why? You've done other significant things in your life, things requiring sustained effort and concentration. You've overcome challenges, personal and professional. You may even be a working creative professional. Somehow that deep and meaningful work that feels central to your ambitions is the one thing you haven't gotten around to doing just yet.

Uncreated works of personal expression are at the top of almost everyone's bucket list. They're also the item most frequently left unchecked when we do kick that bucket. So what's holding you back?

If the problem was a lack of clarity, hopefully we tackled that together in Step I. You should now have a much better sense of what you're actually itching to do.

If the problem was a lack of time and space to do the work, the previous two chapters should have helped you there.

Here comes the hard part. You're out of excuses. Good ones, anyway.

Imagine a child's reaction if you snatched a crayon out of her hand just as she began drawing a picture. Happy toddler? Not quite. But we do something similar to ourselves every time we refuse our creative calling. Tamping down our creative inspirations is existentially distressing. When our creative self rebels against this treatment, we field our go-to excuses: creativity is for kids or trust-funders or people who don't have kids or people who don't have a mortgage. It's for people with successful creative parents, art school degrees, or natural "talent." In short, it's for somebody, anybody, other than *you*. You don't get a crayon.

Here's the truth: each of the creators you admire was where you are now at some point: stuck, afraid, or otherwise trapped in "not me." Yet they all broke through by doing the work. The Cuban American artist Carmen Herrera made groundbreaking abstract work her entire life but didn't have her breakout

New York gallery show until she was eighty-nine. A retrospective at the Whitney followed—when she was 101. Herrera broke through. So will you.

Creativity is like fitness. Developing it to its peak isn't actually all that mysterious, if you're willing to take advice and put in the effort. You can get lost searching all the diet and exercise books for a shortcut, but if you're cast as a superhero and you need to transform your body in three months, the studio will send you to the one Hollywood trainer everyone uses. You will be told what to eat and how to exercise. You will do what you're told because your contract is on the line and you'll be wearing spandex in front of millions of people around the world. Three months later, you will look the part—without the use of a single hack or shortcut to "killer abs." All you have to do is *follow instructions and do the work.*

Ready?

Thinking of a Master Plan

At first, it's frightening to find yourself with the time to be creative. You may wonder whether you should spend your newfound time researching gear, ordering business cards, or updating your website. Anything but actually making new work. And although those endeavors have merit in some realms, when it comes to honing your craft, put first things first. The quantity of your output matters most.

Whatever else you take away from this chapter, remember that you'll get better only once you stop fiddling and start *making.* Quality will come over time, but only if you make a lot of stuff while minimizing self-criticism and not letting yourself fritter away valuable minutes optimizing a workflow with no actual work flowing through it.

Your priority in this new approach to life is to get to work creating. That said, your decisions about *how* you will work will dramatically affect the results of that work.

So what is the Master Plan? This chapter is about setting yourself up to create lots of work. It's about giving yourself assignments, deadlines, and challenges so that you can progress in your craft. You may be a working pro, but maybe you're not being assigned the work you feel you were born to do. If so, you must self-assign it. No one is coming to give you the commission of a lifetime without seeing work from you that's similar enough to the commission that illustrates you can do this work. So how can you avoid this catch-22? You assign yourself work that looks like the work you want to get hired to do. Notice that the discipline required here isn't found under the definition of "creative" anywhere. If you're saying "Wait a minute, I wasn't told there'd be *planning* in creativity," take a deep breath and read further.

By giving yourself deadlines to tackle tough creative challenges that are in tune with your imagination, you'll do your best work. I'm all for small wins, but achieving your next-level vision requires ambition, dedication, and above all—yes—intention. Where do you want to be in your craft in six, twelve, or eighteen months? How are you going to get there? Step by step. Any "overnight success" you've ever read about is really a ten-year master plan coming to fruition. But don't forget, there's a lot of success, a lot of benefit to be experienced and cherished long before your boss notices the extraordinary growth in quality of your output or anyone sees your name in lights.

And remember, it all starts with the *volume* of your work. Repetition is the mother of skill.

Start at the Start

Even if you know exactly what you want to work on, even if you're eager to begin, you might find yourself a little lost. We may know we want to paint or dance or sing, but starting can feel as awkward as signing your name with your nondominant hand. Picking up a camera or a guitar feels weird and uncomfortable. It's effortless to fantasize about what you might do when you don't have the time or space, but now that you're out of excuses, the anxiety of the first step can be very real.

So at the beginning, go gently. If you're just getting started with your creative practice, start small. "Fine, Chase. I'll put aside my epic trilogy of the American West for the time being and focus on a single debut novella."

Even smaller than that. We live in a culture that is obsessed with scale. In your creative practice, what is the smallest thing you could possibly finish and share in some form? Entrepreneurs aim for a "minimum viable product," or MVP, with just enough functionality for customers to actually use it and offer feedback to help improve it.

The same principle applies here. Your first project might be something as simple as completing a tutorial from a manual, if you're learning a new craft such as weaving. For a writer, it might be creating a work of "flash fiction" of only a few hundred words. If you're interested in entrepreneurship, it might be an actual MVP: you could code an app that does one useful thing. It doesn't matter if it's good or beautiful or if anyone pays you a dime for it. The point is that you completed something.

Plan Your Work Sessions

The best creators start work with a plan. Nothing too rigid. They establish a general sense of what they're going to try to do with the time available while leaving room for serendipity. Knowing how to balance structure and flexibility comes only with experience. You don't need a blueprint, just a direction. The plan can change as you adapt to new information or feel a spark of creative inspiration, but walking in without one is almost guaranteed to fail.

What does a session plan look like? It can be a note scribbled on a whiteboard to stoke a brainstorm with a creative collaborator. A to-do in an app. A sketch. A snapshot. The amount of detail depends on the stakes and the players involved. Ideally, a session plan sets out a piece of work you can manageably tackle in the time you have available. Again, estimating this properly takes experience.

The objective of your session depends on the nature of the work. It might be a quantity: five hundred words written, ten composed photos taken during the "golden hour" shortly before sunset. It might be qualitative: finish orchestrating the second movement of your symphony, create the opening credits sequence for your video in Adobe After Effects. Regardless of its content, set your plan down in advance. Don't wait until you're standing at your work space to decide what you're going to work on. Some professional creators I know swear by deciding on a plan the night before. This gives their ideas a bit of time to ferment and coalesce so that when they get down to work, they're ready.

Another critical element is to keep your plan 100 percent creative. Stay out of the back office. Creative work always requires noncreative work to support it: setting up software, testing tools, learning new skills, and so on. Don't get sucked in. Never let the admin get ahead of the real work, the making and the doing. Your prime creative sessions should be devoted to your creative practice. No scrolling Instagram to review similar work, no doing "research," no reviewing the analytics on your website. Scott Belsky, a creativity advocate and Adobe's chief product officer, calls this "insecurity work." It's the work we do as a distraction while telling ourselves it's helpful because it's in line with the goals of the project. *It's not the work.* You're just looking for a quick dopamine hit. So draw clear boundaries, and keep this stuff far away from your session plan, where it belongs.

Beware of Inspiration

The philosopher and boxer Mike Tyson once said, "Everyone has a plan until they get punched in the mouth."

Whatever your creative project, inspiration has a weird way of striking the moment you start working on something else. It's no coincidence that we come up with lots of ideas when we're not in a position to act on them. We do some of our best thinking when we're lightly occupied with another task, whether folding our laundry, taking a shower, or walking to the bus stop. My best ideas tend to come when I'm just waking up, working through my morning routine, cooking meals, lying in my hammock, or enjoying some art.

The inevitable lulls during a work session can, ironically, be very creatively fertile. Those sudden inspirations aren't innocent, though. They are your brain's last-ditch attempts to get you out of doing the work. A fresh idea will always be more appealing than the grind of a project that's already under way. The insidious thing about a new idea is that it feels productive to stop what we're doing and tackle that instead. After all, we're *creative*—we have to act when inspiration strikes, don't we?

The discipline lies in getting the new idea down onto paper and then going back to finish what you originally started. This is just one of the reasons a session plan is important: it helps keep you on task.

Flow, the term coined by the psychologist Mihaly Csikszent-mihalyi, describes the state of effortless concentration we experience when we're "in the zone." Various factors encourage the flow state, but it's not something you can flick on and off like a light switch. It comes and it goes, and you have to keep working either way. It's in the lulls between flow states when we start noticing all the shiny distractions. If we don't develop the discipline of writing those unrelated ideas down and then ignoring them as we continue our work, we will never find our way back into the flow state. We won't finish anything, either.

So set a goal for your session, and hold to it. If inspiration diverts you from your course during your work, scribble it down, sketch it out, get it out of your head. Then return to your plan and finish your work.

Establish a Starting Ritual

Elite athletes and other top performers use mental and physical rituals to prime themselves to begin. So do many creators. Rituals help settle down the conscious mind—the source of all resistance and distraction—and marshal our subconscious creative power. Building an effective ritual that works for you can be a great way to get you into the creative zone. Consider doing the following.

Set a Vision

In chapter 4, I discussed the power of visualization to help achieve goals. Visualization can also aid your creative process. Visualize the work you want to create in your mind's eye before doing the actual work. Research shows that simply picturing a task in your mind before physically doing it reduces errors and improves performance. Since you already have a plan to create something today, this means spending a moment seeing yourself creating the work in as much concrete detail as possible, before you begin. Sitting at the coffee table early in the morning, you might envision yourself hiking to a specific location, unpacking your photo gear on the ridge as the sun rises, and setting up the first shot. Run through all your senses, from the taste of the first sip of coffee to the feeling of the shutter clicking under your finger. Whatever your medium requires. Run through the actions mentally beforehand, and when the time comes to begin, you will experience less resistance and more creative flow.

Tunes

In the previous chapter, I mentioned how effective the right music or ambient sounds can be for entering and maintaining a creative flow state. I *love* a great playlist to get into the right mindset for work. You don't have to choose the same sounds you enjoy when you're actually working. You can crank Nirvana to get energized before a session and switch to Zoë Keating's *Into the Trees* when you're actually working if lyrics would be distracting.

Experiment. Once you've figured out what works for you, use the same playlist each time for a while. This consistency trains your brain to get into gear. The more consistent your starting ritual, the more automatic starting will become.

Tame Distractions

Pare away any digital distractions, preferably so that you can't return to them easily. Activate "Do not disturb" on your phone or turn your phone off and leave it in another room altogether. The simple presence of your phone in the room has been shown to reduce concentration and effectiveness. You can also use dedicated software to block social media sites and other distractions. Whatever your tools and methods of choice, reducing mental noise is key.

Get rid of physical distractions, too. You aren't going to feel like drawing if there is a stack of tax documents spilling off the edge of your desk. Depending on your own state of mind, almost anything in your line of sight has the capacity to trigger thoughts and feelings, so remove distractions and annoyances and replace them with things that are energizing and inspiring.

Log and Clock

I know many designers who put themselves on the clock to both keep work on schedule and learn how to estimate their time (and its value to clients) properly. Keep a log of the time you spend working and what you accomplished in that time. It doesn't take much effort. Just create a text file called "Log," and before you start working, make an entry:

8:15 a.m. Task = ink pages 12 and 13 of my comic book today.

This isn't for everyone, but if you're a creative freelancer who works by the hour, or aspire to be one someday, learning to estimate how long it takes to do your work is important.

At the end of your work session, compare your estimate against what you actually accomplished. We overestimate the duration of certain tasks and underestimate others. This feeds procrastination. Tracking your time will help you organize your schedule, forecast your projects, and price your work. Treat your time like any other valuable investment.

Clocks can be useful in other ways as well. Justin Boreta of the electronic music trio The Glitch Mob turned me onto the Pomodoro Technique, invented by the Italian academic Francesco Cirillo in the 1980s. It's a simple but effective technique to push through creative blocks and keep working on tasks requiring extended concentration, such as writing or composing music. Set a timer for twenty-five minutes, work without interruption, and then take a five-minute break. That's one pomodoro. (The kitchen timer Cirillo used was shaped like a tomato, or *pomodoro* in Italian, hence the name.) Complete four pomodoros, then take a fifteen-minute break. Rinse and repeat.

This method first found wide acceptance in academia, but many creators use it as well. Boreta is a certifiable rock star and says it "works magic." If you find yourself easily interrupted or distracted while you're working, try one of the many pomodoro-based apps available, or investigate some of the many variations on the original technique.

Be Accountable

Some people get to be creative at work. One benefit of having a boss is the built-in accountability. The trade-off is that you don't have control over what you work on. If you're an in-house graphic designer, for example, you're told what you're going to design, its purpose, and when it needs to be done. Whether this sounds fun or not isn't the point. Accountability is hard from either side. Those who get it at work often don't want it. Those who need it to be effective at home have a hard time creating it for themselves.

This doesn't change the fact that *accountability separates professionals from amateurs*. Don't let the word *professional* throw you. It doesn't matter if you get paid for your work. If you want the satisfaction of finishing your work, you're going to need to hold yourself accountable.

Nobody tells Patti Smith what song to write next. Yet she's unbelievably prolific. She holds herself accountable. If she wants to write a new song, she sits down and writes a new song. That is the beauty and the terror of true creative autonomy. No matter what level of fame and success you've achieved in the outside world, as a creator, you're part of a select club of individuals who have to go into a room and figure out what you're going to make next.

This doesn't mean we can't get help if we're stuck or if we're not a full-time paid professional. We can always collaborate with others; more on that in chapter 10. Working creators also frequently socialize with other creators. They spend time talking about what they're working on and discussing their grand creative plans for the future. Whenever we run out of steam on a project, we are spurred on by the knowledge that our friends and peers will be checking in with us about our progress. When someone else knows what we're working on, it becomes embarrassing to drop a project without a very good reason.

An accountability partner can help you stay on track. This can be a friend, spouse, or peer you've asked to stay on your case about a project. It can be a professional partner, such as a book editor, life coach, or cofounder. You might find a group of like-minded artists willing to keep one another accountable in person, via social media, or through any number of accountability apps.

If you're a writer, consider joining a community challenge such as NaNoWriMo, which stands for National Novel Writing Month. For two decades now, thousands of writers around the world have labored to complete 50,000 words of a novel during the month of November. NaNoWriMo features social media groups, in-person meetups, and other events designed to build accountability and encourage every participant to meet the goal. Similar organizations exist for filmmaking, playwriting, poetry, songwriting, even computer programming. If one doesn't exist yet for your medium, start one.

The important thing is that once you have a source of accountability, you need to figure out how to integrate that support into your process. Are you going to text your partner before you start with your goal and then send a follow-up text at the end? Are you going to pop into your Slack channel with regular updates? Are you going to actually create alongside other artists in the same physical location for some of your work sessions? However you build accountability into your workflow is up to you. If you need help holding yourself accountable, get help, and get back to work.

It all boils down to the work itself. Once you've prepared, it's time to *get to work*. In *Bird by Bird*, Anne Lamott offers advice for writers that applies to every creative person: "For me and most of the other writers I know, writing is not rapturous. In fact, the only way I can get anything written at all is to write really, really shitty first drafts."

Shitty first drafts. It's as simple as that: you have to give yourself permission to make *anything*, without judgment, no matter what the critical voice in your head has to say about it. The first photo, the first wireframe of the website, the first stab at that venture pitch—*just starting* is the hardest part.

Pump Up the Volume

When you start making creative work regularly or return to it after a long gap, brilliance will not suddenly spill out of you. Quite the opposite. Picture turning on the kitchen tap in an old, long-vacant apartment. That brown water you see at first is totally normal. Public radio host Ira Glass refers to this disconnect as the creative gap; it's the distance between what we see in our mind's eye—what we *want* to create—and the work we are actually able to create with our current skill set. It's a painful disconnect.

I experienced the gap when I took my grandfather's cameras to Europe with Kate. I had a passion for photography and I knew I had a decent eye, but I hadn't yet developed the photography skills to create images that matched what I saw with that eye. Every time we skipped a meal to develop a roll of film, I was faced with that discouraging disparity. It made me feel like quitting every time: "Annie Leibovitz didn't go through this, did she?" Okay, maybe a handful of people are born with a one-in-a-million genetic knack for a certain medium. For the rest of us, it's about doing the work, logging the reps.

"You gotta know it's normal, and the most important thing you can do is do a lot of work," Glass advises. "It is only by going through a *volume of work* [emphasis mine] that you will close that gap and your work will be as good as your ambitions . . . you've just gotta fight your way through."

Volume of work? It doesn't seem like it can be that simple, but it is. Scientific research, my own anecdotal observations, and the experience of nearly every creator I've ever met agree: when it comes down to it, volume of work is the metric that matters most when it comes to closing the creative gap.

Perversely, we start out by doing everything we can to convince ourselves that something other than volume is more important. We need a new lens to get the right shot. We need to switch to a different writing app with better features. We can't launch our business or build our app until we've gotten an MBA so we know how to monetize it once we build it. The work *before* the work never ends.

For everyone who has succeeded in these pursuits, the old saying proves true: a poor craftsman blames his tools. Tweaking is fine, and trying to improve your process is helpful. Before doing that, however, take some shots with the camera you've got. Write lots of words—with a pencil, if you have to. Begin to recognize those impulses as a form of avoidance. What it really boils down to is this: there's a legitimate fear that if we actually make something, we'll have to face the true state of our skills and accept how much improvement we still have ahead of us.

It sucks, but I've found that simply accepting that it's normal eases the discomfort. The silver lining is that, through creating a quantity of work, you will begin to uncover your own personal, signature style. Style is the bellwether of any established professional. You recognize an Alejandro González Iñárritu film through his style: the kinetic energy; the long, fluid takes; the heightened sense of reality. And whether Lana and Lilly Wachowski are challenging us to question the nature of reality or staging jaw-dropping action scenes, you can recognize their work from a single frame of one of their films. They work with different collaborators on every film, but each film has their fingerprints all over it. Style can be imitated, but your style will emerge only after you've done lots and lots of your own work.

Permission to Suck

Your brain knows you're about to put something out into the world, i.e., become vulnerable. "This is a threat," it says. Cue fight or flight. Pour on the adrenaline. *Why am I sweating?* A voice starts talking:

> *This is stupid.*
> *I'm tired.*
> *I'll do this later when I'm in the mood.*
> *I don't have enough time right now to get anything significant done.*
> *Someone has already done this, but better.*
> *Am I sure about this?*

Though these statements may sound believable, you're really just listening to your primitive biology trying to protect you. This is *not* your intuition at work. Your intuition is what got you excited in the first place. It will help you hone the work after you've produced the shitty first draft. Your only hope to combat this voice is to recognize it as a defensive reflex, a flinch, and nothing more. Then plug your ears against the sound and keep going until you rewire it through sheer persistence.

On my podcast, Jared Leto said, "I only succeed a little because I fail a lot." To find success, lean into failure. Embrace it. Tell yourself that this thing you're about to do is going to need a lot of work and that's okay. In fact, it's normal. Allow yourself Lamott's "shitty first draft" to get something, anything, down. Give yourself permission to suck.

EXECUTE

Execute your strategy and smash through obstacles.

7

Make It Till You Make It

The big secret in life is that there is no big secret. Whatever your goal, you can get there if you're willing to work.

—OPRAH WINFREY

Once you establish the right mindset—declaring yourself a creator, getting to work, starting a new project, opening a new business, whatever—you suddenly perceive the world in a new way.

Your brain is the best pattern-finding machine in the known universe, but it needs a mission. You don't consciously realize it most of the time, but you spend every minute of every day bombarded with input from all your senses. In fact, there are way more senses than the five you learned about in kindergarten. Neurologists have identified at least nine, and there may be as many as twenty or more, from proprioception (knowing where your body is in space) to the cutaneous sense that lets you know when you're blushing. All that input, all the time. Your brain processes billions of bits of information every second, constantly and unconsciously. It sifts through all those data looking for threats and opportunities, filtering out the rest. By changing your mindset, you change the filter.

You can try this right now. Look around the room you're in. Observe it closely, and count as many red things as you can see.

Go ahead, I'll wait.

Now, how many green items did you see?

Wait a minute, weren't we looking for red items, you ask? When you're looking for red, that's all you see. The green things might have been invisible for all they mattered.

If I ask you to notice how colorful your world is, things change again. Once you tell your brain you're on the lookout for all the colors of the spectrum, you begin to perceive hues, tones, richness, and depth—you become hyperaware of color in general. The filter in your brain that normally prevents all that detail from entering your consciousness is lifted, and, thanks to a small shift of intention, your awareness of color explodes. Your unpaid parking tickets aren't taking up brain space in that moment because your brain is actively searching for meaning in and connection around color.

This is the creative mindset at work. The same thing happens when you have a project under way. You can't help but see the world through an entirely new lens. It doesn't have to be visual, either. Working on a screenplay, you might start noticing the musicality of the everyday conversation you overhear on the bus or at the office. You might start writing down the things you hear as you try to figure out the "notes" of everyday dialogue.

The same is true for me right now as I'm in the heart of writing this manuscript. I'm deep in the creative process and simultaneously thinking hard about creativity itself; the short walk I just took outside felt like a tidal wave of sensory overload. Colors, sounds, and scents. Our brains are amazingly good at this stuff, *if we set them to the task.*

Here's the thing: You have to start making, creating, doing creative work to activate this sixth (twenty-first?) sense. Actively working on a creative project unlocks your intuitive power.

While the first half of this book is about imagining and designing your creative calling, this step—and this chapter in particular—is all about the power of *action*. I don't recommend crossing a busy highway before thinking, nor should you jump out of a plane before checking your parachute, but doing ought to precede thinking when it comes to baseline creative work. Too much planning is a trap. Don't fall into it. Instead of trying to plot out the perfect novel before you start writing, accept that it'll take a few shitty drafts to get things sorted out and just start writing. Play. Enjoy the process. Write six different intros and throw five into the trash. You'll figure a lot of it out along the way.

I've discovered that this is a major obstacle for many who aim to begin a creative practice but have very little experience on which to draw. So much of our life is about preparing to act, avoiding judgment, or fitting in. The thought of taking small, bold, radical actions without a plan—even something as innocuous as writing words or making brushstrokes on a blank piece of paper—is frightening. Let's put an end to that. Let's separate crossing a highway and jumping out of a plane from the act of creation.

To act requires making a commitment. It's time to stop dabbling. If you keep walking with your eyes open, you'll course-correct, you'll get to where you want to go. Decide what you're going to try to achieve, and then take the very smallest possible step forward in service of that goal.

I've already discussed how I did this with photography—in an ugly, imprecise, awkward sort of way—but nearly every self-made success has used some variation of this approach. Tim Ferriss, an unknown first-time author at the time, attended tech conferences like South by Southwest and the Consumer Electronics Show when his new book was coming out. He didn't know anybody and nobody knew him. The only thing he had was an ironclad commitment to support his own creation. He'd put the work in. Now it was time to show up for himself and his creative vision. But how?

To start, Tim didn't focus on attending the seminars because that wouldn't have done much to promote his book. Instead, he just went and hung out near the speakers' lounge. Nobody could stop him from mingling with the tech luminaries hanging around. It took persistence and some practice, but over the course of a couple days, he met a number of tech bloggers who were intrigued by the articulate, kinetic author, and, in his own authentic way, Tim was able to naturally circle the conversation around to being a first-time author of a book titled *The Four-Hour Workweek*. Partly because of the evocative title, and partly because of Tim's gift for conversation, many of these bloggers began mentioning the book to others, including it in articles and social feeds. Tim certainly put in a lot of other work to make the book successful, but he credits those early blog mentions as the initial spark that kicked off that now-famous book phenomenon. Tim didn't invent the idea of showing up, doing the work, and letting the results speak for themselves, nor do you have to invent anything new to get your work off the ground.

Andy Warhol was well known for the way he steadfastly kept making work, never letting any one project's success or failure slow him down. "Don't think about making art," he said. "Just get it done. Let everyone else decide if it's good or bad, whether they love it or hate it. While they are deciding, make even more art."

Intuit, Then Do It

As I mentioned earlier, our bodies receive billions of bits of information through our senses, every second of every day. To function, the waking, rational mind has to filter out or suppress most of that information so that we can function at basic tasks, i.e., not walk into walls or fall off cliffs. Other parts of the brain and quite likely even the body still process all this input and store it but in a more holistic, less concrete way. That's why people call it your "gut"—there is a physical kind of intelligence that can "know" or simply feel something that your conscious mind does not perceive. *Don't go down that alley. This book looks interesting. That deal isn't as good as it looks.* Intuition is a tool we don't completely understand, but it's kept our species alive all this time. Ignore it at your peril.

You put your intuition to work whenever you start a creative project. Your intuitive filters become tuned to ideas and inspiration that relate to the goal. Intuition is why visualization and goal setting are so powerful: you have an amazing supercomputer that just needs marching orders and a program to run. The better you get at delegating the right stuff to your gut, the more powerful the results will be.

My gut led me to two of my biggest professional successes: Best Camera and CreativeLive. In neither case did the conscious strategy predate the deep feeling that something interesting was going on, first with mobile photography and then with online learning. I ignored a heavy onslaught of naysayers in both cases because my gut was telling me that there was *something* there.

Going forward felt like being drawn toward a magnet. I was being pulled. In each case, my hunch was confirmed.

So how do we screw up intuition? Simple: by overthinking it. The intellect is a beautiful thing, but you can't let it be your only guide. Going deep and listening to your intuition will inform you whether you're still on the right path. Hear the call, follow your path, execute, and repeat.

When the Going Gets Tough

There is an unavoidable hump along any creative path, a big, steep, muddy hill to climb between the exciting start and the point where you've become a proficient creator. You're going to hit rough patches. There's no thinking your way over this hump. Once you get to it, the time for planning is at an end. Only action will suffice.

Once I'd quit graduate school and started to make decent money as a photographer, I couldn't help but feel as though I had everything figured out. I was self-taught, I didn't know anybody in the industry, and here I was doing the same thing any other pro photographer did: taking pictures and selling them for money. Mission accomplished, right?

Then the honeymoon period ended, and I encountered the dreaded slog. The grind. I realized how far I still had to go and how much work and struggle lay ahead. In reality, I was a total outsider. Nobody knew who I was. I wasn't part of the photography community at all. Sure, I seemed to have the necessary combination of skill and talent to land paying gigs, but it was still really hard. It wasn't the success I'd imagined while daydreaming and eating ramen years before. I wanted more: To work with the best clients. To approach each project with complete creative control. To charge top-of-the-market rates. Access, autonomy, abundance. Sure, I was making some money, but if work had been about a paycheck, I'd have stuck with medical school. The problem was, I didn't see how to get from point A to point B.

This is where so many of us plateau or—worse—quit. We make headway scrambling up a cliff, only to realize we're still at the foot of the mountain. Many times, I've found myself thinking "That mountain is a lot bigger than it looked in the picture." We stand alone and stare upward, trying to think of some shortcut, some way to avoid having to take all those steps to the top. But there they remain.

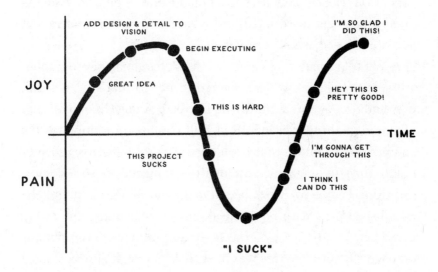

That was a turning point for me. I could easily have spiraled into depression or drifted back out of photography. I'm incredibly grateful that something inside me pushed back. A part of me suggested that it was time to stop thinking so damn much and start doing. The negative voice in my head wasn't very helpful, and I wasn't going to be able to think my way to the next level. If I wanted to be a professional, I might as well act like one first.

I've already mentioned using money from the commercial work I'd done with REI and other clients to buy some baseline professional equipment. I traveled to ski slopes across the country to meet would-be subjects for my portfolio, all at my own expense. It was years before I was granted the industry-standard credentials to stand in the "right" place to get the "right" kinds of photos without having to sneak in ahead of time. None of that mattered. If I'd waited for permission from the gatekeepers, I'd still be waiting.

I leveraged credit card offers for airline miles, slept in rental cars or on friends' couches, and bought film in bulk or even expired film to get discounts. I did whatever it took to put myself as close to my dreams as possible.

A photographer takes photos. A professional photographer sells photos. That's what I wanted to be, so that's what I did, over and over again: at the World Extreme Skiing Championship, Olympic qualifying events, Red Bull contests, anything on the competition calendar that I could get to. I took photos and submitted them to magazines. Suddenly—or maybe not so suddenly, as I think back—my work began to appear alongside photos by established pros with big budgets, press credentials, and swagger. Their photos were on the cover and mine were thumbnails on page 78, but my name was next to each one. It slowly started to work.

The reason it started to work? *I was working.*

There was no thinking my way over the hump. I never just sat at my desk and architected a crafty, gee-whiz plan to get myself to the next level. What changed everything for me was showing up, over and over, wherever my heart and my intuition told me to be—even if my brain was telling me I had no business being there. Taking a thousand tiny, imperfect actions was the only thing that got me from wondering what was possible to experiencing it.

Each action created momentum for more. I embedded myself in action sports, attending meetups, professional conferences, and parties. I shot pics on spec for anyone in the field who asked. All along the way, I asked questions, learning how to get in as I was getting in. I put in the work. I hustled. Then one day I looked up from all that effort and realized that I had somehow made my way over, or perhaps through, the hump.

The work you do when no one is watching is the work that matters most. Pros don't wait until they are pros to act like pros. The people who make it—whatever your definition of success might be—are the ones who are willing to show up and do the work without approval, permission, or praise.

Don't fake it till you make it. *Make* it till you make it.

Escape the Rut

If you'll recall, flow is creativity in action. To do your best work, your job is to get into and maintain the flow state as long as possible. Unfortunately, there is no conveniently located "on" switch for flow. If only there were! As discussed in Step II, there are things you can do to encourage and protect flow, but being a creator means getting down to your work whether flow shows up or not. Before you develop stick-to-itiveness, however, you will end up in a rut, with the internal conviction that you're stuck on the wrong path.

A creative rut is a bit like a finger trap, that little wicker tube that holds your fingers tightly until you stop pulling and bring your fingertips together. Then it slips right off. We get stuck in a rut by trying to think our way out of it: "This project is stalled. Maybe I don't have the talent. I should probably take another class, sharpen my skills. Or just hit 'pause' on this for a few weeks until inspiration returns." You're probably very familiar with that voice. We all hear it whenever the flow comes to a stop. The way to get out of the trap is to relax. The path changes as you walk it. You can pivot only as you move.

Early on, I encountered a rut in my photography. I'd had success, I knew I had an eye for the craft, but part of me suddenly felt uncertain. It was really the only medium I'd explored. Sure, I had a knack for making pictures, but what if the craft of photography wasn't the be-all and end-all for me? What if I went on to spend years mastering the camera only to realize that the "right" medium for me was charcoal or, who knows, needlepoint? How would I ever know if I'd never even tried? (This is the classic sound of a rut being dug.)

I could have put my work down and spent weeks, months, or the rest of my life noodling about what the "right" craft was for me. Thankfully, I defaulted to action over intellect and took oil-painting lessons from a friend. It was close enough to photography that it felt like a worthwhile experiment. And it was; painting taught me a lot. In a practical sense, working with oils showed me how to evoke light and shadow in an image, a lesson I still use in my photography work. In a larger sense, it became clear pretty quickly that although this experiment was part of my path, painting wasn't my true creative calling. My gut told me and, fortunately, I listened.

What if I'd dropped photography and my burgeoning commercial career to make oil paintings instead? Would that mark me as a failure? No—but only if that was what I really wanted. If that was my path. You have to be willing to pivot to stay in tune with yourself. If you go on a hundred auditions and strike out, then decide you actually want to be on the other side and become a casting agent, that doesn't mean you've failed. You've simply succeeded at intuiting the next stretch of your path.

Oils weren't for me, though. Undeterred, I moved forward into acrylics. Acrylic paints are faster and more straightforward than oils, so in a way, I was bending the path back toward what I loved about photography, the immediacy, trying to zero in by listening to my gut. Again, I learned useful things that applied to my photography, but it was also clear that acrylics weren't where I wanted to be focusing my attention. I returned to photography as my primary creative outlet, and now I could say "Hell yeah" to it. I haven't doubted my choice since.

It's important to understand that just sitting down and thinking about whether to pursue oil painting, acrylics, or photography wouldn't have gotten me anywhere. It was only through action that I was able to home in on what worked best for me.

You can't think your way out of a rut. Start by taking action, changing your environment, putting words onto a page, whatever the next step might be. Eventually you'll be back in the flow state.

No matter what's blocking you creatively, your best bet is always to just turn up the volume: *make more stuff.* The default is *action.*

In David Bayles and Ted Orland's book *Art & Fear: Observations on the Perils (and Rewards) of Artmaking,* an apocryphal story is told about a ceramics teacher who divided a class into two groups. Group A would be graded on quality; each student would submit one pot for the teacher to evaluate. Group B would be graded on quantity; all the group's work for the semester would be put on a scale and weighed—the heavier, the better.

If you've been reading along so far, you know where this is going. The students in Group A obsessed about their submission pieces and produced very little work all semester, mostly uninspired, traditional, and "safe." They intellectualized their work. By contrast, Group B created with abandon, free of judgment and expectation, and made many more pieces at a much higher level of quality and aesthetic interest to boot. They prioritized action over intellect.

Earlier in the book, I talked about increasing the volume of your work to develop your skills and as a mechanism to understand your own personal style. Emphasizing volume of output frames creativity as a process. It eliminates the stress and anxiety that often get into the way of starting something when you don't have the "perfect" outcome in mind. It puts you into an iterative mindset that helps you take the risks you need to develop your signature style. Again, action—doing, not thinking—wins the day.

The Art of Done

Your conscious mind is a critic. If you rely on it too much while you're working, you'll struggle to make progress. Instead, stick to a simple, repeatable process:

Day 1: Finish one piece of creative work today, without judgment—whether it's a story, a photo, or a minimum viable product. Just complete the work, create it quickly, and be good with it.

Day 2: Iterate on the work you did yesterday. Do a new draft or update the old one. Put the photo into Photoshop and make it better, add some polish to the lines of yesterday's poem; just take yesterday's baseline and make it better.

Day 3: Repeat Day 2.

Day 4: Repeat Day 3.

Day 5: Decide it's good enough and move on. It's not perfect, not ideal, but *damn, it's pretty good*, right? Good enough to put out into the world.

Finishing brings up emotions about what will happen with the work. Forget about gatekeepers. Forget about money. Forgot about what other people think. They probably don't care. That's a good thing.

Early on especially, do your part, take whatever action you can, and repeat. At this stage of the game, finishing isn't winning a prize. I'm referring specifically to actions that are under your control. Submitting a photo to a magazine is finishing, not getting it onto the cover of the next issue. Hitting "post" on your Instagram photo, not the number of likes it receives, is finishing. Signing your name to a painting, not getting it hung in a gallery, is finishing. I'll talk more about amplifying your work in Step IV. For now, your job is to continue honing your craft.

Stop thinking, take action, and the results will take care of themselves. You imagined a future for yourself in Step I, and you designed the habits to build it in Step II. Now it's time to trust the plan and keep moving forward. Don't get stuck. Choose action over intellect.

8

YOUniversity

People can often do more, change more, and learn more—
often far more—than they ever dreamed possible. Our
potential is hidden in plain sight all around us.

—BARBARA OAKLEY

Learning is the lifeblood of creative work. The more you know how to do and the better you become at doing it, the deeper your understanding of your work and the richer and more interesting it will be. This means you must develop the meta-skill of learning itself. Simple but huge, folks: you've got to learn how to learn to make your best work.

Learning is the core of so many things in life. It's how you stay relevant in any discipline. Necessary skills change over time. It is also how you grow your community. It is how you stay engaged with your work. Moreover, lifelong learning is the unsung hero of nearly every successful creator in the world.

Sure, school can be a valuable resource and an important opportunity for everyone lucky enough to be able to attend. It offers the keys to understanding more complex ideas and opening up to other people's viewpoints. Unfortunately, for too many people, school becomes something you endure in order to get a J.O.B. School can feel like a corral aimed at teaching social conventions instead of a fertile environment for inspiration, growth, and diversity of thought. We show up for class and stick with it through graduation, eager to get our credentials and move on with our lives—the very opposite of a lifelong learning mindset.

It was only when I'd decided to pursue my creative calling to become a photographer that my eyes were opened to an entirely different mode of education. I suddenly had a goal, something I wanted to accomplish. In order to make my vision a reality, I needed knowledge and skills. But I didn't know what I needed to know in order to become a professional photographer. Worse, I didn't even know where to begin.

In the worlds of higher and professional education, they talk about learning paths a lot. Real learning paths are pretty much absent from traditional K–12 education. So many of us show up to whatever class we're told to take, try to remember enough of what we've read and heard to pass the final exam, then forget it all and start from scratch the next semester. Teachers would love it to be otherwise, but that's what happens.

When you're learning for a reason, when you actually have a goal for that knowledge in mind, learning paths become very important. How do you get from A to B? How do you go from not knowing how to develop film to developing film? If you haven't yet acquired the meta-skill of learning how to learn, this process can be very mysterious, even frightening. Without a learning path, you're lost.

I got lost plenty.

Teaching myself to take photographs without a program or any mentors to guide me was a painful process. I progressed in fits and starts, with plenty of dead ends. But it was also more liberating and far more effective than school ever was. Finally, no one was telling me how or what to learn. Instead of being taught a subject according to some textbook's priorities, I could just try to take the photos I wanted to take. When what I tried worked, I'd learned a new technique. When it didn't, I would attack the mistake like a puzzle, going through out-of-print photography books from the library, asking random salespeople at the local camera store, and experimenting diligently until I figured out what had gone wrong. Ultimately, small actions done regularly had a way of showing me what I didn't know. Lightweight failures highlighted techniques I needed to learn and exposed opportunities to deepen my craft.

Slowly, my learning path took shape. I didn't know everything I needed to know yet, but I began to see a rough map of the areas I needed to develop and to understand the logical progression from one thing to the next. Now I could start planning my self-education, taking a deliberate approach to mastering each of the component skills of photography related to my chosen specialty.

This potent mix—books and videos, self-directed practice, and in-the-field experience—dramatically accelerated my progress. I never would have leveled up as quickly in a school environment. Not even close.

Today, I've had the opportunity to talk to hundreds of creative friends and many of the world's top performers about how they've learned best throughout their careers. I've discovered that most share a similar attitude, whether they are athletes, musicians, entrepreneurs, or programmers. The most successful people I know take the reins of their own education, doing what they need to survive school but still investing their heart and soul in mastering their chosen subjects on their own or with outside coaching and training. This learning practice is what drives them to achieve a far higher level of success than their peers.

More important, no matter how much professional success they've seen, regardless of the wealth and the accolades, none of them ever describes being "done" with learning. That idea strikes high performers as absurd. Stop learning? Learning is what brought them success! More learning equals more success. Bring it on!

Every human being has a deep reserve of curiosity, but most of us leave it untapped. In fact, the traditional educational model tends to tamp it right down, so that, when the time comes, we're eager to close the books and go to work at a "normal" job—whatever that means. Sadly, the system is designed to program us for the kinds of lives people lived and the jobs people worked fifty years ago, lives in which creativity and individuality were disruptive and unhelpful. Better to make sure we can sit still and follow instructions, no matter how tedious or illogical. Asking questions slows down the production line. Just memorize these dates, regurgitate them on test day, and make sure to use a number two pencil. Not all classrooms are like this, but far too many still are.

When I started blogging about my experiences as a self-taught photographer, sharing the lessons I learned and the mistakes I made, I began to attract an audience of other people interested in photography, self-discovery, and self-directed learning.

As my professional career progressed, I became more aware of this growing community and its needs. There was so much curiosity there, so much passion. It was nothing like what I'd experienced in high school—people doing their best not to nod off, cribbing notes off each other, doing whatever it took to make the grade—or not. This, by contrast, felt like learning in its purest form. My blog was mostly about photography and, in a larger sense, the professional challenges of a freelance creator, but I had a growing sense that the unshakable thirst for knowledge I saw all around me was only the beginning.

New Learning, New Challenges

In medieval times, the design of education revolved around its delivery mechanism. How did valuable information get from one person's brain into another's? There were two options: face-to-face communication and the written word. Communication required everyone to be in the same physical place. Books could travel in theory, but prior to Gutenberg they were rare and incredibly valuable, each manuscript painstakingly made by hand by skilled artisans. Trade skills such as blacksmithing could be transmitted from parent to child, from master to apprentice. By necessity, all advanced study and exploration had to occur in a single place: within the village or at the university, where books, experts, and students could physically interact.

Today, the challenge of learning delivery has been all but solved. Anyone with a connected device can access knowledge and learn directly from living experts without having to go to a specific place at a specific time at great cost and only with permission from gatekeepers.

But today's learners face new challenges. *Their primary hang-up is understanding what they want to do.* Our career options have expanded so far beyond traditional options that they didn't even exist when you or I were in school. Now a learner can choose to be a firefighter or a coder, an accountant or a YouTuber, a veterinarian or an Etsy seller. With so many possible directions to choose from, so many new skills and new careers and new creative pursuits available, deciding what to explore must come first.

Lots of young people I meet want to learn many different things simultaneously. They want to learn to code their own website, learn to compose theme music for their YouTube channel, and learn copywriting to drive more traffic to their side-hustle website. This is a new attitude. When I grew up, and even as an adult learning photography, pursuing learning was seen as a sign of weakness and vulnerability. Needing to learn something meant admitting you didn't already know it. There was shame there. You tried to keep it quiet. "Hey, if you're a photographer, why do you need to take that Photoshop class? Don't you know your job?"

Since then, willingness to learn has gone from a weakness to a strength. But the number of options can be overwhelming. We may have been told all our lives what *isn't* possible and why we *couldn't* pursue our dreams, but the internet puts the lie to all that. Success stories are everywhere. Just flip through your social feeds. Every day, people all around us are overcoming the greatest of challenges to pursue their passions. It's plain to see that we're living in a new golden era where anything is possible—if you're willing to focus. Our connected lives open a window onto limitless possibility *and* provide the resources to pursue those possibilities.

The new obstacle is figuring out which dream to pursue and then cultivating and applying the necessary energy to engage in that pursuit. The internet provides access to all the world's libraries, but it also provides access to World of Warcraft—limitless knowledge but also limitless distraction.

The first two parts of this book are my attempt to help you overcome these first obstacles. Hopefully, you've done the work to Imagine your own dream, and Design a set of behaviors to support you in pursuing it. Now it's time to leverage your creativity and act in service of your goals. It's time to Execute.

It's always best to begin by doing. School taught me that I'm not ready to learn something properly until I've actually tried it or developed a curiosity so deep that I'm willing to engage with it for hours. As a photographer, I needed to start taking photos *before* I read a pile of books about how lenses work or what depth of field is. Without a body of experience to draw on for context, one f-stop would be just as good as another.

Now that you know what you want to do and you've actually started doing it, it's time to develop the master skill: how to learn. In a way, this is the most important skill of all. Once you understand how *you* learn best, once you figure out how to serve as your own personal academy of higher learning—professor, registrar, and thesis adviser all in one—you can apply that meta-skill to any learning challenge you face for the rest of your life.

Next time you aren't able to do something as well as you'd like, simply enroll yourself in Me University, plan out your semester, master the information, and award yourself a PhD in The Problem You Just Crushed. You'll rarely be intimidated by another learning challenge once you've done this a few times. It's empowering. In fact, it's addictive. It's the secret weapon of the highest performers. There is nothing you can't learn, no matter where you're starting from right now.

Take learning to walk, for example. If you're a parent and your toddler isn't walking yet, you don't just shrug and say, "Oh, well, my kid's just not a natural walker. I'll pull him on a sled from now on." Every able-bodied kid pushes through learning to walk, then run, at her own pace. Everything comes down to crawl, walk, run: anything is learnable, though each person's path will look different. It's true of nearly any skill you can imagine. All you need is motivation, which comes from really wanting to do the thing you're learning how to do. We're learning machines, but to tap into that power you need a purpose. Do you know yours?

Learning How to Learn

If we take learning out of the realm of schools and create an easily repeatable process for learning, we unlock limitless possibility. But where to start? A pattern emerges if you deconstruct the learning process of the highest performers in the world. In this section, I break learning down into three phases: personal, public, and practice. Whether you're learning to cook, play the piano, or write compelling copy to drive more traffic to your website, this pattern applies.

Personal Phase

In the **personal** phase of learning, you're tuning in to your own internal wants, needs, strengths, and motivations. You need to cultivate these things:

- **CURIOSITY.** It doesn't matter what you think you should know or should be able to do. Deciding what to learn—and what not to—are key first steps. What do you actually care about? Learning is a major investment of time and energy. What gets you really excited? Dive in wholeheartedly. If you aren't curious to learn how to do something that may be necessary in your journey, that's fine. Save your investment for the stuff you're excited about, and hire someone to do or barter for the rest. Get clear on what you actually want to know. You don't need to learn everything.
- **TRIAL AND PLAY.** Just get going. Pick up a tool and start. Make a mess. It's okay; you're going to be terrible at first. When I started learning French, my friends who were helping me sat me down and started talking to me in French right

away. I knew about five words, but that didn't matter. Just talking with them face-to-face and struggling to pick those five words out of a stream of others activated a new part of my brain. I realized that I had an ear for accents. I started to internalize the sounds long before I understood the meanings. In photography, my first images were awful, but I found joy in the process and felt confident I could improve. Doing kept me learning, and learning kept me engaged. It was a virtuous cycle. There is no substitute for jumping in at the deep end.

- **INSPIRATION.** As you try things out, oddities will catch your attention. Maybe your wild flailing with a brush led to an interesting effect on the canvas. Maybe one of the settings you played with in Photoshop did something unexpected and compelling. Now you have a question—why did that happen?—and a starting point for investigation. It doesn't have to be wildly significant—it just helps you get into the material. If you approach your new skill in the spirit of whimsy and play, little surprises will pop up frequently.

Public Phase

In the **public** phase of learning, you use outside resources to start answering the questions you're only now ready to ask by using the following resources:

- **SCALED INSTRUCTION.** If something unexpected happened when you did X, why? What was the underlying mechanism? Books have always been a key resource for me at this stage. Now you also have access to visual content: YouTube, learning apps, online experts, platforms such as CreativeLive. A book can't give you the experience of how to direct a photo shoot. "Now tell the model to lift the left hand three inches." But you can learn this in one minute by watching a professional photographer do it. There is no substitute for watching mastery in action. This is the new college. The difference is, you don't just drink from the fire hose; you come to the resource with specific questions in mind based on your experiments. This is a much more effective way to approach new material than "beginner-intermediate-advanced." Let curiosity and inspiration guide your exploration.

- **COMMUNITY.** Seek out other people who are learning the same skill; you can discuss what you've learned and practice together. Whether online or in person, connecting with a community will support your learning efforts. It will also expose you to a diverse set of ideas that will dramatically enrich your perspective on what you're learning. If you weren't in love with your new skill before, this step can tip the balance. Passion is infectious.

- **INDIVIDUAL OR GROUP INSTRUCTION.** If it's feasible, find a teacher. Once you've been trying something on your own for a while and you've been out in the community meeting people farther along than you are, you're going to be much more ready to absorb lessons from a good instructor and you'll be in closer proximity to those who are able to teach the subject. This doesn't have to be one person—you can turn to a small cadre of different instructors, each with a different specialty or viewpoint. One-on-one learning is expensive. That's why it should happen after the other steps. You need to learn enough to understand your own particular needs, interests, and challenges. "Why does this happen every time I do this?" In one-on-one learning, you can have the questions answered that only you would ask.

Practice Phase

In the **practice** phase of learning, you're iterating and honing your skills to a razor's edge by using:

- **REPETITION.** Most skills have conceptual components and mechanical components. To master photography, for example, you have to understand concepts such as exposure and shutter speed. You also have to fiddle with a bunch of knobs and buttons rapidly if you're going to get the shot you want. In the words of the choreographer Twyla Tharp, "Skill gets imprinted through action." Assign yourself daily drills to practice the mechanical basics of the skill, whether reviewing flash cards or working with a kitchen knife. Learning all the recipes in the world won't make you a great chef if you can't chop, dice, and julienne those veggies.
- **JUST DEAR IT.** In chapter 2, I shared the acronym DEAR. It's a form of practice that was my secret weapon for achieving rapid growth in my photography skills and progress in the industry. We're wired to learn through imitation. I put that fact to use by replicating the work of photographers I admired. This doesn't mean copying someone else's style—it means figuring out the way they do things to help build your own approach. It's said that Jack London hand-copied thousands of pages of Rudyard Kipling's works to learn the nuances of story, grammar, and syntax. As you look to your own inspirations, try this: *Deconstruct* other people's methods. *Emulate* the different elements. *Analyze* those parts to see which ones work for you. Then put the winners together and *Repeat* with the new formula.

Learning follows a power-curve distribution, which is a fancy way of saying that you'll make big strides quickly at the beginning and then your progress will slow. How good do you have to be to do what you want to do?

When you're able to complete your own personal objectives, you've learned the material. There is no certificate with an arbitrary set of requirements based on what someone else thinks you should know. Life is too short to "collect" every skill and subskill like a bunch of trading cards. Photoshop has a million tools, but most people can do most everything they need with a handful of them; it takes the above process to figure out *which* handful.

Learn the skill to the level you require it; if that means achieving basic proficiency, fine. You're off to the races now. The beauty of learning this way is that it unlocks unlimited growth potential. Once you've taken a skill from "How do I hold this tool?" to "I made six of these today, would you like one?" you've developed the meta-skill of how to learn. You'll be able to grow and transform your life at a pace you never thought possible.

How You Learn Best

By following the above process, you will achieve proficiency and you'll also start to learn how *you* learn best. I've discovered I'm a visual learner, for example. Painfully visual. When I'm trying to think something through, I need to write it out and draw pictures in order to catapult my thinking. If I'd known that back in school, I would have had a much easier time.

Once I did understand this about myself, I could orient situations to work in my favor. If I was struggling to keep up in a group discussion, I would just grab a marker and take things to the whiteboard. If that wasn't feasible, I'd open my notebook and start mapping out what I was hearing in order to enter my preferred learning modality. Learning stopped being a chore for me.

I'm also a collaborative learner. Once I've absorbed new concepts in quiet reading, I need someone to bounce ideas off to help them sink in. I absorb much better that way than by simply engaging in quiet reflection. This is particular to me. You will have your own preferences, and you may not be aware of them yet—you may be aware only of when you struggle to understand.

As you develop a new skill at your own pace, you'll start to identify your learning preferences. Do you prefer to start with details and work your way up to larger concepts? Or do you need to make a mental map before you can absorb specific facts and figures? You'll have to discover that for yourself. When the information doesn't gel right away, it doesn't mean you're bad or you don't have the necessary talent. It just means you need to try another approach to the material.

Traditional school is often far too rigid; it doesn't allow for variations in learning styles. You're expected to adapt to the teacher's teaching preferences, not the other way around. After all, once you're at the factory, it's rare that allowances will be made for you. You'll just have to adapt to the system. Thankfully, the "take it or leave it" era of traditional education is coming to a close, and new ideas are taking root.

This flexibility has made all the difference to me. One way I like to approach new material is by coming at it from an unexpected angle, putting my own spin on it. This makes it exciting to me and therefore accessible. When I decided to learn how to shoot with Hasselblad medium-format cameras, for example, I started using them for action sports photography right off the bat. People were up in arms. Medium format is a studio tool—you don't take a Hasselblad out on the slopes! But going at it that way hooked my attention in a way that taking photos in a studio never would.

Achieving Mastery

Skills are key in any endeavor and particularly important in pursuing a creative craft and developing a creative practice. They are necessary for real progress to be made. Mastery, however, is something entirely different. While it may sound overwhelming, the act of mastering *anything* will take *all* your learning to an entirely different level, and it is entirely within your reach. Mastery is what you see at the highest levels of any pursuit, in the people I'm suggesting you study, deconstruct, and imitate. It's worth at least understanding how they operate.

Though skills are the fundamental building blocks of mastery, they provide only a fraction of the richness and depth. It's the difference between knowing the basic vocabulary of a language and achieving fluency in it. A few common phrases can take you on amazing adventures when you're on vacation in a foreign land. Your aspirations can stop right there, and you can still have a great trip. But being fluent will allow you to communicate complex ideas with personal flair. Complete command of a language unlocks a new world—friendship, culture, tradition, history. It's important to know that this realm of mastery exists and how it's achieved in case you decide it's worth pursuing as a part of your calling.

If you've watched a lot of martial arts movies, you've probably picked up some beliefs around the idea of mastery. We have this image of a master as an old guy—always a guy—who lives off in the woods or on a mountaintop. After a lifetime of brutal study, practice, and discipline, he's perfected a set of skills. What's the payoff for all that effort? Once the master has passed along his most prized lessons to a talented apprentice, his old rival shows up and kills him. Now his student has a good motive for revenge.

That is not mastery. Mastery is never an end in itself; it is always a by-product.

In fact, if you train in a martial art such as karate, you'll learn that the revered black belt doesn't indicate any sort of perfection or completion at all. Instead, it is only the first step in a whole new progression of learning. It's just another white belt. In the martial arts, every student, no matter her rank, is reminded to approach learning with a beginner's mind. Thinking in terms of some mystical perfect endpoint is an obstacle to growth. Learning is a continual, nurturing, fundamental life process, just like—and deeply entwined with—creativity.

Achieving mastery, as I use the term here, doesn't mean you know it all, only that you know how to navigate the material. You know what you know and what you don't. At the beginning, it's hard to enter a subject because you have to draw a mental map as you explore the territory. Once you've mastered the rudiments, you've drawn the mental map; you don't know everything, but you know where everything goes, how it fits together, and *why*. Your learning accelerates. And the flywheel begins to spin.

Masters know this. Now you do, too.

Learn one thing really well—insanely well, front to back, top to bottom—and the learning experience itself will teach you what mastery feels like, what's required, and why it's so worthwhile to achieve it.

Why are some of the most prominent creators in our culture so good at several things? Mastery begets mastery. Take Lady Gaga, mentioned earlier: she performed at open mics under her real name, Stefani Germanotta, while attending New York University's prestigious Tisch School of Arts. Then she dropped out to play the piano nightly at dive joints on Manhattan's Lower East Side. Only after doing that for *years*, perfecting her craft, did she earn a series of breaks—well after she'd paid her dues—and burst onto the music scene, winning awards, notoriety, and fame. Then she did the same thing with fashion. Then with acting. And she will certainly achieve mastery in other areas before she's done.

Take Nell Painter, a tenured academic and historian. In her memoir, *Old in Art School*, she wrote about enrolling in art school at the age of sixty-four. She made tremendous progress in months, not years, outpacing her much younger peers, because she tackled her learning with the same rigorous discipline she had developed while mastering historical subjects. The painter in her learned how to learn like a historian. The disciplines were different, but the approach to mastery was fundamentally the same.

You're the Answer

No one is coming to save you. Experts are valuable when you're learning new skills, but neither experts nor institutions are going to nurture you, guide you, or make your creative dream a reality. You're on your own path. It's all up to you. This isn't a bad thing, either. Your creativity gives you the capacity to design the life you want.

The world of education has already changed. You no longer need an MFA to paint, publish, or write plays. Venture capitalists don't care where you went to school if your idea is powerful and your code gets the job done. In the most vibrant new industries, college is no longer a requirement for an amazing career. Companies on the cutting edge want knowledge, talent, and passion, not certificates.

Books, blogs, courses, podcasts, and online seminars are now better, cheaper, and more varied than ever before. No money? No problem. CreativeLive has given away literally billions of minutes of video learning from the world's top instructors in dozens of categories. There are lots of similar platforms available. All those inexpensive learning resources are incredibly valuable, but only if you are willing to do the work on your end.

No matter how strong your foundation, how you prefer to learn, or how much money and time you have to invest, you can design and embark on a program of self-directed learning that will get you where you need to go. The knowledge is all out there, ripe for the picking.

You don't need experts. You probably don't need school. What you do need is to create, learn, repeat.

9

You Must Fail to Succeed

When you take risks you learn that there will be times when you succeed and there will be times when you fail, and both are equally important.

—ELLEN DEGENERES

Damn. This was not how I wanted to wake up.

It was early morning on April 9, 2012, and my phone would not stop dinging. Text after text came in. People wanted to talk about the news: Facebook had just acquired Instagram for the eye-popping price of $1 billion, making headlines around the world. Who could have imagined a two-year-old company with a dozen or so employees commanding a ten-figure valuation?

Watching that tech fairy tale unfold, I couldn't help but be amazed at what the Instagram team, starting with founders Kevin Systrom and Mike Krieger, had accomplished in such a short time. I also felt the sting of regret. If things had gone a little bit differently, it might have been my company making headlines that day. It wasn't my imagination, either; the texts flooding my phone within minutes of the news were proof of that. Once I opened my laptop, I encountered an even larger wave of emails, tweets, even blog posts. I was far from the only one who saw the connection. *Yes, I saw the news about Instagram. Yes, I know it could have been us. No, I'm fine. No, I'm not lying about being fine.*

At the time, I shrugged it all off with friends, employees, and colleagues, but my genuine feelings took months to reconcile. My thoughts kept turning toward what might have been. How had a few small mistakes derailed my at-the-time-straightforward path to what ended up becoming a billion-dollar deal?

Everyone's heard the story of the friend's cousin who insists she invented the idea for almond milk only to have "Big Almond" steal her idea. Or the uncle who "had the idea for the iPhone" because he drew a picture on a yellow Post-it once. I'd like to think the story I'm going to tell you is different because I really did make the thing, and it was actually successful—at first.

In 2009, when the iPhone App Store was still new, I launched a photo-sharing app called Best Camera. It went on to be featured by Apple, selected as one of *Wired*'s apps of the year, covered in outlets such as the *New York Times* and *USA Today*, and named *Macworld*'s Top App of 2009. We beat Instagram to market—helped define the market, in fact—and reached a million downloads before most people understood what a photo app really was.

So what happened? How did Best Camera end up on the sidelines?

The truth is, it doesn't matter. This chapter isn't about "the one that got away" or how to stop that from happening. This chapter isn't about fixing anything. The system isn't broken, your creations aren't broken, and you're not broken. Even if you're doing things right, *lots* of opportunities are going to get away. This chapter isn't about avoiding mistakes. That attitude is crippling to creativity. It's about recovery, resilience, and grit. As Richard Branson once told me, "Opportunities are like buses. There's always another one coming." You need to be ready to catch the next bus, not chasing the one you missed. It's gone.

Adversity happens, especially when you are a creator in pursuit of your passions. Failure is baked right into making new stuff. If you let each mistake tear a chunk out of your peace of mind or self-esteem, you'll never last long enough to succeed. Instead, imagine standing in the face of creative trip-ups, squandered opportunities, and epic failures—and *being okay with it.*

Ask any physicist, and she'll tell you it takes *work*—force exerted over a distance—to change any system. Creativity is how we direct that work, whether the system we're trying to change is an industry or a code base.

Talent doesn't emerge without effort. Are you kidding me? Fighting gravity is the hardest thing you can do. It's the brave crew of Virgin SpaceShipTwo returning to the runway after the tragic loss of SpaceShipOne. If you want to achieve escape velocity from Planet Earth, it takes humility, guts, and *rocket fuel.* That is the purpose of this chapter, to help you learn to enjoy the work—all of it, not just the wins. To break through the gravity of Planet No. To give you fuel when your tanks run dry. You *will* make mistakes, run into obstacles, and downright fail at each and every phase of the creative process from idea all the way through launch. Together, let's get better at it. Let's fail better.

My hope is that by explaining how I failed on a global stage with Best Camera, you'll come away not only with insight into a large-scale failure like that one but also a sense of why failing on any scale is better than not trying in the first place. Nothing happens when effort stops.

Solve Real Problems

In photography, as in many other fields, expensive gear is over-rated. After all, what's a photograph? Ignore the tech blogs. What's important is not having a certain number of megapixels with a certain dynamic range. It's capturing a moment, a vanished millisecond of life frozen in time. It's creating a story, at least a thousand words' worth.

When you realize what a photograph can do, when you see what a master—even a proficient amateur—can accomplish with the most basic camera imaginable, the importance of the tech fades. That's why I was one of the very first champions of camera phones in the industry. I became obsessed by the possibilities. I began experimenting with the Palm Treo's camera—absurdly limited, something like 0.3 megapixels—and later with the first iPhone at two whole megapixels. Despite all the limitations, I could clearly see the future from where I stood. What was import-ant wasn't the quality of the camera right then; that would change quickly. It was the ability to take photos anywhere, anytime, and that these devices were connected to the internet. I was in heaven, and I shared my mobile photography experiments widely.

As I experimented and stretched my creativity, sharing what I made online, early on I got nothing but hate. It comes with the territory whenever you try something new. I kept going, and, around 2007, the images I was creating with my phone began to get traction on Twitter and Facebook. As the technology im-proved, it became harder and harder for the average person to distinguish between a camera phone photo and one I'd taken with a professional rig.

Still, as much as I loved the rapidly improving phone cameras, the mechanics of sharing images remained a huge pain point for me, requiring five or even six different apps to capture an image, process, and share it.

That was the "scratch your own itch" moment that occurs at the start of so many businesses. I had encountered a personal pain point that was so obvious, the solution demanded itself: I could fix this!

Make Ideas Real

Apple's brand-new App Store soon made it possible for independent software developers to create and sell their own software for the iPhone and iPad. I decided to develop my own integrated solution for capturing, editing, and sharing photos. In my mind, the best camera isn't the one with the best technical specs, it's the one that's with you when you want to capture that once-in-a-lifetime moment. *The best camera is the one that's with you.* Thus, Best Camera was born.

Everyone I told about the idea insisted that the concept had little value. No one would ever care about two-megapixel photos that weren't worth printing. As for a social network dedicated to sharing mobile photos? Ludicrous.

Maybe you would have seen it differently. Maybe you would have given me an enthusiastic thumbs-up and asked about investing in my new business. You may share the widespread belief that resistance to new ideas is somehow unusual, that if something is truly, unimpeachably terrific, most reasonable people will see and understand its value right away and cheer you to the finish line.

Nope. Quite the opposite, in fact. Good, bad, or ugly, creative ideas are a change to the system. To a system, any change is a threat. The system—and each of us is part of the system—will protect itself. Genuinely new ideas encounter resistance proportional to the size of the change they represent. If you don't believe me, look at the history books. From computers to lightbulbs to the printing press, change has always met resistance, resistance that seems comical a few years later, once the idea has dramatically improved the world.

The nineteenth-century philosopher Arthur Schopenhauer got it right when describing the three stages of truth. First, it's ridiculed. Second, it's violently opposed. Third, it's accepted as self-evident. Thinking in these terms, it's funny to realize that people probably hated the wheel when it first hit the streets. As odd as this might seem, beware: at some point you will have to overcome this systemic resistance to make your ideas reality.

As a part of that system yourself, you are a white blood cell, part of the world's immune response to new ideas. That means that sometimes even you will resist your own ideas as vigorously as the photo industry resisted mobile photography.

Scott Belsky, the author of *The Messy Middle*, warns that "great opportunities never have 'great opportunity' in the subject line." Don't be so quick to shoot yourself, or others, down. Cultivate the discipline of open-mindedness. This is harder than it sounds. Whether it's you against you or you against the world, *overcoming resistance is part of the creative process.* The more others push back—or the more you resist your own idea—the greater the odds that you're pushing into the unknown. The only thing we can ever know about the unknown is that it's where all amazing opportunities await.

You Can't Fail If You Don't Start

I didn't know how to make an app. One approach might have been to put the idea aside and go take a coding class, but this was one of those times when I knew I should delegate the work to an expert. I'd learned to value action over intellect. The time was right for the idea, and I knew exactly what I wanted to build—not the technical details, of course, but the user experience. Since Seattle was a tech hub, I just needed to find local collaborators whose strengths complemented my weaknesses and vice versa. (More on collaboration in chapter 10.)

I started poking around, asking questions of my friends, and making connections within the local developer community. After meeting with a half-dozen groups or so, a friend referred me to a full-service development shop that seemed both capable and interested in my idea. It had built several apps already, a few with modest success. It seemed professional and organized. It was even located only a few blocks from my photo studio, and since the folks there were willing to trade development time for future revenue share, it seemed like an ideal match.

Spoiler alert: the seeds of our failure were sown in the terms of our agreement. Many business and creative failures share a similar story: mistakes or gambles made out of ignorance, enthusiasm, or naiveté in the early stages lead to a project's demise.

The lesson to take from this recurring theme, however, is the opposite of what most people actually do. Too many creators and entrepreneurs decide that for *their* project, the solution is to learn everything about what they're going to do, research all the details exhaustively, and ask every expert for an opinion—*before* starting. Only that way, they think, will their idea be *safe*. Now that risk is out of the way, they can start doing the work. This approach functions about as well as waving your arms around hoping to push the air out of the way before your plane takes off. It's dumb. Even looking back on the experience, I can see that my contract was as good as could be expected at the time, at the dawn of the new business model of app development. Sometimes the only way to learn a lesson is the hard way.

What most of us are really doing when we try to anticipate every possible failure is masticating our once playful, powerful, smart idea into a lifeless paste. As the life of an idea is leached away by "preparation," we become overwhelmed. Trying to avoid every possible pitfall before your idea has any substance either neuters it or leads to its abandonment before anything even gets made.

Most great ideas are never realized because we talk ourselves out of them before we even give them a chance. Give more things a whirl, especially early on. The process of doing something, anything, over doing nothing at all is the path to growth and opportunity.

The Juice Is Worth the Squeeze

Adversity is intrinsic to creative work. You will never be able to avoid it completely. The more you try to avoid problems and optimize your process *before* you do the work, the more distant your goal will become, until it seems almost unbelievable that you'd ever actually start. When facing creative adversity, you could, of course, walk away, but most people walk away too soon. Instead, try leaning in. How? By taking action. Failure may or may not be in your future, but all the growth, opportunity, and reward will be found on the path, not around it.

After several months of work, my badass team, the developers, and I came up with version one of Best Camera app. It was relatively simple, but it was gorgeous. It did exactly what I'd intended: you could take a picture, add a cool effect, and share it with one tap. The user interface was simple but power-ful. We'd borrowed the concept of a "dock" at the bottom of the screen from the Apple desktop ecosystem and combined it with the concept of filters from traditional photography: the effects different kinds of glass could achieve if applied to the front of a camera lens.

In September 2009, Best Camera went live on the App Store and I was thrilled. My 3 a.m. "scratch my own itch" idea had become a fully functional reality. I'd expected a long, slow slog to adoption, but within seventy-two hours, Best Camera was number one in the App Store, quickly making its way through the photography community and then the larger tech community. Then things got weird. I started getting emails and calls: from daytime TV shows, venture capitalists, the *New York Times*, Apple's own PR department—it was nuts. In a very short time, we hit half a million users.

With Best Camera, I knew I'd tapped into something amazing, but it remained to be seen whether I'd be able to stay tapped in. A review in CNET at the time was eerily prescient: "Hopefully, Jarvis and his software-engineering partners . . . will continue to evolve the app and not charge extra for updates." That was certainly my plan.

As amped as I was to push forward, the predominant be-lief at the time was that apps could only ever be a flash in the pan. After all, there were already hundreds of thousands of apps available. How could any single one stay relevant for any amount of time?

In short, the developers didn't share my vision that apps could become huge companies in their own right. I just couldn't convince them otherwise. Meanwhile, Best Camera's success meant a flood of new opportunities for them. Their shop had coded an "App of the Year," and they wanted to chase those new opportunities.

This is the danger of any collaboration. Sometimes the collaborators don't share the same incentives or the same vision. Their vision was based on their experience. At the time, most apps were gimmicks that had their day and then fizzled. Remember apps that turned your phone into a lightsaber or a glass of beer you could tilt and pretend to drink? The developers felt—understandably—that Best Camera would be no different. If I'd had their experiences in the trenches, I might have felt the same way. They'd built the software I'd asked them to build, and they wanted to move on.

Without much leverage with my collaborators, I did the only thing I could: I leaned into promoting mobile photography as the future of not just the photo industry but popular culture itself. I landed a book deal and launched the first book of mobile photos, which landed me on daytime TV talk shows and a book tour. In short, I did everything I could to help people understand that photography is a universal language—it transcends culture, religion, geography, even time. This wasn't about sharing images per se, it was about sharing our lives.

The hustle paid off with more growth—for a time—but the lack of substantive updates started to take a toll and new competitors were on the move. Kevin Systrom had created an app called Burbn that wasn't doing particularly well. He found that users loved the app's photo-sharing features, so he and Mike Krieger pivoted Burbn to something called Instagram. While we'd squandered our growth opportunities, they had built a better version of Best Camera, just taken another $7 million in funding, and were iterating. Fast.

Adversity had reared its head.

Step into the Unknown

Beginnings are tenuous times. Getting anything substantial off the ground means making countless tiny decisions first, any one of which might assume vast importance—*if* you're successful down the road.

The danger is twofold. On the one hand, you can become paralyzed by all the decisions you need to make. They can steal the life from your project—whatever the medium and at whatever the scale—before you've even begun. "What if I don't buy the domain name of every single variation of my business's name and someone squats on one of them? I'll have to pay out thousands of dollars in ransom one day!"

On the other hand, you can rush through the initial decisions in your enthusiasm to get something off the ground, only to realize that you've doomed a promising project out of hastiness.

This dilemma is particularly thorny if you're inexperienced. When you're just starting out, you have little basis on which to decide which initial decisions are critical and which can be tweaked later on if things work out.

This is the point in any project when you have to remind yourself of two important things. First, risk is inevitable in creative work, and no amount of preparation can completely protect you. You'll develop the capacity to make these decisions well only by making lots of them and, yes, failing from time to time. Even failing big.

Second, there is a sane middle ground between leaping off a cliff and hoping there's a net at the bottom and planning the leap for three months before becoming distracted and wandering over to some other chasm. As the French philosopher Voltaire once wrote, "Perfect is the enemy of good." Do enough research, ask enough questions, but remember that action—taking a risk—is the beating heart of creative work.

If you're ever on the fence, unsure of whether you should keep researching or take a leap, that's a clear sign that you've already noodled too much. Get moving, learn something, and take the lessons with you regardless of the outcome.

Plan for Success, Learn from Failure

While I'd anticipated a demand for frequent updates of Best Camera if we succeeded—I'd baked it into the contract—what I had not anticipated was the possibility of such incredibly rapid success. I'd structured an agreement with the developers based on the idea that the app would take a while to achieve liftoff. The revenue split favored me once their initial investment was repaid. That was my failure of imagination. As a result, I hadn't given any thought to the possibility of overnight success removing most of their financial incentive to keep working on it.

As Best Camera stagnated, the online reaction went from the occasional tweeted tirade from a passionate fan to literally thousands of people openly begging for an update. The cold reality was that I couldn't give it to them. I had no access to the code. I couldn't migrate it anywhere else. I couldn't access the App Store to see download data or revenue. I couldn't even update the marketing copy. I was locked out. There I was with an App of the Year award, my vision for the future of mobile photography only partially realized, a huge and passionate user base, and offers to fund the app or even buy it outright for never-work-again amounts of money, and I was dead in the water.

Worse, I was grappling with paralyzing shame for ending up this way. I'd failed.

By the time Facebook bought Instagram, some time had passed. Despite the frustration and sense of loss, I felt strangely calm, almost peaceful. I silenced the torrent of notifications on my phone and sat quietly, letting it all sink in for a minute. I knew I was facing my biggest professional failure—a billion dollars' worth. More than missing out on a big payment, I was missing the joy I would have felt in seeing my work used by damn near every person with a phone.

I failed in several important ways with Best Camera. It was brutal. It hurt. Some days, even ten years later, it still does. Your creative failures will hurt, too. If you're willing to sit with them, however, you'll start to see things a little differently. Time passes. Wounds heal, *if* you allow yourself to feel them. My dear friend Brené Brown put it best: "To strip failure of its real emotional consequence is to scrub the concepts of grit and resilience of the very qualities that make them both so important: toughness, doggedness, and perseverance."

Best Camera was a wild ride. It was not easy, particularly the tedious technical and legal wrangling at the end. My attorneys kept me off Instagram for five years for legal reasons. As all my photographer friends stacked up millions of followers, I watched from the sidelines until late 2016 before joining the fray. That hurt, too. (I'm @chasejarvis, by the way . . . come say hi.)

Yet the experience taught me so many critical things I couldn't have learned any other way. Those lessons were invaluable when I was launching and growing CreativeLive, which has many times more users than Best Camera ever did. I learned how to build a company with aligned incentives, where we work rapidly and iteratively to improve the product based on what the community wants and needs. I learned about the dynamics of Silicon Valley and venture capital. And I learned that technically owning your code and intellectual property isn't enough; you need to be able to put your hands on it. Though I couldn't have known that our very first CreativeLive class would draw 50,000 people, this time I'd anticipated the possibility, and I was ready to ride the wave.

Rejection Therapy

Show up and embrace adversity, in creativity and in life. This has nothing to do with the feel-good "celebrate failure" motto so commonly repeated in our culture today and parroted by entrepreneurs dotting the globe. Failure sucks. It hurts, and you couldn't pay me enough to do it on purpose. But like death and taxes, failure is unavoidable. In fact, our misguided attempts to avoid failure are the most common source of our problems. Each failure is a stepping-stone to your next success. Without being willing to take that step, prepare to do a lot of floundering as you're swept downstream.

I've spent more hours than I care to admit beating myself up over how Best Camera went down, but the honest-to-God truth is that CreativeLive is even more exciting to me. The classes we've given to millions of students around the world—billions of minutes of video streamed to every country on the planet— have already made a tremendous impact. I'll never know how many problems have been solved, how many careers and businesses have been built, and how many lives have been changed for the better because of the way Best Camera's failure helped fuel CreativeLive's success.

The first time you do something, it's hard. In fact, you'll probably screw it up. But let's say you don't, and you strike gold on your first attempt. If Silicon Valley has taught us nothing else, it's that your inexperience with success will probably lead to a more catastrophic failure down the road. We need early failures to develop the skill set to manage success when it comes later on. When you do inevitably face-plant, pick yourself up, brush off the dirt, and don't make the same mistake twice.

There is no magic advice I can give you to help you avoid failure. However, there are many ways you can practice failure with relatively low stakes. Rejection letters are a great example. Whether you're submitting a novel for publication, applying for a grant for your nonprofit, or simply emailing someone you'd like to collaborate with, rejection is unavoidable. Instead of trying and failing to avoid it, lean in. Rack up as many rejections as you can. Instead of laboring over perfecting a single email to a single potential collaborator, send out a hundred and start counting rejections and ignored outreach. Aim for fifty. With rejection as your goal, what's the worst that could happen? That you get more positive responses than you'd hoped?

Jia Jiang, the author of *Rejection Proof: How I Beat Fear and Became Invincible*, decided to leave the corporate world to become an entrepreneur. Unfortunately, his deep-seated fear of rejection held him back from taking the necessary risks to succeed. To overcome that fear, he decided to subject himself to a hundred days of "rejection therapy," doing everything from asking a stranger to loan him a hundred bucks to giving a speech on a random street corner to asking a Krispy Kreme store to whip up custom doughnuts in the shape of the Olympic rings. By the time he'd finished his experiment, he'd learned that rejection was a lot less painful than he'd always feared. The fear of rejection had been what kept him paralyzed.

That incredible experiment allowed Jiang to face his fear while embracing vulnerability. Beyond the personal growth, he created a book and built an enormous following. Success softens the pain of any rejection.

Courage, Confidence, Enthusiasm

If you're stuck at the beginning, afraid to face adversity, take on some scary but low-stakes creative challenges that are just outside your comfort zone. Don't just accept risks, take them on with zest and zeal. Muster *courage, confidence,* and *enthusiasm.* If you're going for a dip in a cold-plunge pool, you don't slink in. That's miserable. Leap in with a shout of joy.

Think small goals, small risks. That way, you can't lose. If you succeed, you've achieved something real. You build momentum for the next thing. If you fail, you've racked up all the useful knowledge and experience of a failure without ending up in an attorney's office as I did with Best Camera.

Try a new recipe every week. Start hosting dinner parties. Arrange a gallery show for your work. Or challenge yourself to write a song or haiku a day for a year. Bring in collaborators and accountability partners. Make failure fun now so you can develop your failure muscles *before* you take out the second mortgage to fund a creative project—only for it to go up in flames, taking your financial stability with it.

Having a few projects cooking at once is another great way to let go of perfect and get unstuck. A single failing project has a way of taking over your life. With a couple of burners going at once, you do what you can for each one, get stuck, move on to another, come back, and repeat. There is a point of diminishing returns when you have too many projects going at one time, but when the stakes are low, it's worth a try. Your work will be better for it.

Overcome Impostor Syndrome

Every creative failure contains the seeds of a future victory, if you're willing to dig for them. You never know where the road will take you. Victories can even masquerade as failures; sometimes it takes years to realize how a long-mourned "loss" was actually a benefit in the long run. (You can see how tragic it is when someone lets a single failure drive him away from creative practice. One failure! Failure is not losing. Failing happens all the time to the winningest of winners.)

Identifying as a creator means choosing to realize your creative aspirations. This requires sitting with fear, coming to terms with self-doubt. You're going to wonder whether you've got what it takes, whether you can make the next project work. That's inevitable. The easiest thing in the world to do with that doubt is choose an extreme: blind faith that everything will work out or relentless doubt that it won't—*other people can turn their ideas into a reality, but I have no agency over my own life.*

Each of us has to find the middle ground between faith and doubt and learn to get comfortable there. Become familiar with the hardships of creativity. Toughen those emotional calluses. When you train hard at the gym, especially at first, you can bet you'll have sore muscles. The second and third sessions are the worst. You're still sore, and now you're back lifting weights, cranking out reps. If you stick with it, you get familiar with the soreness and your awareness of it fades. You know it's just part of the process. It's normal. Meanwhile, your muscles are steadily reknitting themselves. After a few months, you think, hey, I'm a little stronger than when I started.

The same goes for your first few rejection letters. They're going to hurt. Over time, they won't even register. One of the biggest personal benefits I've enjoyed from interviewing hundreds of people for my podcast is learning that *everyone* feels like an impostor sometimes. No one has complete confidence in herself and her abilities. If she did, she'd quickly grow bored with her work and find something else to do. High performers always manage to operate at the edge of their capabilities, whether they consciously intend to or not. They usually feel as though they're out of their element, one way or the other.

When I was awarded a college soccer scholarship, the only freshman that year, I knew that part of the reason was due to the enormous success that prior graduates from my high school program had achieved. That led me to doubt my own abilities. After all, maybe I was just riding on their coattails. Did I actually have what it took to compete at the collegiate level? That attack of impostor syndrome put me into a serious funk. I felt like a fraud. Part of me believed that the other players would laugh me off the field once they learned the "truth."

Once I got to school and started playing, those feelings slowly dissipated. I realized that the system was designed to work that way. Certain high school programs were known for developing strong players. Colleges certainly knew that and banked on it. My participation in my high school program was but one of several factors in my scholarship.

Multiple factors create success in *any* creative pursuit. That's reality. We all want to be discovered and judged on our own, unique merits, but there are always other elements that play a role. It's almost never just about the work itself. Good work is the cost of entry, but breaking through depends on everything from people skills and positioning to serendipity and promotion. Instead of lamenting *this*, embrace it. Step back and consider all the factors that have played a role in the careers of those you seek to emulate. How can you adapt them to create your own approach? This simple shift in mindset may be just the advantage you need to elevate your own game.

Stop Rolling Rocks Downhill

I don't have much empirical evidence that launching a major creative idea or shifting the status quo is ever "easy." It's almost always anything but. A member of the CreativeLive team once expressed frustration about how hard it had been to break through with a particular project we were launching.

"It feels like we're always pushing rocks uphill," he said. Our COO at the time, Mak Azadi, didn't hesitate: "That's why we call it work," he said. "We're not here to make sure things already rolling downhill keep rolling."

You're never going to be that other person who makes it look effortless without starting, finding joy, playing, struggling, pushing through the struggle, and doing it all over again. You've got to practice and stand in the not-knowing and play through the parts where you suck.

Embrace the suck. Have fun on your journey. If you laugh at your mistakes first, whoever laughs at you will be late to the party. If you compare yourself to someone else and find yourself wanting, it's because you're judging yourself by the wrong standard. A poodle is never going to win in the hound category at the Westminster Dog Show. The only way out of this psychological trap is to lean into your unique strengths *and* weaknesses, to admit you don't know everything and accept that you do things your own way. That ancient aphorism "Know thyself" comes to mind. Your goal should always be to become the best you, not a pretty good—or even damn good—version of somebody else.

Years of mindfulness practice have taught me that we are not the voices in our heads. Stop listening to the ones in yours and get back to work.

AMPLIFY

Amplify your vision
to create the impact
you seek.

10

Find Your People

Alone we can do so little, together we can do so much.

—HELEN KELLER

When a megaband like Metallica takes the stage on one of their earthshaking international tours and you're lucky enough to be in the audience, it's easy to fall for the carefully constructed illusion that you're just watching four talented people at work: James Hetfield, Lars Ulrich, Kirk Hammett, and Robert Trujillo. The spotlights help reinforce the illusion.

Though these four musicians are crucial to the experience, they are only one department of a large entertainment organization. More than a hundred highly skilled individuals accompany the band on each and every tour, night after night, month after month, continent after continent. Lighting artists, road crew, special effects technicians, sound engineers—when the members of Metallica talk about getting the band together, that's what they have in mind. It's not a band at all; it's a battalion.

They can perform "For Whom the Bell Tolls" or "Nothing Else Matters" with their instruments, a few mics, and an amp, but they can't be the Metallica we know without all those col-laborators, all top performers in their own way.

You may not be a rock god (yet), but we're all social animals. We thrive on human connection. Creators aren't exempt from this need. Whether you are an introvert or an extrovert, you get through the tough spots with the support and inspiration of people who "get you." Your community.

It can be tough to reconcile this need for support, collaboration, and community with the need to follow your own path. The acid test is this: if you're walking the path but getting nowhere, go find communities of other humans who are passionate about the same things you are and get involved. Roll up your sleeves. Participate. Collaborate. And don't hold back.

The operating principle here is reciprocity, but it's better to think of it as karma: what goes around comes around. Do for others what you would want them to do for you. This doesn't mean do for others in the expectation that they'll promptly re-turn the favor, aka the transactional "You scratch my back, I'll scratch yours" approach. It doesn't work that way. Just do, give, be of service, be visible. This is how the magic of collaboration begins, even if it isn't immediately obvious.

This is another of those creative leaps of faith I'm asking you to take. If you wish you had more comments and likes on your social channels, comment and like on the social channels of people you admire. If you wish that more people came to your events, read your writing, or listened to your songs, then go to events, read contemporary books, and listen to new music—and spread the word about them. *Be the fan you wish you had.*

Community is extremely valuable in creative work. It goes far beyond engaging with your peers and the larger creative ecosystem. By being selective about the creators with whom you collaborate, you can set the bar high on skill but even higher on creative alignment, work style, and the joyfulness of their company. It isn't enough that the first software developer, sound engineer, or choreographer you meet is willing to join forces with you; find a collaborator whose skills and talents are as exciting to you as yours are to them. It takes effort to create a real creative match with one person, let alone several, but the benefits of a good match make up for it. Reciprocal collaboration is a powerful and energizing form of creative work. The right combination will feel less like being a dog walker and more like being in a wolf pack.

Sure, it's scary to trust others this way. It means opening up and revealing your work before it's "perfect." People get all twisted up about this. Sometimes they're afraid someone will run away with their amazing idea. But let me assure you, no one wants your idea. Even on the one-in-a-million chance that they do, it's the execution that matters, so you have almost nothing to fear. We live in an age when novelists make their entire writing process public online and still go on to sell millions of copies of their book. Your ideas are valuable to you because you're the only one who can realize them as you envision them. In the case of an infinitesimally small number of projects, a nondisclosure agreement might be warranted, but in general don't be afraid to share with your collaborators. You need their feedback and support. Putting an NDA into place on a low-level project is like requesting a DNA test before you go on a date.

The idea of a solo creator who goes off to a cabin in the woods for a month and returns with a finished masterpiece? Purely a mirage. If you chase it, you'll be up to your neck in quicksand wondering where those palm trees went. Great artists return from their cabins eager to share their crude first attempts with trusted collaborators and peers. We desperately need to connect with others: those with both similar and radically different influences and interests, those who love what we do, those who will give us honest feedback. We become more fully ourselves when we are in a community of other creators.

Not every acquaintance is a source of encouragement and strength, of course. Some people impede our creative efforts or weigh us down with cynicism and their own limiting beliefs. To become a creator, you have to be willing to forge healthy, supportive relationships with amazing new people *and* reexamine any toxic relationships you're already in. The author and motivational speaker Jim Rohn once said that you are the average of the five people you spend the most time with. Choose wisely.

Choose Your Base Camp

Every community is different. Some will be a better fit for you than others. If you don't experience a warm welcome where you start out, don't give up. Don't beat your head against a wall trying to find acceptance, either. Instead, keep probing. Look for another, more welcoming community to serve as your base camp, the place where you put down stakes and pitch your tent. You can always summit new peaks once you've established your base camp, but you need to start on solid ground.

I first planted my creative flag in the action sports community. Ever since I was a young kid with a skateboard, I'd received a warm welcome there. There was so much encouragement and support to be found in action sports, starting with my very first trip to a skate park. What I loved about skate culture in the mideighties was its purity: although it was growing rapidly, it was still a somewhat underground movement and hadn't yet gone mainstream. We were there because of a love of what we were doing, not because we wanted a sponsorship. We'd spend every day of summer in a creative mode—punk rock for breakfast, lunchtime putting the finishing touches on the vert ramp with borrowed tools, and all afternoon developing a new trick, just happy to share what we'd figured out with our friends.

One of the fundamental skateboarding tricks is an ollie, where you pop yourself and your board into the air without using your hands. Nailing the ollie is essential for doing more advanced tricks, so if you can't learn it, you're stuck. Luckily for me, it was easy to ask for help in a community like that one, given that it was built on principles of creativity, growth, mentorship, and a love of the craft. There's a sense that when one person succeeds, the whole community wins together. So finding older kids or peers willing to help me wasn't just easy, it was encouraged. The world of skateboarding at the time was one of the few places I'd discovered in society where older kids and younger kids were in it together, figuring stuff out and supporting one another's development. Hell, even today, go to any skate park, and you'll likely see a thirty-year age span.

In a community such as skateboarding, you learn how to be present, ask questions, and not annoy people. If you're annoying, it becomes harder to get support from others, so you develop the skill of community building along the way. This is not to say that there aren't rules and a hierarchy. Nor is it to say that everyone is always on his best behavior—it was gritty and tough, and that was fine by me. But the social structure had a foundation of inclusivity and creativity. Today I realize that the skateboarding scene played a huge role in shaping me. It was there I learned that a safe and welcoming base camp, a place in which to develop community and comradery, is just as important as skills.

Years later, when I started taking my camera into the mountains, action sports such as snowboarding were still on the fringe, too. The scene was open, loose, and friendly. You could ask questions of anybody, and they would happily answer them. People were thrilled simply to be doing what they loved in incredibly beautiful places amid a growing global interest. I loved the energy. Action sports made for a dynamic and encouraging base camp for my early work as a photographer, to grow my craft and build my community. Even though there were hundreds of well-known athletes, there were only a few dozen top photographers, which meant there were no kindly photographer mentors to take me under their wing. But that didn't matter, because I'd found my tribe.

As action sports went mainstream, so did my work. I set my sights on expanding into the photography industry community, thinking it would be another great opportunity to learn and be inspired. I naively assumed that all communities based on creativity, self-expression, and a DIY ethos were like action sports. I was wrong. Though I'd anticipated paying my dues to get a seat at the table, I also expected the photography community to welcome me as an eager young pro willing to show up, put in the work, and contribute to the conversation. It didn't happen. Instead, people looked at me like something the cat dragged in. My earnest questions and wide-eyed enthusiasm were met with indifference, even hostility.

At the time I entered it, the world of professional photography was fragmenting and trapped by a fear of change. Wave after wave of technological innovation threatened the cozy status quo. The events I attended featured room after room of curmudgeonly older white guys griping about the future. Sadly, I found very few exceptions to that picture in terms of gender, race, age, or general warmth and friendliness toward fresh faces or fresh ideas. We newbies represented the change that few established veterans wanted to acknowledge, despite the respect we were willing to give them on the merits of their work.

Back then, the industry was paranoid, reactive, clinging to the past. The old pros had decided that there was only so much photography work to go around. The only solution was to hoard techniques, contacts, advice, anything a challenger might use to knock them off their perch. They'd made it up the ladder, and now they were pulling it up after themselves as quickly as they could.

It all seemed shortsighted to me. If people can steal your amazing technique just by looking at one of your photos, your technique is doomed. Customers want to hire *you*—the human being—not some lighting effect or fancy lens. If you're trying to hide your magic tricks from the masses, there is a larger problem to face.

So yeah, I threw a few rocks. But more than that, I shared my photography knowledge—and my opinions—on trade show panels and with aspiring photographers online. I could see which way the wind was blowing, and I wanted to be part of that change. Pretty soon, the establishment pros went from ambivalent to outright hostile. I epitomized the change they dreaded.

Everything changes, and the photography industry would be no exception. After the digital technology wave came crashing through, as communities formed online and information became more widespread, the community became a warmer place, more open and diverse. Over time, I developed a strong sense of empathy about how hard it must have been for established photographers to watch the world they'd known for decades change seemingly overnight. For most of them, it was evolve quickly or die. Despite our differences, I eventually came to call many of those veteran photographers my friends. I learned the history of the craft from them while sharing what I understood about its future.

Community is an essential source of support for any creator. You can participate in at least two right off the bat: your Craft Community (e.g., photography), and the area where you *apply* your craft, your Focus Community (e.g., action sports). At the intersection of these two communities lies your Core Community (e.g., action sports photographers, such as my friend Jimmy

Chin). The people in your Core Community are really good to know because they truly understand your shared niche.

CRAFT
COMMUNITY
(E.G. PHOTOGRAPHY)

FOCUS
COMMUNITY
(E.G. ACTION SPORTS)

CORE
COMMUNITY
(E.G. ACTION SPORTS PHOTOGRAPHY)

For example, if you knit children's sweaters, you might participate in the knitting community or in the community of entrepreneurs selling handmade children's clothing. Instead of seeing other knitters of children's sweaters as competitors, recognize them as your Core Community and develop the strongest relationships there. There are plenty of kids who need sweaters out there. We're stronger together.

Embedding yourself in the knitting community would involve attending knitting conferences and meetups, reading knitting blogs, and participating in knitting communities online. Separately, embedding yourself among the entrepreneurs would involve a parallel but different set of events, blogs, and online communities. The differences between communities in terms of attitude, demographics, popularity, and support might be huge. Each one will offer distinct advantages.

Though you'll probably eventually participate in both your Craft Community and your Focus Community, choose the friendlier, more welcoming one to serve as your base camp. You need that more when you're just starting out.

Become a Joiner

Maybe you're not a joiner. I can't say that joining has ever been easy for me. But it's worth being vulnerable and putting yourself out there. All communities have their warts, and none of them is exactly what we'd like it to be, but they also aren't fixed in stone. They're made of people just like you, and people can change just as you change. Every community has its own life cycle, and your place in each of your communities will evolve over time. In fact, your communities will evolve in part because of your contribution. A quote commonly attributed to Mahatma Gandhi says it well: Be the change you wish to see in the world.

Once you've decided on a base camp community, it's time to participate in that community. No one is going to give you a membership badge or a title, but if you participate in and add value to that community week after week, month after month, you will begin to gain authority among its members. Once you've learned the ropes and established yourself at your base camp, consider expanding into other communities. It's much easier after you've already done it once.

Your role in a new community is to show up, give, support, deliver value authentically, and volunteer whatever you can. Go to events and meet other human beings. In parallel, listen, ask questions, expand your perspective. If you stay active, you'll start to meet collaborators, peers, advisers. It's like joining a band when it holds open auditions; you've got to earn your place as a newcomer. You may need to take a few lumps here and there and prove that you're willing to stick it out with everyone else—whether that's through technology changes, economic downturns, whatever. This helps build a natural and authentic connection that will reward you for the effort you put in.

If you're telling yourself that you don't have time for this, ask yourself, "How badly do I want it?" Because let me tell you, it's essential to have a community to live the creative life you desire. Nothing happens in a vacuum. Actors don't make films alone, startups don't get beta testers without friends, and total strangers won't attend your stand-up shows to give you feedback because they don't know you and don't care. You don't need a lot of people, but you do need *some* who care—especially early on. If you choose to ignore this initially, you'll get a hard dose of reality soon enough, regardless of your level of talent.

When I cofounded CreativeLive, I was well known in photography and had built an app used by more than a million people. In the world of online learning, however, I was the new kid on the block. I knew from experience that it was my responsibility to establish myself in that community. While there was a heavy focus on "ed tech" and massive open online courses, or MOOCs, I could feel the intentions were positive. It was just time for a fresh perspective. Rather than traditional lectures and testing, we could use all the amazing technology available to reimagine education for the better. We could incorporate community, interactivity, live demonstrations, and rich, contextual learning. What I was seeing in the existing online-learning community lay in direct contrast to the revolution we were starting at Creative-Live. I knew that the industry could be so much more.

Thanks to my experience with my other communities, I knew that I could help shape this community's future *if* I was willing to join, participate, and add value. I could help my peers see that "getting the certificate" isn't the only possible objective of a class. We could set our sights higher using technology to make learning deeper, more holistic, and immersive. I wanted us to create valuable resources for learners to explore in their own way and at their own pace.

To drive change and awareness, I needed authority. To gain authority, I needed to participate authentically—for a sustained period of time. So I stopped turning up my nose and dived in headfirst, writing op-eds and other articles, appearing on national TV and elsewhere in the media, and attending and keynoting at conferences all over the world. If I threw rocks from the outside, none of the people building the future of online learning would ever listen to me. If I wanted to help define that vision, I'd have to roll up my sleeves, participate, and add value from within.

This can be both humbling and extremely gratifying. You will have to show up for a while before you're acknowledged, but gradually you'll find your place. And once you've been acknowledged, it's much easier to help shape the landscape in a way that includes your vision.

Participate

Whether you're an entrepreneur, a painter, a model airplane builder, or anything in between, there is a meetup, club, or trade group for you. Human beings organize around shared interests and passions. Check those opportunities out, find the ones you like best, and—here's the important part—talk to lots of people you meet there. Standing in a corner might be less scary, but it's not going to embed you in a community in any meaningful way. And there's something extremely powerful about getting together in person, eyeball to eyeball. If you have social anxiety and need a little help coming out of your shell in group situations, that's okay. It's a process. But it's also not a license to ignore this suggestion. Instead, use this awareness to develop new skills that help you go over, around, or through this obstacle. Again, real-life participation isn't just helpful, it's key.

Of course, you'll also want to engage in the digital side of your community; just don't use doing so as a crutch to avoid social interaction. Use social media to follow the top names in your field as well as your peers. Then jump in and join the conversation online. A thoughtful comment or question that adds to the conversation always goes further than a like or an emoji. This is an easy win, a huge opportunity to expand your network at no cost other than a few minutes of your time each day. It might seem as though you're an anonymous blip among many, but the vast majority of people don't contribute. Thoughtful, helpful comments do get noticed, even if time doesn't permit the person to respond to all of them. The key is to keep adding value over time. Not only does your participation add value to the community, but you will receive a ton of value as well by carefully following the conversation of smart players in the space.

I've met hundreds of people this way, including some people I call my friends now. Each one of them was right where you are now. They started commenting on and sharing my posts. They contributed to the discussion on a regular basis. Even though I had never met them, I started to feel as though I knew them. Eventually I run into one of them at a face-to-face event somewhere, and they say hi. "I'm so-and-so from the internet. Nice to finally meet you in person." Once I hear that familiar username, I know exactly who they are, and I couldn't be more enthusiastic to finally meet them face-to-face.

This is an unbeatable icebreaker with me because I know

they've been participating in and adding value to my community for a long time. In fact, I've done the same to other people I admire, and it's incredibly effective. It's been the start of many interesting friendships and inspiring collaborations over the years. Sustained effort over time is key.

It's simple, really: the way you become interesting is by showing that you're interested. If you want to join a scene, figure out where that scene is, both online and off, and then be there as much as you can.

If you had been a writer, artist, or intellectual in the fifties, you'd have moved to Paris and spent all your free time at Les Deux Magots, the legendary café in Saint-Germain-des-Prés. There you'd have rubbed elbows with the likes of Simone de Beauvoir and Jean-Paul Sartre. They might not have granted you a seat at the table at first, but if you had hung around long enough, you'd eventually have become a part of the scene yourself.

Community isn't rocket science; it just changes over time. Don't fall for the romance and spend your time where your artistic heroes hung out when they were starting out. You need to go where the scene is *now*. And although geography isn't as important as it once was thanks to the internet, there is still no good substitute for meeting other creators in person. Even medium-sized cities can support vibrant artistic communities. Whatever size yours is, help it grow. If there isn't a community for you in your area yet, build one. Start by helping other people make stuff. Volunteer your skills, be willing to do what it takes, and get that karma flowing. You'll learn quickly this way, and, eventually you'll help build the foundation of a more vibrant creative ecosystem to support your own work.

Building community is a creative act in itself. You cannot sustain long-term success without a healthy and supportive community that will advocate for your work and support you through the obstacles we all face as creators.

Collaborate

Joining a community and finding a place in it is only the first step. One of the most valuable dividends is the opportunity to meet and collaborate with others.

A little-known secret that shouldn't be one: creativity is largely about collaboration. My very first creative effort, *Sons of Zorro*, wouldn't have gotten anywhere without the help of the other kids in the neighborhood. I would have ended up like the teenager in *American Beauty* with ten minutes of footage of a plastic bag. I needed collaborators to realize my creative vision, and so do you.

Collaboration is still a significant part of my work and one of my favorite ways to stretch myself as an artist. Whether in my photo studio or at CreativeLive, everyone brings different kinds of expertise to the table. A designer, a developer, a retoucher—every member of the team contributes to the vision in different ways. I literally could not do the work I do without collaborators.

Even as I write this now, my wife, Kate—a brilliant creative force and my longtime collaborator—is helping me maneuver through this manuscript, suggesting smart fixes when I'm stuck, and helping me edit out the rambles.

I also look for ways to collaborate outside my areas of expertise. At one point, curious to go beyond the loose experiments I'd done with the very first video DSLR cameras, I proposed a collaboration with the fantastically talented commercial director Will Hyde and his studio. What about making a music video together? Will's ambition was to pursue more creative, less commercial work to build out his portfolio. This would be just the ticket. We decided to co-direct and co-produce a video for an emerging indie band from Seattle called The Blakes. This would be the perfect low-stakes way to try my hand at a new craft: The Blakes were more than happy to get a free music video out of the experiment and they had no expectations whatsoever. This was good, because at the time I didn't know a grip from a gaffer. First and foremost, I was there to learn.

Collaborating outside your comfort zone is scary but empowering. I have learned to admit when I don't know something as well as my collaborator does, because it will give me the opportunity to learn. All I can offer is what I know. On this gig, we were on an aggressive, high-pressure shooting schedule because of the limited budget. With no paying client, we needed to keep our costs down.

With such an ambitious schedule, Will and I quickly saw that we needed our teams to collaborate in new ways. At the time, video production operated very differently from the world of photography. It was segmented and specialized, a carryover from the hard-core culture of unionized feature film production. As a result, the pace was far too slow for our purposes. My team was coming from the world of location photography, which always required being fast and light. But we lacked experience with audio and video. All of us eventually recognized that we would need to be flexible about the way we worked if we were going to offset each other's weaknesses and augment each other's strengths. Each member became willing to do his job and part of someone else's if necessary. If they were rigging expensive equipment or working with high-voltage gear, they'd protect that role, but otherwise, we all had to get off the stool and pitch in. Instead of a siloed crew where egos were the currency, we became a lightweight, efficient machine suited to the mission, all hands pitching in to get things done.

It was tight, but we made the video on schedule and under budget. The band was blown away—a video like this one would have been far beyond their means. Although the band never broke through to the mainstream, both crews still learned so much from the experience. Will shared with me that he learned the virtues of a streamlined crew when working on a tight budget. In my case, I learned the structure and workflow of a movie set. As a co-director, I got to practice my video skills in real time, often moments after learning them in the first place. Trial by fire. I also had the opportunity to shoot super-duper slow motion using Will's quarter-million-dollar cameras. At the time, he was way ahead of the curve with that technique and the equipment needed to do it. That knowledge helped me land numerous commercial directing jobs worth millions in revenue.

Get out there and collaborate. Work with real people in the real world in any capacity you can and learn from it all. Seek out the best you can find, the people whose work excites you like nothing else. Learn to organize, communicate, and delegate tasks so that each of you can focus on your strengths. Take what you can from every experience but prioritize adding more value to the project through giving.

It can be intimidating to surround yourself with people as good as or better than you are, who care as much or more than you do, but remember this: A-gamers work with A-gamers, B-gamers work with C-gamers. If you want to be great, surround yourself with awesome people doing *their* best work, even if it keeps you on your toes more than you'd like. The best way to level up your own game is to level up the team around you.

The Friends and Family Discount

Of course, all this discussion about finding community leaves out something pretty important. Most of us already have a community or two, including the one that lives in our house. It's time to start looking at your relationship with the communities you're born into and the ones you've grown up in.

Take your friends. You know as well as I do that some people in our lives discourage us and weigh us down with doubt and cynicism. If there's one thing I can't stand, it's cynicism. It's poison; I can't have it in my life anymore. Cynics expect the worst of everyone and predict failure around every corner. It becomes a self-fulfilling prophecy. If we need rocket fuel for our dreams to achieve escape velocity, the cynics in our lives turn on the fire suppression systems and keep us trapped by Earth's gravity. It's outrageous that so many of us tolerate so much hostility and negativity in our personal lives and label it "honesty."

Stop tolerating cynicism and doubt from your so-called friends. Tell them straight up, "This is the new me. I am a creator on a mission. I will fall down and make mistakes along my path, but I'm going to get back up again and again and again until I've made my vision a reality. And when I'm done doing that, I'll be on to the next one. I have room in my life for supporters and cheerleaders and believers. If you can play that role, great, grab your pom-poms. Wet blankets can go back into the drawer and grow mildew."

If they don't get the picture, make new friends.

To achieve your full potential as a creator, you have to be willing to put yourself out there, make yourself vulnerable, and explore life in all its messiness. Toxic relationships make this kind of personal exploration next to impossible. They're insidious. Remember that the resistance you experience from others is directly proportional to how deeply they've stamped out their own creative sparks. The more you try to change, the harder they'll push back because you're reminding them of everything their limiting beliefs prevent them from doing themselves. The thing is, you don't have the spare time or energy to reawaken anybody else's creativity; you're on your own path now.

This is a huge challenge for most new creators. Just as we start going out on a limb, we begin to see with unprecedented clarity how the people we've chosen as friends are trying really hard to pull us out of our tree. Do you *really* want to live by a new set of standards? Befriend people who are already living by them.

Okay, so you can choose new friends and meet new peers in your creative community, but how do you manage your family? In a perfect world, each and every one of your relatives would wholeheartedly and enthusiastically know about, approve, and support your new (or renewed) creative interests. If some or all of them don't get on board, however, cutting them out of your life probably isn't an option—a healthy one, anyway.

The people in your family are an important part of your journey, and you don't want to leave them behind. So do what you can to bring them along instead. Here's how. Instead of telling them about what you're going to do and how great it's going to be, focus on showing them. Go and do the work, whether they pat you on the back or not. Get up before your family does, and go to work at your drawing table. When they wake up, they'll see you there day after day, doing the work. Demonstrate your passion and commitment. Make progress. In writer lingo, "Show, don't tell." The people who love you are far more likely to be convinced by new behaviors than by new declarations of intent.

Once your family see the positive effect your unleashed creativity has on your mental, emotional, and physical well-being, they'll probably come on board. If not, it's time to have a tough conversation. Lead with love and humility, and above all be honest: "This is something I need to do to be happy. I'm pursuing my creative calling. I would like your support."

Collaborators and peers are a miraculous source of strength and support. Accepting that support isn't a sign of weakness; it's a profound human strength. Once you've joined your creative communities and established healthy relationships with people who will support you on your journey, it's time to start thinking about another critical community: the audience you'll build around your own work.

11

Build Your Audience

You get to choose the tribe you will lead. Through your actions
as a leader, you attract a tribe that wants to follow you.

—SETH GODIN

Tell me if this sounds familiar. After spending countless hours
building something—a product, a new website, a piece of art, a
presentation for work—you release it into the world, sharing it
with its intended audience, wherever it's meant to go. You hold
your breath and . . . nothing. Crickets. Tumbleweeds. No one
cares.

Then you start looking at other creators enviously, wondering how *they* manage to get so much traction for their work
when yours—which is just as good if not better—struggles to
get attention.

You rewind the tape to look for mistakes, but there are no obvious ones. You did everything you were supposed to do according to all the experts, books, and industry gurus. You Imagined,

Designed, and Executed your plans well. You banged the promotion drum as loudly as you could, created an account on every social platform on the planet, used all the right hashtags, all of it—and still not a peep. So, what happened? Why is everybody else getting traction while you are not?

It's tempting to make excuses about bigger budgets, larger teams, or other seemingly inadequate resources, but that's not the answer. Sure, those things might be helpful, but the magic ingredient for getting traction is simple: audience.

In the last chapter, we talked about finding communities that already exist in your areas of interest and drawing on them for camaraderie and support, for a peer group from which to grow. These communities are key to nurturing the emerging creator inside you, but they're not the only answer for having an impact on the world. What's missing is your very own audience, one that's specifically interested in *your* work, *your* values, and *your* creativity.

Your very own personal audience can and should be as unique and dynamic as you are. This chapter is all about building that audience and leading it through contribution and service. This is how you form your tribe. It will evolve out of your other communities, but it will take on a character all its own with you at the helm.

Don't worry if nobody knows who you are yet. The beauty of starting out is that you've got nowhere to go but up. Your second follower represents a 100 percent improvement over your first. (You'll likely never see a growth spike like that again.)

Call it your audience, community, tribe, or following—it doesn't matter. To find a home for your ideas and your creative work, you need to cultivate and inspire a group of diverse but like-minded people to receive and ultimately Amplify that work. A creator's audience is your single greatest asset for creating impact. It will bring as much color to your world as creativity brings to your life.

The Other 50 Percent

Your job early on is to make things using all the time and energy you can muster. Learning your craft and honing your voice are nonnegotiables. But not long after you've developed a resilient and productive creative practice, things start to change. As your work grows in quality and quantity, you'll start feeling the itch to share that value with others. It won't be enough to just present your idea to the boss, publish a new blog post for your mom and dad to read, or share what you wrote with your base camp; you're going to want a wider range of people who need to hear your message to start listening.

This isn't simply promoting your work, either. Promotion takes effort and is important if you want to reach people and have an impact, but this widely misunderstood idea of audience goes beyond the cycle of making and promoting to a list of names in a database. In fact, the biggest mistake I see emerging creators make is thinking that their job is to just make stuff and immediately promote it. Sometimes they even skip the creation part altogether and go straight to promoting themselves with the goal of being "influencers." Once you're an influencer—or at least *influential*—people will read or watch or listen to whatever you do, right?

Wrong. Promotion should happen only once you've laid a real foundation. No one knows who you are yet. Why should they?

For your work to make an impact, creation and promotion together should represent half the energy you dedicate to your objective. The other 50 percent should go toward building your audience. To succeed, you need an army of people—don't get too caught up in its size just yet—who love what you do. To build that army, you'll need to engage with individuals thoughtfully and contribute to the larger conversation meaningfully over time.

Don't develop your work on a foundation of creativity, authenticity, and heart only to "aggregate" a hollow "list" of followers via gimmicks and schemes. Build a genuine audience that loves what you do, how you do it, and *why*. All this should happen before, during, and after you've created your new product, website, piece of art, or performance. Community building runs parallel to your creative work, and it requires the same degree of consistency.

Feeling overwhelmed? Take a deep breath. Patience is everything here. You need to be in this for the long haul, so pace yourself. If you're wondering where successful creators found thriving communities, you're wondering the wrong thing. They didn't *find* communities; they built them. In fact, if you consider them successful, they've probably been building their communities for five years or more by now. *This is true even if you've only just heard of them.* All runaway creative successes seem as though they came out of nowhere, but they always represent years of careful effort on the part of the creator. Their community has known about them and their work much longer than the rest of us here in the mainstream have. The anticipation for their big launch has been building up for ages. Their community was the lever that drove the mainstream success you're witnessing now.

Creators create, first and foremost, but if they want someone else to care, they lay the groundwork for future success while they're working. Think of the artists and entrepreneurs who seem to be crushing it right now. There was a time when nobody paid any attention to what they did. They spent years participating in other communities, establishing a base camp, and patiently adding value to it until people started to notice them and their unique contributions. Slowly they built direct connections with those people. Eventually there came a tipping point, and that creator "suddenly" had a thriving community of her own, eager to engage with what she had to share.

It doesn't end there. Even after you succeed in building an audience around yourself and your work, you're never "done." A spark doesn't equal a fire. Success just tells you that your audience-building activity is working—*so keep doing it.* If you sit back and wait for the dollars and accolades to start rolling in or try to leverage the fans and followers of your work as soon as you notice them assembling, you will quickly fade from view. Your community will disperse. Stay hungry, stay humble. Keep doing the work.

Seth Godin blogs each and every day. People take the wrong lesson from this. They think Seth is proof that if you just keep sharing good work consistently for long enough, it'll inevitably get noticed and break through. That isn't true. Ask Seth. He knows the value of community better than anybody else. From his early days as a book packager to his time at Yahoo! to the present, he has always invested effort into building his tribe. He added value to other communities and eventually assembled one around his own work. He never rests on his laurels. To this day, he answers each and every email he receives. He gives talks frequently and launches projects to support his community, such as his altMBA workshop. Yes, he blogs every day and writes book after book, but all that creation and promotion represents only half of the total pie or less.

Though it has evolved, my podcast was originally born out of the desire to add value to the photography community. Nobody else was bringing in successful entrepreneurs and high performers from other communities to help photographers understand success, personal development, and creativity. I knew I could deliver that value, so I started doing interviews with *New York Times* best-selling authors, as well as Pulitzer Prize–, Grammy-, and Oscar-winning artists and renowned entrepreneurs, and posing the kinds of questions I knew the people in my community would ask.

To be clear, audience isn't about being famous. The size of your community—audience, client base, tribe, following—is important only relative to the nature of your calling. If you're a blacksmith and all the good local chefs come to you for their knives, you're golden. Every blow of your hammer has a purpose. If you have a receptive audience for your work and you're fully satisfied by the exchange of value—even if you receive only attention in return—your efforts are working. Keep doing what you're doing.

Every significant creator you know—even the ones who are manically focused on their product or craft—invests disproportionally in cultivating community. None of them just publish and hope for the best. They know the *why* behind their work and they *do* a lot of great work, but they're also tuned into *who* their work resonates with, *where* that community spends its time and attention, and *how* to get their work into those spaces.

If you've prepared an epic feast, the big question is, *Who's going to eat all this food?*

Establish Your Point of View

As we saw back in chapter 3, the first step in standing out is to be unapologetically you. It's one thing to understand this concept, quite another to actually put yourself into the public sphere as a [insert your calling here]. Once you've done that and established yourself in a few preexisting communities such as your base camp, it's time to become the locus of an entirely new community, sustained and driven by *you*. It requires that you *lead*.

This is uncomfortable. I mentioned my cold-plunge habit back in chapter 4. If you've built a cold-water habit of your own, you'll be well prepared to take this plunge and actually say something you mean. Again, you can't slink in to stand out. Courage, at least *some* confidence, and a minimum level of enthusiasm are required.

Around 2004, I created a Blogger account to share my creative journey. Surviving an avalanche had taught me that I wanted to use whatever time I had on Earth to do more; I wanted to help others on their creative journey the way I'd always wished someone would have helped me. The blog would also be an opportunity to practice putting out my point of view. Even then, I understood that a point of view—not a technique—would be the foundation of my creative success. The blog would give me a place to exercise my point of view as an artist, even though my words played a larger role there than my photos did. I needed to get comfortable speaking my truth.

The site wasn't beautiful, it wasn't optimized for photography, but it served the purpose. I didn't need the perfect tool, just an available one.

I'd done plenty of academic writing in grad school, but I needed to learn how to communicate my beliefs in plain English, no BS. That didn't come easily. At first I didn't know quite what to write about or how. Everything felt awkward and stilted. I finally got started by discussing specific problems I encountered: a misunderstanding on set, technical difficulties with a particular shot, a client management lesson I'd learned the hard way.

Over time, my writing improved. I started sharing about all my experiences as a photographer. I wrote about my frustrations with the then-stifling photo industry—every day, I'd reach out to pros I admired to connect and collaborate, and I'd never hear back. I wrote about the industry-wide reluctance to share "trade secrets" and how I was relying on the card catalog at the local library to dig up out-of-print photography books just to learn my trade.

My point of view slowly took shape. Through writing, I started to figure out who I was and what I was all about. I believed that the creative industries were failing to support creators. I enjoyed helping other creators succeed. I believed in figuring stuff out for yourself and learning through action. Things in the industry were so claustrophobic; I wanted to be as open and transparent as possible.

I discovered all of this through the process of writing and sharing, oftentimes in awkward, esoteric, and imprecise ways. I didn't come up with ideas in a cave somewhere and then come back into the light to scatter them about. I learned my point of view through doing my work and—importantly—connecting with others around what I was thinking and feeling.

It was never about promoting my photography studio. Even as my audience grew, I had no illusions that potential clients were reading any of my stuff. I focused on adding value and being of service to the people who needed it—my people. What did I know that others might find useful? I shared about taking digital photography into the field, taking state-of-the-art cameras to mountain peaks. Everyone used digital cameras in the studio, but I demonstrated how it was possible to take those delicate tools on the road in unique and—for the time—unexpected ways. The equipment manufacturers took notice. They could see I was breaking new ground and expanding the market for new products, from medium-format digital cameras to durable memory cards to field-hardened laptop computer cases. It was all an experiment for me, but by documenting and sharing that journey—featuring both the glory moments and the learning moments along the way—my little laboratory became a place for fellow creators to gather virtually and bond.

Meanwhile, the technology evolved. Soon I was sharing how-to videos on Google Video, Viddler, and other early tools (YouTube wasn't a standout yet). As the scope of my creative work expanded, I was able to share information you really couldn't find anywhere else. For example, I showed my audience the travel photo kit I used for international shoots. If you forget a piece of important equipment for a gig in the Himalayas, you're out of luck.

I also shared a glimpse of my lifestyle as a photographer trying to learn, grow, and experience all that life had to offer—while still building my business. By 2005, I had a small but mighty staff that included a full-time videographer to capture the ups and downs of doing our work. We'd travel to exotic locations, sleep in our cars, camp out, then find ourselves in a chartered helicopter headed to an extraordinary vantage point. We recorded and shared so many of those moments, it started to have a major impact among fellow creators and the people who hired them.

At the time there were limited sources of lifestyle, adventure, and advice like this. And as YouTube, Facebook, and other tools started emerging, I experimented with them all—whatever it took to spread the message widely.

If I'd just kept my head down and done client work like most other photographers at the time, I'd probably still be a working photographer, but I would never have scratched beyond the surface of my creative potential. Sharing my work taught me to take criticism. It led to future collaborations with companies around the world. Thanks to the blog, I received all kinds of interesting offers. "Can we fly you to Hong Kong to be in our video?" Hell yeah, you can. Slowly a community of my own grew up around my point of view, attracted by the value I offered. That audience became the core pillar of everything I would subsequently build, from Best Camera to CreativeLive and beyond. A few years later, *Wired* magazine cofounder Kevin Kelly made the claim that you need only a thousand true fans to be a successful creator today. Many people scoffed, but I had already stumbled into that experience and found it to be true.

As I worked on larger projects with clients of greater stature, I kept looking for ways to bring those brands and their products to meet my audience, which was more important to me than any one job. I treated it with absolute integrity, bringing my followers into the picture only with products and services I could fully stand behind.

Launching the Nikon D90 is one example of this—once I saw the value in a DSLR camera with the groundbreaking capacity to create video, I was over the moon to share my experience with my audience. In fact, it was a thrill to be the first pro photographer in the world to get to use this technology. They shared my excitement. The product was genuinely interesting and valuable to them and my videos and stories took them behind the scenes in a new way. They were more than happy to help spread the word.

The way I saw it, my community was one big dinner party, and I wanted to bring the most fascinating and delightful guests to my table to meet the regulars. No bores. No stiffs. All insight and entertainment. Naturally, this meant turning away many brands clamoring for access. But as a result, my community could see how hard I worked to bring value to them, and the brands I did invite saw how enthusiastically my community responded to authentic partnerships and collaborations. It was a classic win-win.

A combination of authenticity, authority, and vulnerability created my brand and grew my tribe. That tribe gave me unique and valuable opportunities with my client base. In fact, it became a vehicle for not needing clients at all. It gave me the power to say no. When you don't need your clients, your clients get way more excited about working with you. You can be really picky. I could say no to jobs I otherwise would have taken, which meant I could double down on doing what I loved and making things in support of my audience—a powerful virtuous cycle.

The Trust Battery

Nothing is more valuable than the trust your community places in you. You have to earn it and then you have to protect it with all your might.

Tobias Lütke, founder and CEO of Shopify, likens trust to a battery. When new people enter your community, their trust in you, their trust battery, is at a 50 percent charge. Anyone knows a half-charged phone won't last all day. You need to plug that thing in soon or the battery will run out just when you need it most. As Tobi describes it, every single interaction you have with the people in your community either charges their battery or drains it. How, then, do you charge that trust battery? In *Rising Strong*, Brené Brown points to a number of key factors that build trust, including reliability, accountability, integrity, and generosity. Every action you take with your community is an opportunity to build this trust or damage it.

So what does this mean for a creator? First and foremost, tell the truth. Tell. The. Truth. If you're telling them about something even remotely related to a client, let them know, even if what you're saying is coming from a genuine place of offering value.

It means show up and be seen. The people in your community show up to be a part of your world because your values align with theirs. Stay true to who you are in every interaction, just as you would with a close friend.

It means keep your promises. If you say you're going to do something for the community, follow through. If you fail, hold yourself accountable.

It means give, give, and give some more. Your audience isn't something you leverage. It's something you *cultivate, nourish, and sustain.* How do you sustain your audience? Value. Nowadays, people get a hundred Instagram followers and immediately try to sell them something or become a sponsored influencer. I wrote more than a thousand blog posts and racked up millions of page views before I even considered "pushing" or "selling" anything. Best Camera—a $3 photo app—was the first time I ever "monetized" my audience. Meanwhile, I commented regularly on other people's blogs and otherwise engaged on social media without any links back to my own stuff. I just patiently, steadfastly provided value to my small but growing community over a significant period of time.

The details of execution are always changing as new tools spring up and fade away, but the philosophy of community building remains the same: give. CreativeLive has always poured an incredible amount of value into its community. We broadcast top-notch creative classes with world-class photographers, designers, and entrepreneurs. Anyone in the world can watch most of them, beginning to end, for free. It isn't quite "You get a car, you get a car, *everybody* gets a car" like on *Oprah*—but it's still awesome. It's no accident that CreativeLive has such a large and highly engaged community.

Whether your craft is singing, dancing, knitting, or cooking doesn't matter. What you give doesn't have to be educational, but it does have to provide value to others. Giving like this isn't easy, but once you see it working, you'll be motivated to keep doing it. The most effective way to improve the effectiveness of your community-building efforts is to look at the people who are succeeding and then DEAR it: deconstruct, emulate, analyze and repeat (see chapter 2). What tactics do the highest performers in your space share? This has nothing to do with your worth as a human being. It's just about learning from people further along the path than you are. Keep your voice. Don't be the next Rihanna, be the first you. Don't imitate anyone else's message or point of view. Just study the mechanisms, the tactics that might make your efforts easier and more effective.

Since it's necessary to deliver value to sustain your audience, I choose to see it as an opportunity for my own learning and growth. I always seek a balance between commercial work and personal work. The personal work becomes a playground to see which ideas get traction, and the commercial work pays for my ability to play in my desired domain. Put another way: *I don't create art to land high-dollar commercial projects, I do high-dollar projects so I can create more art.* Doing stuff just for my own curiosity and my community lets me fool around without having to worry about clients and deadlines and just see where things go. If something doesn't click in my heart or resonate with my community, I shift to something else that might.

Creating work for your community also builds your portfolio. If you want to get a certain kind of paying gig, you will most likely need to demonstrate your ability first. Clients in any industry rarely like to make big bets on unknowns. I made hundreds of videos and self-directed short films before I was ever paid a dollar to make them for clients. That required significant time, investment, and attention, but it opened up entirely new possibilities for me as a creator. Personal work like this has led to all my biggest professional breakthroughs. Don't expect anyone to take a chance on you just because you've expressed an interest or added a bullet point to the "Services" page of your website. If you shoot portraits and you want to start shooting cars, go do a car shoot. That's how you invest in your business today. Show the world what you can do. Your community becomes your laboratory.

The attention of your audience is never going to get any easier to capture than right this minute. Remind yourself of this whenever you find yourself saying that you'll start building an audience tomorrow. Every day things get more crowded. Of course, you'll know when the time is right for you, and there will always be an audience for your work, even if it's small. But it's probably true that the best time to start is right now.

Your community is an insanely valuable asset. Treat it well, with the utmost integrity. I bring my clients to meet my audience, not the other way around. You have to be careful. Most corporations are kryptonite for communities. That's not on purpose; it's a by-product of the way they operate in service of profit margins and exploitation of resources. The irony is that communities are what they seek. Some exceptional corporations understand this and have built thriving communities around their products.

Keep charging those trust batteries. You will never, ever regret charging up your community's trust. And you will *always* regret draining it—trust me. My team has an expression for when a potential gig raises a red flag: "Don't squish the puppy!" The puppy is the beautiful idea, the creative concept, the authenticity that will resonate with our tribe of millions. If you've ever read *Of Mice and Men*, you'll know that not everyone who wants to pet the puppy can be allowed to do so, even if they really, really, *really* want to. All too often, I do a deal with a company that guarantees me creative control and, partway through, it starts crossing that line. I sit the client down immediately: "You hired me to do something unique. If you don't let me do that, you won't get what you paid for. You won't get the outcomes you seek. And my community won't be any part of it."

Don't squish the puppy.

Determine Your Smallest Viable Tribe

When you're starting out with your audience, think small. Really small. Ask yourself: What's the most narrow, most focused tribe I could build around my work? How can I engage with that tribe consistently, every day if possible? Do only what you can commit to doing regularly. When sustaining your community, keep it sustainable. Keep a laser focus on establishing authority and authenticity with a small group of people who love what you do. Get that right, and more will gravitate to you and your work over time.

Is it okay to advertise? Look, there's no shame in an ad or a sponsored post. You can do amazing things with targeting, and if you know exactly the type of people who would like your stuff, it can be a very useful way of getting the message directly to them. That said, ads are a parallel activity that don't belong in your thinking about community. Most people turn to ads far too early in the process, as though you can somehow *buy* a community. You can't. You can buy temporary attention, but you cannot buy a community member. If you're not sure whether or not you should advertise, the answer is probably no.

Trust your gut. If you're thinking of running an ad, telling your community about a product, or monetizing things in some way and your intuition is ringing a bell: DON'T DO IT.

And if things do start to work, don't let your ego take the

reins. If you've never had the experience of getting a lot of attention before, it can be intoxicating. Keep your eye on what matters: your authenticity and integrity. This means you have to stay true to your vision even if that means deviating from your community. *You've got to stay on your path.* That inevitably means that some of your followers aren't going to come along for the ride. They're going to get stuck on the old you, the version they saw that initially drew them in, despite the fact that you're growing. That's okay. You are a creator, not an influencer. Influencers become anything they need to be to hold on to their audience. A creator holds to his or her path, and the right people come along for the journey.

Even as your community grows, don't forget your base camp. Your other communities are still important; you can't afford to bounce them. Keep showing up, keep finding new ways to contribute and collaborate with others, and those communities will continue to fuel your success and feed into your future.

In Real Life

People will tell you that social media make it possible to do all your community building from the comfort of your living room with the right social media strategy. That just ain't true. We've seen plenty of politicians learn this lesson the hard way. You have to get out in front of people in the real world. You have to take the stage. There is no substitute.

After REI purchased my photos to decorate its flagship store in Seattle, the managers asked me to come speak to the community they were building around the store. They knew how deeply embedded in outdoor action sports I'd already become. That was why I worked in a ski shop, to be around people who ski and snowboard all day! I wanted to be a living, breathing part of that community.

I accepted the gig, and my team and I created a fun event to raise funds for the Northwest Avalanche Center to help raise awareness about avalanche danger. Every year, I'd do a slide-show of my work, compiling the best images of all the fly fish-ing, climbing, skiing, and snowboarding Kate and I had done throughout the previous year. To promote each event, I'd put fly-ers everywhere; we filled the house on pure hustle. I'd tell stories of our adventures and then show photos while a live DJ played in the background. We got to have a ton of fun, connect in per-son with a couple hundred friends, and raise money for a very important cause.

Get in front of people in your community however you can. Go to events, from big conferences to coffee shop meetups. If you connect with someone online in your area, invite them to meet face-to-face. Join Toastmasters International to hone your public speaking. Get involved with local entrepreneurs. Create events of your own, and help bring people together.

Attend. Talk. Ask questions and answer them. Add value. Slowly but surely, your community will take shape.

Make Your Own Mentor

There is one more benefit to the audience you build around yourself and your ideas: it becomes an invaluable source of ad-vice and support.

After we'd wrapped our fifth or sixth CreativeLive workshop, I took the crew out for pizza. We were all thrilled, high-fiving each other over another successful live broadcast.

"Let's talk about our vision. What's the future of CreativeLive?"

I asked them. "Where can we take it from here? Who would be a dream instructor?" Their first suggestions were all-star photographers like Annie Leibovitz and Anne Geddes.

"Yes, we absolutely want instructors like that on the platform," I said. "We are CreativeLive. Creativity is a huge umbrella. And think bigger." Someone said Richard Branson. "*Now* you're talking." Branson had already been a huge inspiration to me as an entrepreneur. A rebel from the start, he'd launched Virgin Records as a complete industry outsider and then built it by signing controversial but promising bands I loved, ones the established record companies wouldn't touch, such as the Sex Pistols.

Cut to a few years later. As part of my ongoing effort to build my community, I'd said yes to an invitation to a gathering for creators and entrepreneurs in London. I didn't know much about the event ahead of time, so I was a bit shocked to find myself seated between Peter Gabriel and Richard Branson. I didn't immediately engage in conversation. They already knew each other, so I mostly listened. Later on at the event, I chatted with Peter about photography, and Richard, always curious, started asking questions. Before I knew it, I'd been connected to the guy who oversees his investments. Eventually Richard became an investor in CreativeLive and a trusted adviser. To this day, I know I can call on him and his team for ideas and support.

Everyone wants a mentor, the wise little green creature who will teach us how to swing a lightsaber and use the Force. I was no exception when I started out in photography. I thought someone was going to take my outstretched hand and guide me along the path to greatness. They'd tell me what to learn, how to learn it, and what to do once I'd done so.

As I've progressed along my creative path and become a person whom other aspiring photographers ask to serve as their own mentor, I've come to realize that mentorship as we think of it is a pernicious fairy tale.

When I realized that no one was going to mentor me the way I'd always imagined, I turned to books. It was actually pretty simple. To learn how to run my photography business, I read *The Business Guide to Photography*. Lo and behold, I found the answers to most of my questions. I didn't need to corner a celebrity photographer at a party and demand her help. Books are mentorship at scale. The best part is, you can be mentored by the greatest minds in history if you're willing to crack the pages of a book. Over the years, I've assembled a sort of Franken-mentor made up not only of books but also of the words of advice from many different people I've met along the way. It isn't the romantic notion you might have of mentorship, but it's mentorship as it exists in the real world.

When I was sitting next to Richard Branson, every instinct told me to start up a chat right away. *He wants to help the next generation of entrepreneurs, doesn't he?* Instead, I was patient and ran into him again later at the event. Which led to an introduction to his team. When the time was right and I had a compelling but competitive investment opportunity for CreativeLive's Series B round of venture funding, I was able to *offer* it to Richard. At that moment I was adding value and being of service to the Virgin team, letting it into an exclusive opportunity, analogous to what I'd done for years with my own community around photography.

I've learned to connect with people I respect by offering value first, whether that's through creating connections, providing creative ideas, or simply being interested in and helpful about whatever someone is creating. I met my earliest advisers by writing thoughtfully about their ideas on my blog. All that attention caught their attention in return. This is still a phenomenal way to build community. I can rattle off ten people I've never met who participate almost every day. They're out there supporting me and adding value. I notice. (If one of you is reading this right now, and sharing on your social channels yet again, thanks for the support.)

Even if you're sitting in your sweats in your house in Ohio, go online and retweet the creator whose business you admire. Leave a thoughtful comment and share her message every day for two years. Not in a creepy way, in a thoughtful one. By that point, I don't care who she is, she'll know who you are. And if you happen to meet in real life one day? You'll have something authentic to speak about. You can reference specific moments in her creative career arc that you have admired or learned from. That will connect the two of you, however briefly, in a simple but meaningful way. And that's what this is all about.

I don't have a Yoda; I have a web of advisers in my community. I draw advice from all kinds of people, each with a distinct and valuable perspective. I've built and nurtured those relationships over years, just as I've built the rest of my community. Even when I don't have a relationship with someone, I can just follow that person on social media or read her books. It's a beautiful thing that so many top performers share their advice, ideas, and inspiration so freely. I can't believe how often I meet people who fail to take advantage of a book or a blog post but wonder bitterly why so-and-so isn't replying to their emails. So-and-so is busy writing the next book or blog post, that's why.

A devoted, real-life human mentor falling into your lap would be an amazing thing if it happened. But don't hold your breath. This is exactly the kind of grasping, take-before-you-give mentality that poisons a new community. Today, the greatest performers on Earth make their knowledge and advice public, often for free. And you can get more if you are willing to go further. For example, when a student volunteers to be in the audience of a CreativeLive course, he gets to spend two or three days in close proximity with the instructor and only a handful of other students. Bonds form, believe me. Though being in our audience is always free, there are many similar opportunities that are pay-to-play, such as courses, seminars, and masterminds. You won't find a better opportunity for building lasting relationships with the people you most admire.

Another aspect of the mentor illusion is the idea that someone is going to come along to provide structure and accountability for your work. If you're waiting for a mentor to do this for you, go back and reread Step II. We're always looking for an opportunity to hand the keys over to someone else. That's a one-way ticket back to where you started. You're walking your own path now. You can't escape doing the work and managing your career, deciding where you want to go and then going there.

Be smart. Make your own mentor. Read, listen, and learn—the resources are limitless. Then, be of service, add value, and forge connections with the people you admire. Instead of putting all your faith in a person you haven't even met, create a web of advice and advisers that will bolster you for years to come.

Building your audience and then cultivating it—no matter its size and no matter how far your own star rises—is the missing ingredient for 99 percent of the creators I meet who feel that they're not succeeding.

Only once you've built a vibrant community of your own will you be ready to take your creative work to the next stage, to get out there and not simply share but *launch*. This goes beyond putting your stuff out there. This is about taking the stage and standing out for all the world to see. With your community holding you up, there's a good chance you'll be seen above the crowd.

It's go time.

12

Launch!

You have something important to contribute, and you have to take the risk to contribute it.

—MAE JEMISON

It's time to take the stage in a major way. This isn't about putting out another blog post, song, or story. It's about creating something transformational, of standout significance to you, your community, and your creative path: a new novel, album, or business. A big swing. A project representing months or even years of dedicated effort.

To be clear, *whatever* you do with the results of your creative efforts, doing the work itself is intrinsically valuable and fulfilling. Hang your painting on your own damn wall. It's a joyful thing to be surrounded by the things you've made. That said, if you're willing to take the next step, the possibilities are truly endless.

When it came time to launch CreativeLive, I was already an old hand at the process. I'd put big things out in front of my community so many times that my launch calluses had calluses. I was still nervous as hell, though. I still have photos from that period: empty coffee cups everywhere, everyone's hair sticking up at odd angles, whiteboards with lists such as "Shit that's gonna break." We were all frenetic, bleary-eyed. It's just the nature of any big push. I find it helps to know that this is normal during creative crunch time.

This chapter is all about launching big things that matter. We get better at it through practice—but those jitters never go away completely. As Kelly McGonigal explained in her book *The Upside of Stress: Why Stress Is Good and How to Get Good at It*, we feel nervous at times like these because we're invested in them. We care about the outcome, and our body tries to help us achieve our goal by going into high-alert mode. If I don't have jitters before a launch, it's a sign to me that the work isn't ready because I'm not fully invested in it yet. I've got to believe in what I'm launching if I expect anyone else to pay attention.

This chapter is the culmination of Step IV. You've found your peers and collaborators. You've built a community of your own, a tribe oriented around your work. Now it's time to find the courage to hit send on something that has pushed you to your creative limit. The work isn't done until you walk away—or, far better, share it with the world.

But here's the secret nobody's bothered to tell you: this step isn't the end. It's just the beginning of another exciting chapter in your life as a creator. This is the part where your creation does work out in the world and where the impact of your creativity starts to make itself more widely known.

Sharing and Shame

If we're proud of what we've made, and we've built an audience in tune with our ideas and beliefs, what's the problem with sharing?

They're going to love what we've got to offer, right? Yet we still often feel an overpowering desire to hide. We might drop our work limply onto the floor and slink away, instead of holding it up for everyone to see.

When you resist sharing proudly, you're listening to shame. Shame is the insidious voice telling you that you're not good enough. That if you make a mistake, it means that you're a mistake. That if people don't like your work, they don't like you. Shame can be crippling for any creator. Some of us grapple with deeper feelings of shame than others, but none of us is completely immune. You're not born with it. Shame is something you put on early in life and then it *sticks*, like a sweaty shirt. Unexamined, it will stifle your ambitions and choke the life out of your creativity.

One early memory comes to my mind: We're at a family wedding. I'm about eight years old and having a blast. I marvel during the cutting of the cake, the removal of the garter, all the little wedding rituals—I'm fascinated by all of it. Now I see that the bride is going to throw a bouquet of flowers over her shoulder. A crowd gathers behind her. (I don't pay much attention to its composition.) Everyone's so excited. This is *fun*. The bride is looking over her shoulder, faking like she's going to throw it any second. The crowd leans forward anxiously.

I get it—it's a game! This is my moment! I play sports, so this is a perfect opportunity to get some of that attention and praise I'm always craving. They'll never believe how fast I can go and how high I can leap. Sprinting twenty feet from stage left, I make a textbook dive, timed perfectly, and snatch the flowers in midair, land on my side, and slide to a stop on the dance floor, much to the disappointment of all the unmarried women and hundreds of onlookers.

Triumphant, I dust myself off, stand up in front of the wedding guests, and hold the bouquet up at arm's length like a trophy, grinning from ear to ear.

Crickets. Then laughter. Pointing.

My face turns scarlet. After what feels like an eternity but is probably only a few seconds, my dad makes his way over to me, grabs the bouquet, and hands it back to the bride with a smile and a nod. As the festivities in the room ramp back up for a redo of the bouquet toss, he walks me off to the side of the room, tears welling up in my eyes. I'm not sure what just happened, but I know I did something wrong.

My dad could have come down hard on me—it wouldn't have been completely out of character. But that's not what he did. Instead, he kneeled down, looked me in the eyes, and complimented me on my catch. That helped. Then he explained where I had gone wrong and what the whole bouquet tradition was all about. I still felt embarrassed, but the feeling underneath that was guilt, not shame. I'd done something wrong, but *I* wasn't wrong. I was okay. I'd simply made a mistake.

That wasn't always how things worked out, though. I've experienced shame many times, just as you have. But if it weren't for the way my dad handled that situation, I probably wouldn't have volunteered to breakdance in front of two thousand strangers on a family trip a few years later. I'm grateful.

If you put something out there and people don't like it or ignore it, the shame we carry says, "You are bad." But here's the thing: *you are not your work.* This is difficult to reconcile because your work does reflect you, your skills, tastes, values, and beliefs. You have to become vulnerable to create and even more vulnerable to share your creations with others. But it gets easier with practice. And every time you share in the face of fear, your work has a chance to become exponentially more valuable.

I've faced shame many times. I felt ashamed telling my parents

I was giving up on professional soccer; later, on med school, and again on grad school. Both Kate and my family supported my decisions to quit, which helped, but that didn't make the feelings go away completely. I had to work through that shame myself, lance it, and let it heal, something I've gotten better and better at doing through practice.

As creators, each of us has to learn to nurture and parent ourselves, particularly where creativity is concerned. I'd love for you to think of this entire book as a manual for doing this. The tools I've given you are intended to do for you what my dad did for me at that wedding: give you a pat on the back, show you what to do differently, and send you back out onto the dance floor, where there's a whole new layer of upside to doing the creative work you were meant to do.

When we are operating in shame, we too easily believe the awful thoughts about ourselves that we hear in our head. But that is not who we are. Meditation has taught me that I am not my thoughts. Practicing meditation over the years has made it much easier for me to observe and identify the voice of shame and call it out for the fraud it is.

There are many different ways to cope with the vulnerability of sharing and the shame that can sometimes result. In a podcast conversation, Brené Brown shared with me that she keeps a tiny list in her wallet with the names of a handful of people who matter most to her. Whenever she feels the weight of other people's opinions too strongly, she consults the list. "Have I let any of these people down? No? Then I'll be okay."

You're never going to get everyone you know (let alone every random person on social media) on board with your decision to pursue creativity. You're certainly never going to have unanimous positive feedback for everything you make. In fact, if the work you put out is *only* celebrated, beware. Your best work will evoke a strong reaction, positive *and* negative. As Aesop says, trying to please everyone ends up pleasing no one—especially yourself.

Depending on what you make and how much you charge for it, you can build a lucrative career out of doing work that pleases only a tiny fraction of the people who see it. Once you've found your true fans, forget the rest of the damn internet and all the haters out there. Focus on making work you love and putting that work into the right channels, where your people will find it. Of course, it requires work to make that happen—more on that in a minute—but that's not the point here. The key is to develop a sharing mindset, regardless of the response from everyone else.

Once you have cultivated a vulnerable and sharing mindset and put your work into the world, the rest of it—the responses from those who receive your work—is just the weather. It's here today, gone tomorrow. Your work will remain.

Build a Sharing Mindset

In chapter 4, we learned to cultivate the creative mindset, face down our insecurities, sidestep impostor syndrome, and follow the pull of our passions instead of pushing ourselves to where we think we ought to be. If you haven't read chapter 4 yet because you were eager to get to this part of the book, go back there, read it, and put the recommendations into practice. You've got to get your mind right for this work.

Sharing our work requires the same resilience, the same discipline, the same attention to self-care as creating it in the first place. The cool thing is, you've already been building this capacity like a muscle by practicing your craft. Now it's time to develop the next layer of resilience. You develop the sharing mindset with practice and by starting small. If you want to do a mainstage TED talk, don't jump straight to sending in your application. Join a local improv group to work on your speaking skills. Find short, unpaid speaking opportunities at smaller conferences in your community. Do an open-mic night—anything to get in front of a bunch of strangers and rack up experience.

It's natural to be scared when you begin to share your creative work habitually, even with your spouse or your peers at work. Start small and be consistent. If you want to publish a book, don't just lock yourself in your room for six months and write. Start by sharing your initial ideas with friends and mentors or on social media. Then graduate to short stories or long blog posts. It's like lifting weights: work your way up to it, or risk pulling a muscle. By hitting send on something small regularly, not only do you flex your creative muscles, you will get better and better at sharing and tackling stuff higher up on the food chain, the riskiest but most rewarding work you will ever do in your life.

Success is fleeting; failure is never permanent. Whatever response your work elicits, even if it's a thunderous success, remind yourself: this, too, shall pass.

When developing a sharing mindset, think authenticity and vulnerability. Learning to embrace both takes time and practice. Success doesn't just happen. Not for anybody. People who think success is like winning the lottery have no idea how much work happens *before* someone becomes widely recognized for her craft. Brené Brown was practicing her craft and building her own community long before the TED talk that led to "viral" fame. (There have been thousands of TED and TEDx talks; how many of those speakers went on to match Brené?) Tim Ferriss plans every step of each book launch months in advance, lining up dozens of podcast interviews, planning every step of his strategy, and otherwise doing everything in his power to support the fruits of his labor. He becomes his own best ally.

So should you. The success you see is always just the tip of the iceberg. This chapter is about what goes on under the surface.

Cultivate Support

When you summit a mountain, you're only halfway there.

This isn't just a platitude, either. I went up Mount Kilimanjaro, Africa's highest peak, with Melissa Arnot Reid, the first American woman to summit Mount Everest and survive the descent without supplemental oxygen. As exciting as it was to reach the top, she reminded me just as we reached the summit that I still faced a tremendous challenge.

Maybe it was the thin air I was breathing, but I just hadn't put it together that I still had half of the journey left to travel. Likewise, you can create your art all on your own, but sharing it requires another level of effort rarely seen by the casual observer. If you want what you create to make an impact on the world, you must advocate for yourself and create a supportive community— a launchpad—to help your work make that impact.

My advice? Be soft and vulnerable in creating; ferocious and bold in sharing.

We've already talked about what to do if your family and friends don't support you on your creative path. You may even find that your existing communities don't go all in on what you create or don't support it to the extent that you'd like. And that's okay. One of the biggest mistakes we make, however, is in trying to win over the haters. Forget them! Focusing on the people who respond positively to what you do is the name of this game. Nurture those connections. Even if only a handful of people cheer you on, that's fine. Remember Brandon Stanton from Humans of New York? Today he has more than 20 million followers. The first portrait he posted got zero likes and one comment from a college friend. It's always worth reminding yourself that if you take the long view, these are simply the early seeds of your community. You will learn more by paying attention to the few positive lights than by worrying about the millions of others who are still unaware of you—let alone any haters.

This isn't easy, of course. It takes a strong internal compass.

I'm reminded of my experience launching Best Camera. I've rarely felt more lonely than I did in those early months. Not because of my team or our community—we had tons of raving fans almost immediately—but because my collaborators on the project had essentially abandoned me right from the start. It would have been very easy to focus on the developers' lack of support and let that completely derail me into self-pity and surrender. I struggled but I still put myself out there time after time, in the media, on TV, online—wherever I could to advocate for a project I passionately believed in. The end result would have been the same if I hadn't, but I showed up for myself and my work when it mattered. Each time we show up for our work, we make it easier for ourselves the next time.

The Sharing Cycle

Some will tell you that simply doing the work is enough, but I believe that sharing and promoting your work aren't simply "marketing." These are profoundly nourishing and necessary functions of your creativity. They are a way of showing yourself that you value your own work. In fact, there's a circular flow you'll find in the life of any healthy and productive creative person: Create > Share > Promote > Cultivate Community > Create (Again). The most prolific, successful, and prominent professional creators are always working their way around this loop, sometimes doing several different loops for different projects concurrently.

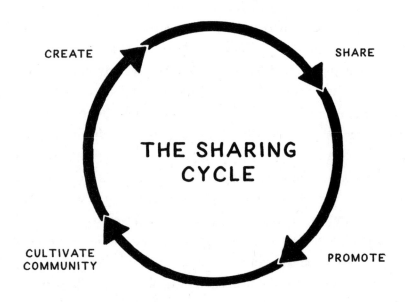

There is more to sharing than just pressing send. Promoting and cultivating community are two active, hands-on processes, as all-consuming as making the work itself can be. You can spend years making a masterpiece, but the promotional effort needs to be scheduled carefully if you're going to build momentum. Over time, you'll learn how to make the mental and emotional transition to promoting, but it takes practice. The nice thing is that once you're promoting, you can start to think of yourself as assisting people who might be helped or inspired by your work. Rather than pitching someone a product, you're a guide. You will be much more effective when you don't feel so wrapped up in your work.

Everyone does this. No one, no matter how famous or successful, gets to bow out of the sharing phase and just create all day. A feature film isn't "done" on opening night. Watch those celebrity actors. As charmed as their lives are, they work. They spend months before shooting getting into HD-ready physical condition. They spend months on a grueling film shoot. Then you'll see them back at work preparing for opening night: doing an international media tour, using their social channels to drive engagement, recording special interviews and other features for the video release, whatever it takes to back up all the hard work they've invested in the film itself. This honors the work. You can celebrate the work while remaining authentic to your identity as a creator.

Consider your favorite band. The show they performed in your hometown last summer? That's a promotion to sell copies of their latest album. It's interesting when viewed through this lens to see how simple—and acceptable—promotion becomes. We love our rock stars. From the stage, they are loving their art and sharing it with you. Regardless of the medium, the same opportunity is there for you to share *your* work. Yes, it's convenient that music has an element of performance to it that might be less obvious with other creative crafts—but there's no reason you can't adopt the same mentality when it comes time to share what you have made.

Sure, if you're a creator who gets all the value you want from creating in your studio, if the creative process in and of itself is enough for you, then yes, this cycle of sharing might not be for you. No judgment from me. But outside of the rare exception, publicly celebrating your work is a lively, helpful, beneficial part of the creative process in every medium. In fact, I would argue that the great artists achieved that greatness in part because they spent time and energy inviting you to experience their work. The effort required to spread the message in our work is an extension of the work, a factor in our growth and development as creators. Talking about your work, explaining it, navigating questions about it, and standing next to it out in the world can all be understood as *internal acts* that help you understand the work better than if you had just set it on a shelf and walked away.

If You Don't Want to Share

Rest assured, no one is born knowing how to share. It's always uncomfortable at first. That said, if you strongly resist promoting your work, it's time to ask yourself: Are you working on the right stuff? If you've worked your way through the book sequentially, you'll already have done a lot of work to dial in on the work that you truly want to make. If you've skipped some sections, now is the time to fill in those blanks, because you may not really be in touch with your creative calling.

Back in graduate school, I tried every way I could to incorporate my creativity into my academic writing. Despite all the effort, I never wanted to share my work with anyone in my circle of friends. Eventually I realized that it was because I wasn't proud of it. Those weren't the photos I actually wanted to make. I was doing what I could to make the best of my situation, but I was not walking my path. I had different aspirations that I was ignoring. I was pursuing my art with the limited autonomy I had at the time, and it was better than not creating at all, but half-measures weren't going to do it. Ultimately, that resistance was a good thing. It was in not feeling proud enough to share my work that I realized that I was working on the wrong stuff altogether and that I'd need to leave grad school behind for good.

When you love your work, there's a feeling that it needs to be in the world. It doesn't feel like "selling" if you believe your stuff will make people happier, make them think, drive social change, help people feel more fulfilled, entertained, whatever. It isn't dirty or selfish to promote, share, or invite others to your work when you're truly proud of it. In that case, it's not really just the eyeballs you're after anyway; it's hearts and minds and human connection.

The desire to drive attention to your work can be fed by the love you have for it. In the same way we have to learn to love and be kind to ourselves, we need to learn to love what we make. Of course, you'll always see something you might do better next time. That feeling never goes away, and it strikes in this minute as I write this book to you. But I see it as a sign that I'm still engaged and growing as a creator.

Regardless of your project or your process, it's essential to cultivate a love for what you've made and recognize the value in it for others. If you're not feeling it, it's a sign to recalibrate. Go back to Step I of the book. Reread it if you have to. Once you're making the work you were born to make, that resistance will fade into the background.

Acknowledge Your Ambition

Creative expression is as important to human health as exercise and mindfulness. A few decades ago, "jogging" was an oddball fad. As a society, however, we've collectively figured out that regular physical activity isn't weird at all. In an era of modern conveniences, we'd simply forgotten that movement is crucial to our well-being. We are on the verge of rediscovering this about creativity as well.

Assuming that's true, you might be wondering why it isn't enough to make your work and put it into a drawer. After all, you can meditate regularly without going on a silent retreat, and you can certainly do the seven-minute workout every morning without running a marathon or going to the CrossFit games.

You're manifesting your creative power for a reason. Making work just to maintain your creative abilities, to be more human, is fine. Tapping into your creative mojo feels good, like huffing pure oxygen. It's life sustaining and practical in and of itself. I've observed, however, that there are *always* fun and fulfilling ways you can make your work an integral part of your life, whether through starting a business or just sharing funny videos with friends. Showing your work cultivates connection, hones your craft, and allows you to become stronger and better at what you love. Launching your creations into the world is part of the cycle. It closes the loop and provides access to a next-level sense of satisfaction.

My experience and what I've learned in talking to thousands of creators around the world is that as we improve, as we fall in love with our work, we naturally find ourselves wanting to find it an audience and help it make an impact. We all understand our work more as we share the work because it's in the sharing process that our work's potential more fully reveals itself.

If your work is about pain you've experienced, sharing it can help you process your emotions *and* help comfort others or even help them avoid the same mistakes. As a way to grieve the loss of her brother, Mariangela Abeo began creating portraits of people touched by suicide. Her project, Faces of Fortitude, provides a safe, stigma-free space to talk about mental health and share stories of loss and survival. That space was desperately needed. By sharing your experience—in any form it might take—you can experience healing, connect with others, process your pain, inspire others, or some combination of all these.

Don't let any of this overwhelm you at the start. Just as when you begin to flex your creative muscles, this growth happens naturally—if you're willing to begin with small actions. For example, at the start of a new mindfulness practice, the idea of a ten-day silent retreat might sound off-putting, even scary, but nobody's saying you have to do that to see a benefit from meditation. My wife, Kate, started meditating after being inspired by a friend and, over time, went from a five-minute daily sit to multi-day retreats to becoming a mindfulness teacher herself. (Teaching meditation would have struck her as absurd the first time she sat down to meditate years ago.)

Become proactive. Don't lie to yourself. If your secret vision is to become a *New York Times* bestselling author, lean into all of it: join writing groups, write a blog, submit stories for publication, rack up as many rejection letters as possible.

You may just be starting out on the path. If you shy away from sharing and you want to make work just for yourself for now, that's totally fine. You may find that as your practice grows, your feelings change. If you start cooking, you may enjoy making elaborate meals for yourself or your family for quite a while. Over time, though, you might start to wonder whether you have the capacity to tackle another layer of complexity: throwing a multi-course dinner party. Once you've mastered that challenge, a catering business might suddenly seem appealing. Or not.

It doesn't have to be big. The hobby of charcoal drawing might lead to a new annual tradition of sending a handmade holiday card to all your family and friends. *South Park* started as a video holiday card, after all.

Here's the truth, though: I think you do have ambition. Many of us learn to keep it locked up inside. We're afraid even to admit it. But what if you could manifest your ambition in all its glory? *How alive would you feel?*

Develop the Energy to Share

None of this is easy. This is why you need energy, the physical and emotional capacity to do the work. Physical fitness, nutrition, and mindfulness are especially important to creators because both creating work and promoting it place huge demands on us. If you allow yourself to become depleted, you will be undermined when you try to launch your business, present your vision at a big meeting, or publish your book. Even more energy is required anytime you tackle something new—and sharing may be a completely new experience for you.

Tony Robbins gets incredible results for the people who attend his seminars. I've had the privilege of working with Tony in those settings on a few occasions. I always came away with new clarity. The most impressive part, however, is watching Tony activate energy in others (and teach them to activate it themselves). He understands how much energy is required to make real change in your life, whether that means adopting a new habit or taking a major risk. That's what all the jumping around and fire walking is about. Techniques like these are just the first and most visible steps in rewiring our nervous systems. They remind us what real energy feels like in the body and that it's available to us on demand.

I'm not suggesting throwing a dance party every time you need to share your work. But it wouldn't hurt.

In a conversation on my podcast, the Swiss designer Tina Roth

Eisenberg shared an amazing nugget of wisdom I'll never forget: Enthusiasm is more powerful—and ultimately more valuable— than confidence. Confidence is all about yourself—you develop it by repeatedly orchestrating successful outcomes. As you complete and share your work, your confidence grows even if the work doesn't become outwardly successful. You learn that you have agency and that you can complete what you start. This is obviously an important and helpful trait to possess.

Enthusiasm inspires confidence and energy in others. Its effects, therefore, are potentially far more valuable. If you can get ten or even a hundred other people excited, think of the network effects, value, and energy that are possible to create around your work.

With enthusiasm and confidence on your side, all that's missing is a bit of courage. Courage is the thing you need to get started—before confidence is built through repetition and before enthusiasm is there to inspire you. It's the ability to do what frightens you. If you combine these three forces? Watch out.

Confidence, courage, and enthusiasm play a central role in anyone's success. They affect the way you carry yourself in the world. It's the difference between "Um, here's my work? I, uh, hope you like it? Bye." and "Here's my work. I'd love some feedback." Sharing with courage, confidence, and enthusiasm starts things out on the right foot.

Success Is Not Necessary

Sharing successfully doesn't mean the work will be a "success." But *it doesn't have to succeed*. This is important. You can do everything right and still get things wrong. The mindset and energy you bring will keep you resilient through all the failures you'll face as a creator. Without them, you will crumble right away. Do you have any idea how many shots Michael Jordan *missed* during his career? More than nine thousand. Take baseball: a legendary hitter bats a .300 average, which means he succeeds only one in three times at bat. Take any famous entrepreneur, and her (true) biography will serve mostly as an index of failures with a few big wins mixed in. We think otherwise only because of our tendency to minimize failure and dwell on success when telling the story afterward.

You can do everything right, in both making the work and sharing it, and there is still no guarantee of success. Best Camera became wildly successful, but ultimately it was my biggest failure. So much lost potential. The lessons I learned from that failure became key factors in the success of CreativeLive. You learn from every failure. You build confidence in failure, you begin to trust that every failure contains a lesson or an opportunity. It's the universe's way of telling you something you haven't figured out yet.

The goal of this book isn't to teach you *what* to think about creativity but *how*. A well-filled mind takes second place to a well-formed mind. As you consistently put your creativity to work, share that work, and grapple with the results, you'll see how important these lessons are.

You can do this right now. Think back to an old failure, five years or more in the past: losing a job, ending a relationship, suffering through a financial catastrophe. Chances are you're at the point where you can see that failure as what it truly was: a stepping-stone to where you are today.

If whatever you're facing isn't making sense yet, if you can't see the lesson in it, you haven't zoomed out far enough. When you're in the middle of a mess, it can be chaotic and frightening, but if you can adopt a wider view, even laugh in the face of struggle, that sense of perspective will save you and keep you going through anything.

When you create, you're not just creating art or a product or a business, you're creating *possibilities*. You won't be aware of all of them, but they're there. It's a virtuous cycle. Only by embracing your innate creativity will you begin to see the life you are truly capable of creating for yourself. It'll be scary at first, but if you learn to label your fear as what it really is—a sign that you care about the outcome—you'll begin to unlock a whole new world.

Read This Last

Stevens Pass is a small but mighty ski resort situated in a mountain pass a couple of hours east of Seattle. I skied there growing up, taking the "Saturday ski bus" most winter weekends. Later, I spent many happy days there honing my photography skills with friends.

What a pleasure, then, when the resort put me on retainer for my photography services. Over the course of the next five years, I would be helping it with a visual rebranding effort aimed at attracting an energetic mix of customers—from young families to top skiers and snowboarders.

Though my photography at the time took me all over the world—New Zealand, Europe, Asia—to work with colossal brands, Stevens Pass was a gem of a client. I relished each opportunity to photograph local heroes and work with the new friends I was making at the resort. It was just my kind of challenge: solving problems creatively with people I liked, in a place with personal meaning for me, surrounded by the natural beauty of the Cascade Mountains. I was in my element and couldn't have been happier. If you do a lot of client work, you learn to appreciate the delightful clients. I never take it for granted when I'm among good people doing something I love.

As the project progressed, I grew close to Chris Rudolph, the resort's young director of marketing, known among his friends as "the ambassador of all things rad." He was my kind of guy: scrappy, joyful, indomitable. Chris embodied creativity. He did everything he could to make his life and the life of those around him the very best, right down to the bumper sticker on his truck that read, "Be the person your dog thinks you are."

It was a long shot because the competition was tough, but he'd landed a highly creative job at Stevens, and through grit and ingenuity, he'd seemingly overnight elevated that little ski area up in the corner of the country to a secret destination for the winter sport elite: athletes, photographers, and filmmakers. Chris and I hit it off right away. When I wasn't in the area, we stayed in touch in case heavy snowfall was predicted. Then I'd catch a plane with my production crew from wherever we'd been working to return and capture those perfect days at Stevens.

The more time we spent up there, the closer Kate and I became with Chris and his longtime girlfriend, Anne. Whenever we'd come swooping in so I could capture the slopes in pristine condition, we'd hang around together after the shoot to share a meal and catch up over beers by the fire.

At one point during the winter of 2012, I left a shoot in Venice for a quick trip to Barcelona to recruit a potential hire for CreativeLive. The evening after I arrived in Spain, I was in my hotel room, on the phone with Kate back in Seattle and reading encouraging news of a winter storm dumping a blanket of fresh snow on Stevens Pass. Nothing would have made me happier than to drop everything and head to the resort to catch the ideal conditions.

As we were talking, an ominous tweet popped up: "Avalanche at Stevens Pass. Skiers caught." I felt a chill. As more updates posted in quick succession, I learned that the slope in question was in the backcountry area of the resort, relatively inaccessible to most people—with the exception of those who knew the area well. With all the time I'd spent there, and with the breadth of my relationships across the action sports community, the chances were high that Kate and I knew those skiers. Still on the phone, we anxiously scanned social media and news sites for more updates but found nothing substantial. I texted Chris, who, as director of marketing, would know the details of any rescue effort: "Holy shit, dude. Thinking of you—hope everything's OK."

I felt helpless watching the events unfold from halfway around the world. Late that night in Barcelona, I learned the terrible news. Three skiers had died in the avalanche: my dear friend Chris Rudolph, another friend from the Freeskiing World Tour, Jim Jack, and a third skier I'd met a few times named Johnny Brennan. Elyse Saugstad, another pro skier I'd met, had also been caught in the slide, but thankfully she'd survived against tremendous odds.

The news left me devastated. I was completely gutted.

I also couldn't help but recognize that had it not been for my last-minute trip to Europe, my production team and I would probably have been out on the slopes on that fateful day. I'd miraculously survived a massive avalanche just a handful of years earlier; somehow that made me feel closer to those who hadn't survived. I had felt a sliver of the terror they must have experienced in their final moments.

I took stock in a way I hadn't done since my last brush with death: What would have flashed through my mind as that wall of snow ripped down the mountain at sixty miles per hour? Pure fear? Regret? Acceptance? Staring vacantly out the window on my early-morning flight back to Seattle, I asked myself: Was I truly living the life I'd intended? Was I fulfilling my true calling?

A year later, the *New York Times* told the story of the Stevens Pass avalanche using a groundbreaking online multimedia approach. Images, video, animations, and audio recordings from the day were blended into the first interactive reporting of its kind. When the *Times* called me about contributing to the piece, titled "Snow Fall," I was honored and humbled to provide them with the material Chris and I had created together over several years, from aerial images to epic skiing shots to portraits of Chris himself. It felt like a way to honor his memory and get his creative thumbprint on the story, which went on to win a Pulitzer Prize and became the most viewed online *New York Times* story to date. I can only hope the story's popularity helped to raise awareness around avalanche safety.

Chris, my friend—you walked your own path until the very moment it was cut short. Thank you for allowing me to walk with you for a while. I will always cherish our journey together.

I relate this story here at the end of this book as a reminder to both you and me.

I didn't write this book just to share some helpful creative hacks or to egg you into finally "finishing that novel" or taking that jewelry-making class at the local community college you keep thinking about. Those would be outstanding secondary outcomes, but that's not my primary purpose.

I wrote this book to help you unlock a hidden part of yourself, a critical space sorely neglected in our culture. So many of us live our lives with a nagging sense that something important is missing. We finish school, build a career, start a family, buy a house, build friendships, and do all the other things society tells us make for a happy and fulfilling existence. And we still often don't feel fulfilled. I've come to believe that creative expression is the missing element in a life well lived.

Creativity is a critical human function. It imbues every incident we experience in life—every sight, sound, and texture—with profound meaning. Without acknowledging and exercising our creativity in small, consistent ways, we're undermining our natural capacity to Imagine, Design, Execute, and Amplify the life we're meant to be living. A life without creativity lacks intention, shape, and connection to our own humanity. Without creativity to reveal our own agency, we become a cork bouncing in the tide.

Looking at the text as a whole, I realize I've written the book that I myself needed. This is the book I wished I could have read at the start of my own creative journey. Like everyone else, I just wanted to be happy. It took some time to realize that the only way to have a chance at everything I wanted from my life was by taking ownership for creating it: hearing the call and walking my creative path. This is true for each and every one of us. It's true for you.

Happiness isn't an accident. The science is clear on this: human happiness isn't gained from achievement. It's chosen. We decide to be happy, and then that decision helps drive the achievement that brings us fulfillment, not the other way around. Winning the lottery won't make you happy, and neither will the fact that Mercury is finally out of retrograde. Happiness is a decision.

Yes, there are things in life that you have no control over, from natural disasters such as avalanches to serious health problems to everyday annoyances such as traffic jams and leaky faucets. And nobody can avoid the whims of fate. Born with privilege or without, you're not responsible for the hand you've been dealt, only for how you take the precious gifts you *have* been given and make them into something through your creativity. That's all anyone can do. In fact, that's what we're here to do.

I'm a relentless optimist. I've made a deliberate effort to hold positivity as a core personal trait. It serves my life and the lives of those around me. We get stuck because we think happiness and positivity are things that are handed to a lucky few. No. The ones who have happiness chose to take it. Being positive is not blind optimism, corny platitudes, glossing over facts, or burying your head in the sand. It's finding the good in any given situation. Allocating attention to opportunities and upside, rather than challenges and downside. Positivity means approaching life with the belief that anything is possible.

It is.

Negativity can feel familiar if that's where you're used to living. If you expect that things won't work out, you can't be disappointed, right? In fact, the mind is wired to emphasize negativity. The brain evolved to prioritize the sight of a predator over the aesthetic perfection of the sunset framing that predator as it bounds toward you with supper in mind. By default, we watch for predators and miss the sunsets entirely.

This hardwired instinct is a liability in the modern world. It's literally poisonous. Negative thinking releases stress hormones, raises blood pressure, suppresses your immune system, and leads to a host of other health problems. Negative thinking impairs your cognitive ability and memory. Worst of all, negativity becomes a self-fulfilling prophecy. When you expect a negative outcome, you tune your intuition to act accordingly, creating the dreaded outcome and reinforcing that negative response: "See? I told you it was going to turn out like this!" It's a downward spiral that's also contagious. When you take a cynical view of life, your toxic outlook infects everyone around you, at home and at work.

The best antidote to negative thinking is creative doing. Or, as the legendary investor Ben Horowitz puts it, "There is no silver bullet that's going to fix that. No, we are going to have to use a lot of lead bullets."

Small, daily creative actions bolster positivity and inspire resolute thinking. In my own career, relentless positivity and creativity have always been my secret weapons. Don't believe me?

Think about the kindest person you've ever met. Positive or negative disposition?

Think about the most successful person you've ever met. Positive or negative disposition?

Think about the happiest person you've ever met. Positive or negative disposition?

If this doesn't come naturally to you, don't sweat it. You're fighting against your biology. You have the capacity to rewire the neural pathways in your brain. Choosing to be positive, choosing to be happy, will literally change your mind over time. To make it stick, however, you're going to need a system, a set of habits and behaviors. That's what I hope I've provided in these pages.

That's what my secret mission is. That's what the IDEA framework is intended to do. By teaching yourself to *imagine* what's possible for your life, you're wiring yourself for success. By continuously *designing* your life and iterating on that design, you discover what works for you and what doesn't. *Executing* on that vision becomes so much easier after you've charted a path. Choosing to *amplify* your creativity makes you rich in spirit and more grounded in your community. Your example becomes a beacon for others.

Not everything here will be a fit for you. That's okay. Just as I assembled my own approach to life by deconstructing the lives of the creators, skate punks, world-class performers, and philosophers I've studied, I encourage you to take what works, integrate it into your own life, and ditch the rest. If you are simply willing to accept that you *are* a creator, responsible for designing and living your own dream, I will consider my job done. As your creative practice deepens and expands, you will experience a greater sense of direction over your own life. You will prove to yourself, over and over, that you have the power to turn your ideas into reality. This sense of agency and autonomy will bring you happiness and satisfaction like nothing else.

Pursue your creative calling.

Acknowledgments

At the beginning of chapter 10, I lay out the idea that nothing happens in a vacuum, that every project requires an orchestra of collaborators behind the scenes to make it possible. This book proves that idea in spades.

First to my wife, Kate: This book would probably still be a pile of scribbles, lists, sticky notes, sketches, docs on hard drives, pull quotes, and notebook pages all over the floor without you, babe. There were stretches in the process of creating all this where I fell apart and you glued me—and this book—back together. There were times when you worked harder than I did: nudging me, suggesting changes, reworking the garbage I'd scribbled out on a scrap of paper into the idea it was meant to be. I'll never forget the sacrifices you made. I think you even missed a few episodes of *Game of Thrones* for this book. I'm so grateful. You are my love and my light, my muse and my rock.

To my family, core and extended: your unending support has been a driving force in my life. I love you. To my friends who are always there, even on the occasion that I'm not: Thanks for keeping it real, for keeping me real, for knowing more than just my highlight reel and still caring. You know all the good, the bad, and the ugly work—personal and otherwise—that's gone into these pages . . . thank you. You are so awesome.

To my agent, Steve Hanselman—you're simply the best. Your vision is spectacular. Thanks for your guidance over the years and for helping me choose the best path when this book inside me had to get out. Here's to this one, and the next, and the next. I see a long and joyful path working together, far into the future.

To my team that worked on this book day in, day out, thank

you. Hollis Heimbouch: I knew from the first minute we met that you'd be the one to bring this book to life. Thank you for helping me make the book I wanted to make. I know you fought for it, and that matters to me. You and the rest of your team at Harper: Rebecca, Brian, Rachel, and too many others to name, behind the scenes—thank you. David Moldawer, thank you for helping pull this book out of my brain, my heart, and my soul and onto paper; for the research; and for ensuring we captured fleeting ideas, told the right stories, cut the cruft, and hit the deadlines. To everyone in the trenches making this happen, thank you. I'm over the moon with what we've created together. It took a village.

To my dear writing-guru friends who got early, *early* drafts and made suggestions that really shaped the arc of this project: thank you. Brené Brown, Tim Ferriss, Seth Godin, Robert Greene, Ryan Holiday, Scott Aumont, Rozen Noguellou, Megan Jasper, Cal McAllister, Alex Hillinger, and Taylor Winters . . . the time you spent with me on this was such a gift. Thanks for having my back. Eternally grateful.

To the icons, inspirations, stars, leaders, heroes, friends, and collaborators who appear in the pages herein; to everyone whose experiences, wisdom, and stories you shared with me over dinner, in an interview—recorded or not—in business, in lore, and in life, thank you. For every nugget or shining example that found its way into the book, there were three or five others that found the cutting-room floor. But rest assured I'll share those in future books, podcasts, interviews, the book tour, and endless other venues that the universe permits. Thank you for being the shining examples that you are in the world, for me, for the readers of this book, and for the lives you've already touched in pursuit of your very own creative calling. You rock.

To Milan Bozic, Lou Maxon, Vasco Morelli, Matt Queen,

Andrew van Leeuwen, and Norton Zanini—the posse who helped wrangle the design aspects of this beast. Obviously, we couldn't make a book about creativity without properly pushing the standard book package further than typically allowed, as we have here. Thank you for the nights, weekends, and in-between times. I love where it ended up.

To my work family at CreativeLive and CJI past, present, and future: what a crazy ride it's been. Too many collaborators and co-conspirators to name in my ride-or-die posse, across thousands of hours, grinding day in and out—doing things every day that people said were impossible. Watching the teamwork, the individual effort—all of it—I learned so much from you, and you profoundly inspired the making of this book. Although I know you thought I was crazy at various times along our path—perhaps rightly so on occasion—I hope you've found some delight that we've made it this far. I know I have. And I hope you share the same excitement I have for whatever's up around the bend.

Lastly, to all: what matters most is that we didn't just talk about it, we did it.

About the Author

Chase Jarvis is an award-winning artist and entrepreneur. One of the most influential photographers of the past decade, he has created campaigns for Apple, Nike, Red Bull, and many other major brands. Galleries have exhibited his work in the United States, Europe, and the Middle East. He was a contributor to the Pulitzer Prize–winning *New York Times* story "Snow Fall," and he earned an Emmy nomination for his documentary *Portrait of a City*. He created Best Camera, the first photo app to share images to social networks. He is also the cofounder of Creative-Live, where more than 10 million students learn photography, video, design, music, and business from the world's top creators and entrepreneurs.

Chase has been a keynote speaker on six continents, an adviser to *Fortune* 100 brands, and a guest at the Obama White House, the United Nations, the Library of Congress, 10 Downing Street, Buckingham Palace, and the DIFC in Dubai. He lives with his wife, Kate, in Seattle, Washington, where he serves as a volunteer director for several nonprofit boards. He is @chasejarvis across social media platforms.

www.creativecalling.com
www.chasejarvis.com
www.creativelive.com